FAMILY THERAPY AND SYSTEMIC PRACTICE

Readings on Child Protection, Clinical Techniques and Empirical Foundations

Alan Carr

University Press of America,® Inc.
Lanham • New York • Oxford

Copyright © 1997 by
University Press of America,® Inc.
4720 Boston Way
Lanham, Maryland 20706

12 Hid's Copse Rd.
Cummor Hill, Oxford OX2 9JJ

Library of Congress Cataloging-in-Publication Data

Carr, Alan, Dr.
Family therapy and systemic practice : reading of child protection,
clinical techniques, and empirical foundations / Alan Carr.
p. cm.
l. Family psychotherapy. 2. Child psychotherapy. I. Title.
RC488.5.C366 1997 616.89'156--dc21 97-33579 CIP

ISBN 0-7618-0912-0 (cloth: alk. ppr.)
ISBN 0-7618-0913-9 (pk : alk. ppr.)

♾™ The paper used in this publication meets the minimum
requirements of American National Standard for information
Sciences—Permanence of Paper for Printed Library Materials,
ANSI Z39.48—1984

World is crazier and more of it than we think,
Incorrigibly plural. I peel and portion
A tangerine and spit the pips and feel
The drunkenness of things being various

Louis MacNeice (1940) *Snow*

CONTENTS

PREFACE

In this volume I have attempted to draw together a selection of essays or readings about one approach to the practice in family therapy and systemic consultation. The particular approach that has been taken, I have referred to as *Positive Practice* in a treatment manual that was published by Harwood Academic press in 1995. Indeed it was in response to the many inquiries about the development of the approach described in *Positive Practice: A Step by Step Guide to Family Therapy*, that the present volume was compiled. The main questions that have been asked were

- How did *Positive Practice* evolve?
- With what types of cases did the approach develop
- Why did this approach evolve?
- What other approaches were considered along the way?

It would be very convenient to be able to say that the approach was developed in a systematic and carefully planned way to solve specific problems and the development of the approach was structured and progressive. This, of course was not the case. Rather, at different points in time a variety of factors influenced the piecemeal and somewhat chaotic formation of the approach. These factors included the needs and requirements of clients, the synergy between colleagues, the available training and reading opportunities and the systemic contexts within which practice was conducted and personal lifecycle experiences.

At various points along this meandering itinerary which spanned more than 10 years I attempted with colleagues to crystallise certain aspects of practice in brief essays and articles which were published largely in family therapy journals. It is these papers published between 1986 and 1997 that have been collected and presented in this volume.

In retrospect it has been possible to discern three distinct stages in the evolution of *Positive Practice* and these stages are described in Chapter 1.

It has also been possible to segregate the papers into three broad groupings. The first group deal with systemic consultation and child protection related issues. The second group of papers deal largely with specific clinical techniques. The remaining papers focus on empirical research of particular relevance to the practice of family therapy.

Inevitably, as a collection of essays, this volume lacks the continuity which characterized the *Positive Practice* treatment manual. However, what it lacks in continuity, it makes up for, I hope, in diversity.

I am grateful to the many people who have helped me develop the ideas presented in these papers. In particular I would like to thank the group at the Mater Hospital in Dublin who introduced me to family therapy: Imelda McCarthy, Nollaig Byrne, Koos Mandos, Jim Sheehan and Paul McQuaid.

I am also grateful to Chris Cooper, Peter Simms and Carol Elisabeth Burra in Kingston, Ontario with whom I worked while living in Canada.

In the UK my gratitude goes to the group with whom I practiced while at Thurlow House in King's Lynn: Dermot McDonnell, Chris Wood, George Gawlinski, Shiela Docking, Sue Grant, Nick Irving, Shahin Afnan, Jonathan Dossetor, Dennis Barter, Denise Sherwood, Mike Cliffe, Paul Berry, Anne and Martin Haliday, Fiona Grey, Amanda Ekdawai and Elaine Rudd.

Thanks to Anne Osborne for her help with the many literature searches conducted at the Queen Elisabeth Hospital Library in Kings Lynn and to Penny Owen for her collaboration on the audit project. Thanks to Pat Taylor, Chris Ashton, Helen Maskell and Joy Meyers for administrative back-up for the multidisciplinary programmes. Thanks to Andrew Marchant for rating the videotapes of the individual sessions in the case of elective mutism reported in Chapter 6.

Thanks to Barry Mason, Jim Wilson, Elsa Jones, Jeff Farris, Jan, Ben Kennedy, and Eddy Street for their comments on the review of empirical studies of Milan systemic family Therapy (Chapter 18) which was presented at the Family Institute Cardiff in December 1990. Thanks also to Lel Simpson, Panos Vostanis, John Burnham, Queenie Harris, and Oded Manor for permitting the inclusion of research which was unpublished at the time in the review.

My colleagues at UCD, particularly Professor Ciarán Benson, Dr Patricia Noonan Walsh and Frances Osborne have been very supportive of my efforts to edit this book and I am grateful to them for their patience and encouragement.

Thanks are also due to colleagues at the Clanwilliam Institute in Dublin where I practice: Ed McHale, Phil Kearney, Cory deJong, Declan Roche, Bernadette O'Sullivan and Clive Garland.

Writing about practice is a tricky business. Bryan Lask at Great Ormond Street Children's Hospital, while editor of the *Journal of Family Therapy*, played a particularly significant role in encouraging me to persist with my very early attempts in this area. I am grateful for his assistance. Thanks also to John Carpenter and Bebe Speed, current editors of the *Journal of Family Therapy* for their ongoing encouragement. Gratitude also goes to Peter Stratton, editor of *Human Systems*, and especially to Terry Trepper, editor of the *Journal of Family Psychotherapy*, who has been extaordinary supportive.

Thanks to Gill Randell for illustrations which speak louder than words in Chapters 4 and 16.

The more important aspects of what I know about family life, I have learned from my own family and to them I am particularly grateful. *Go raibh míle maith agaibh go léir.*

Alan Carr, May 1997.

EDITORIAL ACKNOWLEDGEMENTS

Thanks to John Carpenter, editor of the *Journal of Family Therapy*, and Blackwell Press for permission to reproduce the following papers which were previously published in the *Journal of Family Therapy*:

Chapter 4. Countertransference reactions to families where child abuse has occurred. *Journal of Family Therapy, 11,* 87-97, 1989.

Chapter 6. Concurrent individual and family therapy in a case of elective mutism. *Journal of Family Therapy, 11,* 29-44,1989, with S. Afnan.

Chapter 7. Anorexia Nervosa: The treatment of a male case with combined behavioural and family therapy. *Journal of Family Therapy, 11,* 335-351, 1989. With D. MacDonnell & S. Afnan.

Chapter 9. Failure in family therapy: A catalogue of engagement mistakes. *Journal of Family Therapy, 12,* 371-386, 1990.

Chapter 15. Three techniques for the solo-family therapist. *Journal of Family Therapy, 8,* 373-382, 1986.

Chapter 17. Audit and family systems consultation: Evaluation of practice at a child and family centre. *Journal of Family Therapy, 16,* 143-157, 1994, with D. McDonnell & P. Owen.

Chapter 18. Milan Systemic Family Therapy: A review of 10 empirical investigations. *Journal of Family Therapy, 3,* 237-264, 1991.

Thanks to Peter Stratton , editor of *Human Systems: The Journal of Systemic Consultation and Management*, for permission to reproduce the following papers which were previously published in *Human Systems: The Journal of Systemic Consultation and Management*:

Chapter 2. Child abuse, rehabilitation and poverty: A quintet of Problems. *Human Systems :The Journal of Systemic Consultation and management, 5,* 283-292, 1995.

Chapter 3. Power and influence in systemic consultation. *Human Systems: Journal of Systemic Consultation and Management, 2,* 15-30 1991.

Chapter 11. Systemic consultation and goal setting. *Human Systems: The Journal of Systemic Consultation and management, 4,* 49-59,1993.

Chapter 12. Giving directives effectively: The implications of research on compliance with doctor's orders for family therapy. *Human Systems: Journal of Systemic Consultation and Management, 1,* 115-127, 1990.

Chapter 16. Carrying parcels and making puddings: Two co-operative styles. *Human Systems: The Journal of Systemic Consultation and Management, 3,* 111-136,1993.

Thanks to Terry Trepper, editor of *Journal of Family Psychotherapy* and Haworth Press for permission to reproduce the following papers in this volume.

Chapter 13. Involving children in family therapy and systemic consultation. *Journal of Family Psychotherapy, 5*(1), 41-59,1994.

Chapter 14. Resistance, dilemmas and crises in family therapy: A framework for positive practice. *Journal of Family Psychotherapy, 6,* 29-42, 1995.

Thanks to Maureen Crago, editor of *The Australian and New Zealand Journal of Family Therapy,* for permission to reproduce the following papers in this volume.

Chapter 10. A formulation model for use in family therapy. The *Australian and New Zealand Journal of Family Therapy,* 11, 85-92, 1990.

Thanks to Laura Middleton, editor of *Practice,* for permission to reproduce the following papers in this volume.

Chapter 5. Thurlow House Assessment Programme for Families with Physically Abused Children. *Practice, 2*(3), 208-220, 1988, with G. Gawlinski, D. MacDonnell, & N. Irving.

Chapter 8. Thurlow House Adolescent Assessment Programme. Practice, 2, 60-190,1989, with G. Gawlinski, D. MacDonnell, N. Irving, & S. Docking.

Thanks to Patricia Kennedy, Editor of *Éisteacht: Journal of the Irish Association of Counselling and Therapy,* for permission to reproduce the following paper in this volume.
Chapter 1. Three stages in the development of an integrative approach to working with families. *Éisteacht: Journal of the Irish Association of Counselling and Therapy,* 1 (40), 9-15, 1997.

Thanks to Mary Montaut, editor of *Inside Out: A Quarterly Publication for Humanistic and Integrative Psychotherapy* for permission to reproduce the following paper in this volume.
Chapter 19. Psychotherapy Research. *Inside Out. Quarterly Publication for Humanistic and Integrative Psychotherapy ,* 27, 20-32, 1996.

Thanks to the Psychological Society at University College Dublin and the editors of the *Thornfield Journal* for permission to reproduce the following papers in this volume.
Chapter 20. Family Psychology. The emergence of a new field. Thornfield *Journal,* 17, 1-8, 1994.

AC
May 1997

SECTION 1

CHILD PROTECTION

In this section a series of five papers have been drawn together which deal with practice in cases where child protection is the central concern. The papers arose from the work of the multidisciplinary team at Thurlow House (an NHS Child and Family Clinic) in Norfolk between 1984 and 1991. The team's composition changed over that period. Core members for the greater part of that period included George Gawlinski, the late Dermot MacDonnell, Nick Irving, Chris Wood, Shiela Docking and Sue Grant. (Other members have been listed in the Acknowledgements.)

This section opens with Chapter 1 (Three stages in the development of an integrative approach to working with families) which shows how the approach to formulating systemic problems described in the *Positive Practice* textbook (Carr, 1995) evolved and the relevance of formulation model presented in the textbook to management of child protection cases. Initially there was an exclusive focus on current repetitive behaviour patterns in the here-and-now. Later, account was taken of these patterns and related belief systems which prevented participants from breaking out of these rigid cycles of interaction. In the third and most recent stage in the evolution of positive practice, historical and contextual risk factors that underpin constraining belief systems and rigid problem maintaining interaction cycles have been incorporated into our conceptual framework in the form of a three column formulation model. This most recent approach to formulation, unlike its two predecessors, allows important risk factors which have a bearing on statutory case management to be taken into account in assessment and intervention in cases where child protection is a central concern.

Five key issues which compromise the effectiveness of treatment programmes for families in which child abuse is a central concern are summarized in Chapter 2 (Child abuse, rehabilitation and poverty: A quintet of Problems). These are the problems associated with denial of abuse; non-co-operation with treatment plans; non-conformity with the role of a client in treatment; confusion about professionals roles in offering statutory control or therapeutic support; and counter-transference reactions to families where child abuse has occurred. Finally, the way in which poverty potentiates the impact of these problems is explored.

During the mid-1980's it was becoming increasingly difficult to reconcile the concept of neutrality in systemic practice (particularly as articulated by the Milan school) with the reality of child abuse and family violence. It became clear to me that with families where violence is a central concern, a framework for conceptualizing the issue of power and influence within family systems and within systems comprising families and professionals was required. Such a framework is present in Chapter 3 (Power and influence in systemic consultation).

In many of the child protection cases with which I was involved, I found that strong differences of opinion occurred among colleagues in the wider professional system. In Chapter 4 (Countertransference reactions to families where child abuse has occurred) a preliminary attempt to explain these intense emotional reactions and related behaviour patterns is offered.

The complexity of the challenging cases which were referred to the Thurlow House team and the limited resources available to us, forced us to develop a highly systematic approach to evaluating these families so that realistic long term plans could be made. Chapter 5 (Thurlow House Assessment Programme for Families with Physically Abused Children) offers a description of the programme that the team at Thurlow House developed for evaluating families where violence towards children had occurred.

REFERENCES
Carr, A. (1995). *Positive Practice: A Step-By-Step Guide to Family Therapy.* Reading: Harwood.

CHAPTER 1

THREE STAGES IN THE DEVELOPMENT OF A BRIEF INTEGRATIVE APPROACH TO CLINICAL WORK WITH FAMILIES

ABSTRACT

Three phases are identified in the development of brief integrative approach to consultation with families who require help with child-focused psychosocial difficulties in this paper. In the first phase, therapy focused on uncovering recursive patterns of interaction around problems and coaching family members in ways of changing these problem-maintaining patterns. In the second phase, the focus was widened to included both the patterns of interaction around problems and the belief-systems and scripts which prevented some families from benefiting from simple coaching as a way of disrupting problem maintaining interaction patterns. During this phase a variety of methods to help families develop less constraining belief systems were used. Cases where child protection was the central issues led to the inclusion of risk factors in the framework in its third phase of development. Risk factors that predispose family members to hold constraining beliefs and participate in problems maintaining interaction patterns were incorporated into the framework for conceptualizing family problems and methods for managing risk factors were included in therapeutic packages. In addition, the process of engagement, assessment, therapy and disengagement was conceptualized as a recursive stage-based process, with particular tasks associated with each stage. This development arose from therapeutic failures arising out of problems with the contracting process.

HISTORY OF POSITIVE PRACTICE

Positive Practice, a brief integrative approach to consultation with families who require help with child-focused psychosocial difficulties, evolved over 15 years of clinical work in North America, the UK and Ireland in a wide variety of clinical contexts with a number of multidisciplinary teams. It was crystallized while working in the UK in an NHS outpatient clinic for child-focused problems in the 1980's. Most of our work there was with multiproblem families whose problems occurred in multiple contexts and who were involved with multiple agencies. The intention was to develop an approach that was suitable for most referrals, effective, brief and explicit so others could be easily trained to use the model.

THE EARLY PERIOD. TRACKING EPISODES AND COACHING

In the early period, clinical practice involved simply tracking episodes of problem occurrence and coaching family members in how to break patterns of interaction around presenting problems. In the assessment phase of consultation most inquires would focus on clarifying the pattern of interaction around the presenting problem. Here are some typical questions from this phase.

Figure 1.1. Behaviour pattern around a problem

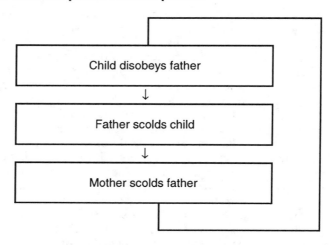

- *Imagine we were watching a video of what happened last time the problem occurred. Tell me in detail what we would see?*
- *Imagine the problem is happening right now and I am blind. Tell*

> me everything that is going on before the problem during the
> problem and after the problem. What is everyone in the family
> doing?
> • Imagine a typical day where the problem occurs. Describe it to me
> from the time everyone gets up in the morning?

Of course family members typically disagreed about the exact nature of
an episode of the problem and much time was spent carefully cross
checking with all family members until a consensus was reached on
what an episode of the problem looked like. Once such an agreement
was reached, therapy would focus on coaching parents in child
management skills or helping parents to develop child management
plans and monitoring their progress in implementing these. For
example, parents who disagreed about child management would be
coached to agree on a particular strategy for managing a problem or to
agree-to-disagree and take turns in applying their own particular
solution to the problem. Figure 1.1 shows a simplified episode of
problem maintaining behaviour. In this example, the parents would be
coached in how to agree to implement a child management programme.
Figure 1.2 summarises the main features of the approach to clinical
practice used during this first phase of development.

This approach to practice drew ideas and practices from
structural (Colapinto, 1991), strategic (Madanes, 1991), MRI (Segal,
1991), brief therapy (Cade & Hudson-O'Hanlon, 1993) and behavioural
(Falloon, 1991) models of family therapy. Central to this style of
practice was the idea that with detailed interviewing problems could be
clearly defined. A related idea was that, by tracking a behavioural
sequence in an interview a pattern of interaction around a clearly
defined problem could be constructed. For each person participating in
the pattern the costs and benefits of participation could be identified.
Such patterns might be characterized by relationship patterns that could
be described as symmetrical or complementary; enmeshed or
disengaged; and rigid or flexible. These patterns might also entail
triangulation, coercive patterns of mutual negative reinforcement and
attempted solutions that maintained the problems they aimed to solve.
Interventions, during this early stage of the development aimed to
disrupt the pattern of interaction around the presenting problem. They
included, symptom monitoring, skill development, role changing and
exception amplifying. While often these interventions were successful,
sometimes there were problems with families not carrying out
homework assignments. In response to these therapeutic failures
guidelines for goal setting (Carr, 1993) and inviting family members to
undertake tasks (Carr, 1990a) were developed. This approach was
found to be useful for solving common child-management problems

like disobedience, fighting, early teenage drug problems, homework-related problems, toileting difficulties, childhood sleep problems and unusual syndromes like elective mutism (Carr et al, 1989a).

Figure 1. 2. Summary of ideas and practice during early period of positive practice

Consultation process	• Track pattern around problem • Coach family in new behaviours
Schools	• Structural • Strategic • MRI • Brief Therapy • Behavioural approaches
Constructs	• Clear problem definition • Pattern of interaction around problem • Costs and benefits for each person participating in the pattern • Symmetrical and complementary relationship patterns • Enmeshment and disengagement • Rigidity & flexibility • Triangulation • Coercive patterns of mutual negative reinforcement • Solutions that are problems
Interventions	• Symptom-monitoring • Skill-development • Role-changing • Exception-amplifying
Application	• Applicable to families and wider problem-systems with chaotic roles and routines that prevent problem resolution, but where belief systems underpinning these roles and routines are not entrenched. • Useful with conduct problems, toileting and sleep problems

THE MIDDLE PERIOD. EXPLORING BELIEF SYSTEMS
Even with refinements in task-giving and goal-setting, the approach
used in the early period often did not work for a distinct group of
families. This was because family members stayed stuck in patterns of
interaction due to beliefs that they held about problems and solutions,
child development or family relationships. For example, parents,
adolescents and professionals dealing with problems associated with
school non-attendance and somatic symptoms often had great difficulty
resolving problems because one faction would define the problem as a
discipline issue. Another faction would define the problem as a health
issue. These differing belief systems locked members of the problem-
system into rigid problem-maintaining patterns of interaction. Figure
1.3 shows how the factions involved in a case of school non-attendance
and recurrent-abdominal-pain were trapped in a problem-maintaining
pattern of interaction by their belief systems. When attempts were made
to coach such families out of their rigid patterns of interaction, on many
occasions following progress, relapses would occur because the belief
systems that underpinned the problem-maintaining patterns of
interaction had not been addressed.

During this middle-stage of development, the clinical approach
to practice involved tracking patterns of interaction around the
presenting problem and then identifying beliefs that locked members of
the problem-system into these rigid problem-maintaining roles. Therapy
focused on helping members of the problem-system to evolve less
constraining belief systems that would allow them to solve the problem
rather than maintain it. While coaching was still used, most of the
emphasis was on changing belief systems.

A distinct therapeutic technique was developed for identifying
belief systems and scripts that prevented problem resolution. Initially
the therapist would help family members identify the problem and the
pattern of interaction around it. This would be followed by inquires
about beliefs concerning problems and solutions. Here are some
common questions used at this stage to pinpoint deeply held beliefs
about problems and solutions.

- *Imagine the everyone in the family was sorting out this problem
  your way. What would I see them doing ?*
- *Guess what your husband (or wife or daughter or son) would say
  the solution is and what would you see if everyone tried to sort it
  out their way?*
- *What advice would your mother (or father or granny or grandad)
  give you if they were here and doing their best to help you solve
  this problem?*

Figure 1.3. A pattern of behaviour around problem and related belief systems

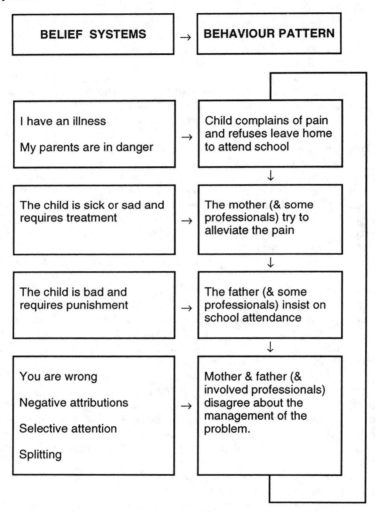

Once all family members had articulated their beliefs about problems and solutions, these would be summarized and their differences emphasised. For example, in the case set out in Figure 1.3, the mother viewed the child's recurrent abdominal pain and school non-attendance as a reflection of illness and so the appropriate solution in her view was to diagnose and treat the underlying illness. The father, on the other hand, viewed the problem as one of disobedience and saws the imposition of strict discipline as the solution. Once conflicting belief systems have been articulated, each is explored with each family member describing their fantasies about the awful things which would happen if everyone tried to solve the problem using their belief system as the guiding framework. Inquires at this stage may take the following forms.

- *What would prevent you (or your mother or your father or your husband or your wife) from following through and sorting the problem out your way?*
- *What is the awful thing that might happen if everyone tried to do it your way?*
- *What is the awful thing that would happen if you tried to do it your way and other family members didn't go along with you?*
- *What beliefs about being a parent (or husband or wife or son or daughter) prevent you from trying to sort the problem out your way?*

Usually these types of questions bring forth beliefs centring on the themes of conflict, aggression, self-harm, unpredictability, abandonment and engulfment. An exploration of these themes in many cases provided much new information and offered fertile ground from which the therapist and family may constructed a new and more useful framing of the problem that pointed to a solution that did not entail catastrophic consequences. For example in the case presented in Figure 1.3, the child's abdominal pains and non-attendance were framed as a reaction to parental disagreement about the meaning and significance of the problem and the lack of a consensus about how to manage it which in turn arose from parents concerns not to undermine the quite different interpretations that each parent held of the problem. Such reframings and therapeutic dialogue between family members about their implications in many instances led to sufficient change in family members' belief systems for problem resolution to occur. In other instances, parents required coaching interventions also.

The main features of this approach to practice are set out in Figure 1.4. This approach is appropriate to cases where the family is over-organized and have rigid belief systems. It drew on ideas from the Milan schools of family therapy (Campbell et al, 1991), psychodynamic therapy (Malan, 1979), cognitive therapy (Beck, 1976), constructivist psychotherapy (Kelly, 1955) and social constructionism (Pearce, 1994). In attempting to map out family belief-systems we used constructs such as schemas, scripts, personal and family construct systems, hierarchically organized belief determining contexts, attributional styles and defense mechanisms.

Figure 1.4. Ideas and practices used during the middle period

Consultation process	• Track pattern around problem • Identify constraining belief systems • Change constraining beliefs
Schools	• Milan schools of family therapy • Psychodynamic therapy • Cognitive therapy • Constructivism • Social constructionism
Constructs	• Belief systems • Schemas and scripts • Attributional styles • Cognitive distortions • Defense mechanisms • Personal and family construct systems • Hierarchically organized belief determining contexts
Interventions	• Circular questioning • Belief exploration tasks • Rituals • Paradoxical tasks
Application	• Applicable to families and wider problem-systems where entrenched belief systems underpin rigid problem maintaining interaction patterns • Useful with school refusal and somatization problems

Interventions included circular questioning, belief-exploration tasks, rituals, positive connotation and defiance based paradoxical prescriptions.

For many cases that did not respond to the coaching approach described earlier, this approach, which focused on belief systems as well as patterns of interaction was effective. It appeared to be useful in cases where the pattern of interaction around the problem was maintained by entrenched beliefs. Common problems that responded to this approach were chronic school refusal, somatization problems and childhood anorexia (e.g. Carr et al 1989b).

THE LATER PERIOD: MANAGING RISK

The model went through a final stage of evolution and it is this that is described in the text Positive Practice (Carr, 1995a). Cases where suicide risk, child protection risks, physical disability or learning difficulties are present, pose a problem for the approaches to practice outlined so far because they have no place in them for risk factors. A good model for family therapy practice must include some method for incorporating risk factors into it and for managing risk and abuses of power in an ethically responsible way (Carr, 1991). A three column formulation taking account of risk factors is presented in Figure 1.5. In the right hand column, the pattern of interaction around the problem of child abuse is set out. In the left hand column, risk factors that predispose the mother, the father and the child to participating in this pattern are presented. In the central column, the belief systems that link the predisposing risk factors to the problem-maintaining behaviour patterns are noted. This formulation suggests certain components that might be included in a multisystemic intervention package. In this case of physical child abuse, the overall case management plan might involve coaching the parents in the management of bouts of excessive crying on the part of the child; exploring maternal beliefs about the baby's episodes of crying and relating these to her early attachment experiences; increasing social support for the mother; and referring the father for treatment of his alcohol problem.

This formulation is an example of the types of formulations that can be constructed using the three column model set out in Figure 1.6 (Carr, 1990). Various categories of predisposing risk factors are listed in the left column. Constructs from various schools of family therapy that are useful in describing problem maintaining interaction patterns are listed in the right hand column. Constructs that are useful for describing belief systems that link risk factors to patterns of interaction around problems are listed n the middle column. Of course these three lists are not exhaustive. However they offer clinicians, particularly trainee clinicians, a cognitively economical way of categorizing important constructs that may be used in developing formulations for particular cases such as that formulated in Figure 1.5.

Clinical practice using this approach involves co-constructing such a formulation with members of the problem-system and then working to resolve the problem by coaching, exploring belief systems

Figure 1. 5. A three column formulation linking risk factors to a behaviour pattern and identifying mediating belief systems

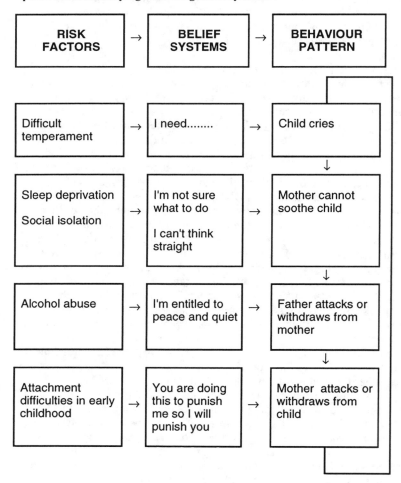

and managing risk factors. Detailed exploration of socialization histories of family members using genograms and detailed developmental history reconstruction are routine ways of identifying certain historical risk factors. Inquires about current living and working arrangements, observations of clients home settings and interviews with member of the wider professional network involved with the family allow for contemporary risk factors such as isolation, crowding, work related stresses and so forth to be assessed. Useful categories of interventions for risk management include stress reduction; increasing social support; networking with other professionals; co-ordinating service delivery; and providing individual therapy focusing on processing of stressful early and recent life events. While some of these interventions may seem to be non-systemic or linear, they are conceptualized as targeting particular aspects of the problem-system as mapped out in a three column formulation. That is, they are linear interventions offered within the context of a systemic conceptualization. The three column formulation model allows therapists to routinely integrate conceptual ideas and empirical findings from the literature into their daily practice. Most of the ideas on risk factors that we have used in Positive Practice have been drawn from developmental psychopathology (e.g., Rutter, Taylor and Hersov, 1994), the child protection literature (e.g., Cicchetti & Carlson, 1989), and health psychology (e.g., Sarafino, 1994).

THE CENTRALITY OF THE CONSULTATION CONTRACT AND STAGES OF THE CONSULTATION PROCESS
So far, the consultation process has been described as one where clients are willing and eager to co-operate with the process of mapping out their problems and then working to change them. This is not always the case. An analysis of a series of therapeutic failures clearly showed that problems with the contracting process were common in many therapeutic failures (Carr, 1990c). For example, in cases of school-based conduct problems or early childhood difficulties, the customer for therapy is the teacher or the social worker not a family member. Difficulties arise when therapists proceed on the assumption family members want to form a therapeutic contract. A second difficulty related to contracting is that of resistance. This is where ambivalence about the contract between the therapist and the family occurs during the process of therapy. For example, parents may have difficulty following through on a child management plan (Carr, 1995b). A third difficulty related to contracting arises where a relapse in the presenting problem occurs because of another unresolved problem. For example, a couple who have successfully resolved a child-focused problem may relapse because of unresolved marital problems.

In Positive Practice all of these difficulties are delt with by conceptualizing the consultation process as a series of stages and stipulating that the tasks associated with each stage must be completed before progressing to the next stage if therapeutic failure is to be avoided.

Figure 1.6. Three column formulation model

PREDISPOSING FACTORS	BELIEF SYSTEMS	BEHAVIOUR PATTERN
• Remote & recent stressful life events (e.g. bereavement, social isolation; crowding) • Membership of stressful social systems outside the family (e.g. work) • Debilitating somatic states (e.g. diabetes) • Personality traits & abilities (e.g. low IQ, impulsivity) • Genetic vulnerabilities (e.g. family history of mood disorders)	**Beliefs systems** • Personal, familial and cultural schemas, scripts and construct systems containing • Beliefs about problems and solutions • Beliefs about parenting and family relationships **Styles of information processing** • Attributional styles • Cognitive distortions • Defense mechanisms	• Clear problem definition • Pattern of interaction around problem • Costs and benefits for each person participating in the pattern • Symmetrical and complementary relationship patterns • Enmeshment and disengagement • Rigidity & flexibility • Triangulation • Coercive patterns of mutual negative reinforcement • Solutions that are problems

So before a family assessment, a network analysis must be conducted to identify the customer for therapy and other members of the problem system, so that a decision can be made about who to invite to the first meeting. A preliminary set of hypotheses must also be drawn up to decide what lines of inquire to follow in the preliminary consultation. Failure to complete these tasks may lead to non-attendance problems or confusion about what areas to focus on in the preliminary consultation. Families must contract for assessment and when this phase of the consultation process is complete, the formulation must be explained sufficiently so that a rationale for therapeutic goals and a contract for a number of therapy sessions offered. If therapists attempt to progress from assessment to therapy without making a contract, difficulties may occur when ambivalence arises about aspects of mid-therapy tasks and processes. In the final sessions of an episode of therapy, failure to deal with relapse management and to clarify how further episodes of consultation may be set up can lead to long term problems. For example relapses may lead families to sink once more into problem-maintaining patterns which engender helplessness and hopelessness. The consultation process in Positive Practice is conceptualized as the recursive loop set out in Figure 1.7, and the relationship between the therapist and the client may involve one or more cycles of this loop. That is, one or more episodes of therapy.

Episodes of consultation are usually brief involving between five and ten sessions of therapy. Therapeutic relationships may be ongoing over years and involve a series of episodes. Thus, while Positive Practice is premised on a brief approach to therapy, it may be used with cases that require both short and long-term intervention. While it appears to place much emphasis only on the technical aspects of the therapeutic process, there is a recognition of the centrality of the therapeutic relationship to the process of therapy. By placing the therapist into a map of the therapeutic process (in Figure 1.7), Positive Practice has evolved from an approach based on ideas drawn largely form first order cybernetics in the early phase to one that holds much in common with second-order approaches. Finally, there is an acceptance that formulations used within Positive Practice are no more than social constructions evolved by the clinician and the family, and the primary criterion for selecting one formulation over another is how useful it is in helping families solve problems (Pearce, 1994).

DISCUSSION

The approach to practice, the evolution of which is described in this paper is not intended to represent yet another new school of family therapy. Rather it is part of the current integrationist trend which is sweeping the fields of psychotherapy and family therapy in both the US (Norcross & Goldfried, 1992; Sprenkle & Bischof, 1994; Breunlin, 1992; Pinsof, 1994) and the UK (Dryden, 1992; Carpenter & Treacher, 1993).

Figure 1.7. Stages of the consultation process

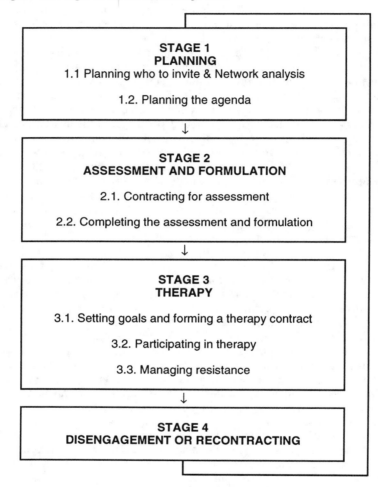

It is quite distinct from eclectic approaches to the practice of psychotherapy or family therapy which offer no clear rationale for inclusion of new ideas and techniques or of selecting between specific ideas or techniques under specific circumstances.

Positive Practice offers a useful 'first framework' for novice clinicians. At University College Dublin, our clinical psychology trainees find that the highly structured unifying framework of Positive Practice enhances clinical confidence and competence. The confused eclecticism that arises from exposure to multiple models without any unifying framework is avoided.

While, the approach to practice described in this paper was developed explicitly for use in cases referred for child-focused problems, it may probably be used for a wide variety of cases. Recently, I have been using a version of the model for working with individual adults and couples facing midlife dilemmas. Finally, an empirical evaluation of this approach is currently being planned.

REFERENCES

Beck, A. (1976). *Cognitive Therapy and the Emotional Disorders.* New York: International Universities Press

Breunlin, D. D., Schwartz, R. & MacKune-Karrer, B. (1992). *Meta frameworks Transcending the Models of Family Therapy.* San Francisco: Jossey-Bass.

Cade, B. & Hudson O'Hanlon, B. (1993). *A Brief Guide to Brief Therapy.* New York: Norton

Campbell, D., Draper, R. and Crutchley, E. (1991). The Milan Systemic Approach to Family Therapy (pp. 325-362). In A. Gurman & D. Kniskern (eds.), *Handbook of Family Therapy . Volume 2.* New York: Brunner/Mazel.

Carpenter, J. and Treacher, A. (eds.). (1993). *Using Family Therapy in the 90s.* Oxford: Basil Blackwell.

Carr, A. & Afnan, S. (1989a). Concurrent individual and family therapy in a case of elective mutism. *Journal of Family Therapy 11:* 29-44.

Carr, A. MacDonnell, D., & Afnan, S. (1989b). Anorexia Nervosa: The treatment of a male case with combined behavioural and family therapy. *Journal of Family Therapy, 11:* 335-351.

Carr, A. (1990a). Giving directives effectively: The implications of research on compliance with doctor's orders for family therapy. *Human Systems: Journal of Systemic Consultation and Management 1:* 115-127.

Carr, A. (1990b) A formulation model for use in family therapy. *The Australian and New Zealand Journal of Family Therapy 11:* 85-92.

Carr, A. (1990c). Failure in family therapy: A catalogue of engagement mistakes. *Journal of Family Therapy 12:* 371-386.

Carr, A. (1991). Power and influence in systemic consultation. *Human Systems: Journal of Systemic Consultation and Management 2:* 15-30.

Carr, A. (1993). Systemic consultation and goal setting. *Human Systems :The Journal of Systemic Consultation and Management 4:* 49-59.

Carr, A. (1995a). *Positive Practice: A Step-by-Step-Guide to Family Therapy.* Reading: Harwood.

Carr, A. (1995b). Resistance, dilemmas and crises in family therapy: A framework for positive practice. *Journal of Family psychotherapy 6:* 29-42.

Cicchetti, D. & Carlson, V. (1989). *Child Maltreatment.* Cambridge: Cambridge University Press.

Colapinto, J. (1991). Structural Family Therapy (pp. 417-443). In A. Gurman & D. Kniskern (eds.), *Handbook of Family Therapy . Volume 2.* New York:

Brunner/Mazel.

Dryden, W. (ed.). (1992). *Integrative and eclectic Therapy - A Handbook.* Buckingham: O.U.

Falloon, I. (1991). Behavioural Family Therapy (pp. 65-94). In A. Gurman & D. Kniskern (eds.), *Handbook of Family Therapy . Volume 2.* New York: Brunner/Mazel.

Fowler, H. & Fowler, F. (1964).*The Concise Oxford Dictionary. Oxford:* Clarendon.

Kelly, G. (1955). *The Psychology of Personal Constructs.* New York: Norton.

Madanes, C. (1991). Strategic Family Therapy (pp. 396-416) In A. Gurman & D. Kniskern (eds.), *Handbook of Family Therapy . Volume 2.* New York: Brunner/Mazel.

Malan, D. (1979). *Individual Psychotherapy and the Science of Psychodynamics.* London: Butterworths.

Norcross, J. & Goldfried, M. (eds.). (1992). *Handbook of Psychotherapy Integration.* New York: Basic Books.

Pearce, B. (1994). *Interpersonal Communication: Making Social Worlds.* New York: HarperCollins.

Pinsof, W. (1994). An overview of integrative problem centred therapy: A synthesis of family and individual psychotherapies. *Journal of Family Therapy 16:* 103-120

Rutter, E. Taylor & L. Hersov (eds.). (1994).*Child and Adolescent Psychiatry: Modern Approaches (Third edition).* Oxford: Blackwell.

Sarafino, E. (1994). *Health Psychology. Biopsychosocial Interactions. (Second edition.)* New York: Wiley.

Segal, L. (1991). Brief Therapy: The MRI approach (pp. 171-199). In A. Gurman & D. Kniskern (eds.), *Handbook of Family Therapy . Volume 2.* New York: Brunner/Mazel.

Sprenkle, D. & Bischof, G. (1994). Contemporary family therapy in the United States. *Journal of Family Therapy 16 :* 5-23.

CHAPTER 2

REHABILITATION, CHILD ABUSE AND POVERTY: A QUINTET OF PROBLEMS ENTAILED BY THE DOMINANT DISCOURSE

ABSTRACT
Available empirical evidence shows that rehabilitation programmes for families at risk for child abuse do not prevent further abuse in the majority of cases. In this paper five problems that may account for this are discussed. These are the problems of denial, co-operation, conformity, role confusion and countertransference. It is argued that this quintet of problems is partially rooted in the way in which risk and rehabilitation have been socially constructed within the dominant discourse concerning child protection. Finally, the way in which poverty potentiates the impact of these problems is explored.

THE ROAD TO REHABILITATION
In Ireland, the UK and the US, the road to rehabilitation, following child abuse is clearly charted and socially constructed as follows. Where physical or sexual child abuse has occurred and statutory agents are satisfied that the injuries or testimony of the child or other family members warrant a designation of child abuse, the statutory agent is required by the state to take steps to reduce the risk of further abuse occurring. The two most common strategies are to arrange for the child to be placed in care or to require the alleged abuser to leave the household of the abused child.

Once the immediate risk of re-abuse has been dealt with through one of these strategies, statutory agents are then required to arrange for the risks of re-abuse within the child's family to be reduced if possible. This will enable the child to live with both parents again without risk of further abuse. Usually the process of risk reduction involves the parents and the child engaging in some form of psycho-social consultation with an expert mental health professional. Often the mental health professional is selected by the statutory agent.

THE AIM OF CHILD PROTECTION SYSTEMS

Within this dominant discourse concerning child abuse, the primary aim of child protection systems is to minimize harm to children. Harm, in this context, includes both short term difficulties and long term sequalae. It also refers to a wide variety of well documented difficulties in the physical, psychological, familial and broader social domains that result from the occurrence of child abuse. Risk factors for the occurrence of physical and sexual child abuse have been clearly established by thorough and rigorous research conducted within a positivist framework. These have been integrated into a number of multifactorial systemic models. These models and the research on which they are based inform the practice of many professionals working with families at risk (Cicchetti & Carlson, 1989). In particular, they inform the way in which rehabilitation programmes for families at risk are conducted. According to this body of knowledge, risks may be reduced by giving families (1) practical help with housing and household management (2) social help with child care or child management and (3) counselling or psychosocial consultations to help with intrapsychic or interpersonal difficulties. Different combinations of these interventions are offered depending upon the risk factors present in any particular case.

REHABILITATION DOESN'T WORK

Available evidence suggests that the majority of family rehabilitation programmes developed as part of child protection systems are ineffective in reducing risk and injury (Cohn & Daro, 1987). In a major review of treatment studies involving over 3000 families, it was found that between 20% and 87% of children who suffered physical abuse were re-abused following treatment and for sexual abuse re-abuse occurred in 16% -38% of cases (Jones, 1987). These studies spanned more than a decade and included projects on both sides of the Atlantic.

In this essay some of the reasons for this are explored. These explorations are based on my reading of the mainstream child protection literature and clinical observations made over a seven year period (1984-1991). During this time I was working as part of a multidisciplinary team offering assessment and rehabilitation services to families where child abuse had occurred. The team operated within an NHS outpatient Child & Family Clinic. Accounts of this work have been described elsewhere (Carr, 1989, 1990;1991; 1994; Gawlinski, Carr et al., 1988; Irving, Carr et al, 1988;)

Five problems seem to me to be entailed by rehabilitation programmes informed by the dominant discourse which has evolved around child protection. I have termed these the problems of denial, co-operation, conformity, role confusion and countertransference. These problems are elaborated below. All five problems are potentiated by poverty. More specifically they are exacerbated by the social exclusion, colonzation and marginalization entailed by poverty. Members of poor families are excluded from participation in many valued social processes and institutions. Through accepting assistance within the context of the welfare state they are colonized and their autonomy is eroded. With eroded autonomy and without participation in important social process and institutions they become marginalized. What follows is an exploration of the impact of poverty and these associated processes on a quintet of problems which characterize practice in the child protection field.

THE PROBLEM OF DENIAL

A core requirement for the viability of rehabilitation programmes, according to statutory agents, is that abusers must accept responsibility for abuse. Two other requirements are that parents accept that the way their family life is organized poses a risk to their child and that they are responsible for the risk and its reduction. Parents who cannot accept these responsibilities are unsuitable for rehabilitation. In short, for rehabilitation to work, statutory agents must be satisfied that parents are not locked into a *process of denial.*

The argument within the dominant discourse is that by giving up denial the abuser is agreeing to accept a new self-definition: that of an abuser. Once this problem-saturated identity (White, 1993) has been accepted, then rehabilitation can proceed.

For many abuser's the costs of giving up the process of denial are very high. It lead's inevitably to punishment for a criminal offence. Rehabilitation is rarely an alternative to punishment. (Although there are exceptions to this, for example Giaretto, 1982). At a broader cultural level, giving up the process of denial leads to stigmatization and ostracization rather than acceptance and understanding. Within the family, giving up the process of denial has negative consequences for abusers because they face the possibility of rejection, anger and lack of forgiveness from other family members. At personal level, giving up the process of denial and jettisoning the rationalizations that allow the abuser to justify his or her violence, creates the risk of extreme self-criticism. This lack of self-acceptance may lead to personal disintegration.

For victims of abuse, when the abuser gives up the process of denial there are many benefits. The abuse stops and there is a sense of safety. However, there are many hidden costs. The victim has to grapple with conflicting feelings of anger and loyalty towards the abuser and towards those family members who denied the abuse also.

Giving up the process of denial also has negative consequences for family members uninvolved in the abuse. They must accept that one of their kin whom they trusted is capable of betrayal and violence and that they have failed to recognized this or to protect the victimized child. They must also deal with suspicions that the victimized child provoked that parent into the abuse and that the victim has been tarnished by the experience. These issues give rise to conflicting feelings of anger and loyalty towards the abuser and the abused child along with feelings of personal guilt.

The benefits of giving up the process of denial are the possibility of public and familial forgiveness and personal atonement. However, the route from giving up the process of denial to these benefits is rarely clear and the way in which the abuser can move to a position where he or she is a person with a problem rather than a problem-person within the family and society is usually obscure.

From this analysis it is obvious that the costs of giving up the process of denial are high and the benefits are unclearly defined. When child abuse occurs within a poor family the process of denial is strengthened by an awareness that giving up this process will lead to further social exclusion and marginalization for the family as a whole, but particularly for the abusing parent. There is also an awareness that the level of colonization will increase if the process of denial is given up and rehabilitation embarked upon.

The problem of denial, in my view, is a major factor contributing to the failure of rehabilitation programmes. A discussion of the reasons why child abuse is constructed in such a way as to facilitate the denial process will be reserved for the final section of this paper.

THE PROBLEM OF CO-OPERATION

For a rehabilitation programme to be viable, a second requirement is that the parents and/or the child co-operate with the statutory agents by arranging for risk reduction.

Within the dominant discourse, the argument is that once the parents have given up the process of denial, they will want to co-operate with statutory agents in reducing the risk of child abuse. There is also an assumption that co-operation will be possible within the context of a statutory framework such as a care order or wardship.

However, there are problems with this social-construction of co-operation. Co-operation typically requires trust on both sides. The relationship between statutory agents and parents who have had their authority usurped by the state is based on mis-trust. The state does not trust the parents to meet the child's needs and the parents do not trust the state who have disintegrated their family. Mis-trust is the core of the problem of co-operation.

Because of their marginalized position, members of poor families are more likely to be mistrustful of professionals who they construe as powerful contributors to their marginalized position. This mistrust makes co-operation in rehabilitation problematic.

Parents and children may act as if they trust statutory agents so that they may become reunited. However, the risk of abuse may remain. The problem of co-operation is a second factor contributing to the failure of rehabilitation programmes.

THE PROBLEM OF CONFORMITY
A third requirement of rehabilitation programmes is that the parents and/or the child demonstrate that the strategy for risk reduction that they have chosen conforms to prevailing ideas about how best risks may be reduced. It has already been mentioned that within the dominant discourse it is accepted that the risks of child abused may be reduced by offering families practical help with household management; social help with child management; and psychosocial therapy for intrapsychic and interpersonal difficulties.

Usually families have little difficulty conforming when they are required to accept practical help or social assistance with child care. Many have considerable difficulty co-operating with counselling and various forms of therapy. This is in part a skills problem and in part a motivational problem. Often parents of families where child abuse has occurred have not got the skills to benefit from office based talking therapies. It is also difficult for anyone to benefit from counselling or therapy when they are threatened with the continued disintegration of their family if they refuse to conform.

Verbal skill-deficits and coercion into verbal psychotherapy are two faces of the problem of conformity. The assumption within the dominant discourse is that psychotherapy is accessible to people regardless of their verbal facility and that a coercive context does not compromise markedly the effectiveness of such interventions. In my view, these assumptions are problematic and may account in part for the failure of rehabilitation programmes.

Verbally based psychotherapy and counselling has been shown to be relatively inaccessible to people who live in a context characterized by poverty (Lorion, 1978). Thus families who live in such contexts may have particular difficulty conforming with rehabilitation programmes that entail such therapy. Furthermore, conforming to the requirement of mandatory therapy may be particularly problematic for families living in poverty since it reflects further colonization. It is not surprising that such families attend therapy erratically and often with an agenda that differs from that of the treatment team. Typically, frustrated rehabilitation teams allude to these conformity problems by describing the family as *manipulative* or *resistant*.

THE PROBLEM OF ROLE CONFUSION

Within the dominant discourse, the terms *monitoring* and *support* are often mentioned as the dual function of social workers in child care cases. There is an assumption that families at risk may be monitored by statutory social workers and also supported or rehabilitated by them or their closely aligned colleagues in the health service.

Our own clinical experience shows that most families have considerable difficulty in accepting support or rehabilitative consultation from professionals whom they also construe as fulfilling a statutory risk monitoring role. Indeed, parents and children in multi-problem families may have difficulty drawing a distinction between the roles of statutory agent and therapeutic agent. Both are seen as fulfilling a statutory monitoring role. In the minds of such family members the coalitions between the statutory agents and therapeutic agencies may appear far stronger than those between the therapeutic agencies and themselves. In the face of such role-confusion, families have difficulties participating in rehabilitation programmes.

Families socially excluded and marginalized by poverty are uniquely prone to the problem of role confusion. Because they are on the periphery of society, the main distinction they make is between families like themselves who are marginalized and powerless on the one hand and powerful professionals from official agencies on the other. With this as the superordinate distinction, often the subordinate distinction between the roles of statutory agent and therapeutic agent is not drawn (Crowther et al., 1990).

THE PROBLEM OF COUNTERTRANSFERENCE

A major problem faced by professionals and non-professionals in helping families reduce risk is retaining a non-aligned and relatively neutral position with respect to each member of the family. Workers involved in the rehabilitation of child abuse find themselves experiencing extremely strong and disturbing sets of emotions. Within the literature on child protection practice these experiences have been referred to as countertransference reactions (Carr, 1989)[1].

In cases of physical child abuse the two commonest countertransference reactions are *rescuing the child* and *rescuing the parents.* In the former reaction, the urge is to protect the child at all costs and to deny any loyalty that the child may have to the parents or any competence or potential for therapeutic change on the part of the parents. In the latter reaction the urge is to protect the parents from criticism raised by other professionals and to deny any parental shortcomings. Professionals within the same system adopting these two countertransference reactions tend to polarise and have difficulty co-operating with each other and the family with whom they are working.

In cases of intrafamilial child sexual abuse *rescuing the father* is one common countertransference reaction. The other is *rescuing the mother and child while persecuting the father.* The first reaction leads therapists to deny evidence pointing to the father's culpability and to highlight the fathers strengths as a parent. The second reaction is associated with an urge to split the father off from the rest of the family and to deny any loyalties that other members may have to him. These two countertransference reactions are complimentary and professionals experiencing them may tend to polarise each other thus compromising their ability to work co-operatively in the service of the clients.

If therapists act out their countertransference reactions their emotionally driven aggressive or protective behaviour interferes with their capacity to help the families with which they work to change the way they organise their lives so as to reduce the risk of child abuse. The problem of countertransference is therefore yet another factor which accounts for the failure of rehabilitation programmes.

Child protection workers' countertransference reactions (Carr, 1989) to families where child abuse has occurred may be intensified when such families live in poverty. Abused children from poverty-stricken families may be construed by some child protection professionals as doubly victimized: victimized by poverty and victimized by the abusing parent. In these instances the intensity of these professional's countertransference reactions to the abuse (notably *rescuing the child* or *rescuing the mother and child and persecuting the father*) may be potentiated by the additional perceived victimization of the child through living in an impoverished family.

Parents who have abused their children or who are alleged to have done so may be construed by some child protection workers to be doubly victimised: victimized by poverty and then victimized for being a child abuser (which such professionals construe as an uncontrollable response to the constraints imposed by poverty.) The poverty of such families potentiates countertransference reactions (like *rescuing the parents* or *rescuing the father*) that such child protection professionals experience.

CONCLUDING COMMENTS

The five problems discussed in this paper are not trivial difficulties requiring technical solutions. Rather, they are serious difficulties that are rooted in they way child protection has been constructed within the dominant discourse.

With the problem of denial, it is clear that many parents who have abused their children would be prepared to give up the process of denial if ostracization was not inevitable. This leads us to question why, as a society, we need to ostracize people who abuse their children, particularly if they are impoverished?   One explanation for this ostracization rests on the process of projection. In our westernized culture we deny our own aggressive and destructive impulses and project them into abusers whom we then ostracize. This process of projection may be further facilitated if the abuser is already a member of a marginalized group such as the unemployed or the impoverished. This process of projection protects us from a more fundamental re-examination of the way in which we participate in the abuse of children on a daily basis. We do this, for example, by creating a judicial system which is fundamentally distrustful of children's testimony. We do it by propagating values that maintain a family ethos which permits violence and secrecy. For example in Ireland two common aphorisms are: *Children should be seen and not heard* and *Spare the rod and spoil the child.*   There is a paradox here that subserves the problem of denial. The state and its citizens will not give up the denial of their participation in the abuse of children, yet they expect identified child abusers to give up their denial before admission to a rehabilitation programme. If, as a society we took steps to acknowledge our own daily abuse of children and our need to examine and change this we would be less likely to see abusers as problem-people requiring ostracization and more likely to see them as people like ourselves with problems requiring help.

Of course their are factions within society and within our own mental health professions who have begun both personal and political re-examinations of their culpability in relation to child abuse. When such professionals find themselves working shoulder to shoulder with colleagues who have not embarked upon this process, existing countertransference reactions may be intensified and polarization may occur.

Underlying the problems of co-operation, conformity and role confusion is the idea that abusers (unlike ourselves) can be coerced into mandatory psychotherapy and that psychologically they are capable of forging intrapsychic and interpersonal changes within a climate of mistrust. In short, as a society we are construing people who abuse children, particularly those who live in poverty, as different from ourselves, as intrinsically mad or bad, and therefore subject to a different psychology than ourselves, a psychology that allows them to make therapeutic gains under coercion.

In this paper I have argued that the failure of child protection rehabilitation programmes may be due, in part, to the problems of denial, co-operation, conformity, role confusion and countertransference. These problems, which are potentiated by poverty, stem from us construing abusers as fundamentally different from ourselves. Similar arguments have been made by the Fifth Province Associates (Mc Carthy & Byrne, 1988; Byrne & McCarthy, 1988).

FOOTNOTES
1. Within the psychoanalytic tradition countertransference refers specifically to those aspects of therapists' emotional reactions to clients which replicate or resonate with their reactions to parental figures during infancy. However, the term is used within discussions of the doctor-patient relationship and in the child protection field in a broader way to refer to professionals' *overall* emotional responses to patients or clients. It is in this broadened sense that the term is used here and in our previous discussions of this issue (Carr,1989).

REFERENCES
Byrne, N. O'R. & McCarthy, I.C. (1988). Moving statutes: Re-questing ambivalence through ambiguous discourse. *Irish Journal of Psychology,* 173-182.

Carr, A. (1989), Countertransference reactions to families where child abuse has occurred. *Journal of Family Therapy,* 11, 87-97.

Carr, A. (1990). Failure in family therapy: A catalogue of engagement mistakes. *Journal of Family Therapy,* 12, 371-386.

Carr, A. (1991). Power and influence in systemic consultation. *Human Systems: Journal of Systemic Consultation and Management,* 2, 15-30.

Carr, A. (1994). *Positive Practice: A step-by-Step Guide to Family Therapy.* Berkshire. Harwood.

Cicchetti, D. & Carlson, V. (1989). *Child Maltreatment.* Cambridge: Cambridge University Press.

Cohn, A. & Daro, D. (1987). Is treatment too late: What ten years of evaluative research tells us. *Child Abuse & Neglect,* 11, 443-442.

Crowther, C., Dare., C. & Wilson, J. (1990). Why should we talk to you? You'll only tell the court? On being an informer and a family therapist. *Journal of Family Therapy,* 12, 105-122.

Gawlinski, G. Carr, A., MacDonnell, D., & Irving, N. (1988). Thurlow House Assessment Programme for Families with Physically Abused Children. *Practice,* 2(3), 208-220.

Giaretto, H,. (1982). *Integrated Treatment of Child Sexual Abuse.* Palo Alto: CA, Science and Behaviour.

Irving, N., Carr, A., Gawlinski, G., & MacDonnell, D. (1988).Thurlow House Child Abuse Programme: Residential family evaluation. British *Journal of Occupational Therapy,* 51, 116-119.

Jones, D. (1987). The untreatable family. *Child Abuse & Neglect,* 11, 409-420.
Lorion, , R. (1978). Research on psychotherapy and behaviour change with the disadvantaged. In S. L. Garfield and A. E. Bergin (Eds.). *Handbook of Psychotherapy and Behaviour Change.* New York. Wiley
McCarthy, I.C., & Byrne, N.O'R. (1988). Mis-taken love: Conversations on the problem of incest in an Irish context. *Family Process*, 27, 181-199.
White, M. (1993). Deconstruction and therapy. In S. Gilligan & R. Price (Eds.) *Therapeutic Conversations.* New York. Norton.

CHAPTER 3

POWER AND INFLUENCE IN SYSTEMS CONSULTATION

ABSTRACT

The disagreement between Haley and Bateson over the usefulness of the concept of power in accounting for problems in human systems is described. Seven propositions which address the main issues raised by the Haley-Bateson debate are then set out. Finally some clinical and ethical implications of these propositions are presented.

INTRODUCTION

The Haley-Bateson Disagreement. Controversy over the concept of power has characterized the development of systems consultation and family therapy from the earliest days (Dell, 1989; Fish, 1990; Hoffman, 1990; Simon, 1982). It may have begun with the division between Bateson and Haley during the Double-Bind Project (Bateson, 1976; Haley, 1976).

Haley's Position. Haley argued that all human relationships were characterized by attempts of one party to influence another (Haley, 1976a; Haley, 1976b; Simon, 1982). Humans invariably organize themselves into a hierarchy. Some power-struggles result in the emergence of symptoms, e.g. psychosis or intrafamilial violence. Therapists are influence experts who use their power to ameliorate symptoms. Therapy is a power struggle between the therapist and those aspects of the client-system which resist change. The therapist's job is to map out the power game surrounding the symptom and then develop strategy to influence the members of this game to behave differently. The responsibility for changing the client-system rests squarely on the shoulders of the therapist. The therapist may sometimes prescribe apparently paradoxical tasks in discharging this responsibility. Providing clients with an opportunity to develop insight into the game surrounding the symptom is not the responsibility of the therapist, although such insight may occur as a result of behavioural change. Therapists who do not take responsibility for ameliorating their clients symptoms through the use carefully selected influence strategies are viewed by from this perspective as being unethical, insofar as they are often ineffective helpers (Haley, 1976a, Chapter 8). Some avowedly non-strategic therapists use therapeutic style which does not involve conscious attempts at influencing clients. Such therapists believe that this style is an effective way of helping clients resolve presenting problems. In such situations, from Haley's perspective, the use of the non-directive style within sessions is paradoxically a strategic intervention since the style is adopted with the overall intention of influencing the family in the long term.

Bateson's Position. In contrast to Haley, Bateson argued that power was a myth (Bateson, 1972). He said: "The idea of power corrupts... Perhaps there is no such thing as unilateral power. The man in power depends on receiving information all the time from outside. He responds to this information just as much as he causes things to happen...It is an interaction and not a lineal situation." (1972, p. 486). It is not the case, argued Bateson, that the non-symptomatic members of a family exclusively and unilaterally influence and victimise the symptomatic member. The symptomatic member of a family also influences the non-symptomatic member. No one member of the client system can be held fully accountable for the symptom or problem. No one can be exclusively blamed. The notion of mutual influence holds for the therapeutic system also. For Bateson, a systemic model of therapy must view the therapist and family as members of a single therapeutic system in which the therapist influences the family and the family influence the therapist.

Therapists who endorse the myth of power and attempt to unilaterally influence their clients run the risk of harming their clients by coercing them into patterns of behaviour which reduce the flexibility, potentiality and complexity of their social ecosystem. The therapists job is to construct with clients, new and different ways of looking at the symptoms and the social context in which they are embedded. These new punctuations of the situation must be perceptibly different from the clients' original way of construing the symptom and its context. The new ways of looking at the problem situation provides clients with opportunities to choose alternative ways of dealing with the presenting problem or symptom. These new ways of handling the problem should not be prescribed by the therapist but should be chosen by the clients. Good therapy leads to solutions which entail the resolution of the presenting problem in a way that fits with the clients social ecosystem.

　　　　The Current Status of the debate. The power-debate, left unresolved by Haley and Bateson, continues to the present. For example, the split in the Milan Team may be viewed, in part, as a disagreement about power and influence in therapy. Selvini-Palazzoli's (1986) paper on dirty games is reminiscent of Haley's position. The constructivist position of Cecchin and Boscolo is distinctly Batesonian (Hoffman et al, 1989). Clinicians and researchers concerned primarily with problems that involve social inequality or physical violence often take up a position similar to Haley's. For example, both feminists (McKinnon and Miller, 1987) and child protection advocates (Will, 1989) have roundly criticized Batesonian ideology. They have argued that clinicians must include the concept of power and its abuse within their theories and prescribe methods for dealing with inequality and abuse of power in clinical practice. Batesonians have responded by insisting that clinicians must distinguish between contexts where therapy is appropriate and contexts where social control is called for. The therapist must then offer therapy or exercise statutory power depending upon the requirements of the case (Hoffman, 1985, p. 394). In clinical practice, the criteria by which such distinctions can be made usually entail reference to concepts such as risk, dangerousness, capacity for self-protection or illness which fall outside of Batesonian theory. Insofar as this is the case, a Batesonian approach to systems consultation falls short of the needs of both practitioners and clients.

SEVEN PROPOSITIONS
The issues raised by the power debate permeate daily clinical practice and research. In the remainder of this essay a number of propositions are presented which offer a solution to some of these issues.

　　　　1. Actions have the power to influence others, in part, because of their meaning. The outcome of an attempt to exert power over another person and influence that person to act in a particular way may be due to the physical properties of the act of influence, or to the meaning of this act, or both. For example, if Tim hits Sue and she becomes unconscious, it is the physical properties of Tim's action that have influenced Sue to become unconscious. If, on the other hand, Tim threatens to hit Sue unless she has sex with him and she complies with Tim's wishes, then it is the meaning of Tim's actions that influence Sue to comply. The meaning which Tim's threats have for the couple will be determined by the social context within which they occur. This social context may have multiple levels including the meaning of the individual words; the meaning of the episode as one of a series of episodes; the meaning of the episode within the context of Sue and Tim's life scripts; and the significance of the episode *vis-a-vis* the couple's relationship, their family myths and the overall culture in which they live (Cronen and Pearse, 1985).

2. Power to influence others depends, in part, upon the immediate interactional context. Implicit in Haley's position is the view that power is a personal attribute which enables a person to influence another to do something which he or she would not otherwise do. Bateson's position is that such a conception of power is a myth. Influence is always bi-directional. The view taken here, is that power is not a personal attribute, nor is it a myth. Rather, the potential one has to influence others is context dependent. In any given situation a person may attempt to influence another to do some thing which he or she would not otherwise do. The situation or context in question will place certain constraints and certain affordances on the person who wishes to influence others. Furthermore, attempts to influence others will alter the context and change the constraints and affordances which the context entails (Cronen, 1990).

For example, a father wants his son, who is watching TV, to go to bed. In this context the father is constrained by variety of factors from influencing the son to comply with his wishes. These include the boy's reluctance to miss the end of the TV programme; the fathers wish to end the day with his son on a positive note; and the father's reluctance to wake the baby, humiliate the son or upset his wife by using physical force to achieve his end. The situation also entails a number of affordances which empower the father to influence the boy. The boy loves and respects the father and has a habit of carrying out most of his requests; the boy is tired and would like to go to sleep; and the father is prepared to video-record the end of the programme the boy is watching so that he can see it next morning. Once the father asks the boy to go to bed and promises to video the end of the programme for the boy, the boy's response will create a new set of constraints and affordances for the father.

3. Power to influence others depends, in part, upon enduring features of a person's social, psychological and physical context. Swimming upstream against a tide of trait theorists, Bateson argued that social influence was best explained in terms of patterns of social interaction only, without reference to personal attributes. He said :"It is nonsense to talk about 'dependency' or 'aggressiveness' .. All such words have their roots in what happens between persons... Explanations which shift attention from the interpersonal field to a factitious inner tendency .. is I suggest very great nonsense" (Bateson, 1979, p.133).

Unfortunately this position has often led to the neglect of the importance of relatively enduring features of a person's social, psychological and physical context upon his or her capacity to influence others. Enduring features of a person's context may tip the scales, such that more often than not, the constraints against influencing others significantly outweigh the affordances. Such enduring contextual inequalities between people may be identified in the social, psychological and physical spheres. For example inequality in social power is in part explained by differences in wealth, Socio-Economic-Status, ethnicity and gender. Differences in psychological power may be attributable to variations in IQ or life skills. Differences in physical power may be attributed to level of physical maturity, and the presence or absence of disease or genetic vulnerability. At the cutting edge of clinical practice and research in the field of systemic consultation a central task is establishing the linkages between relatively enduring features of a person's physical, psychological and social context (including those that enhance or diminish their power) and patterns of social interaction within the problem system. Exemplary clinical projects typifying this approach are Falloon's (1985) work with families of schizophrenics, Lask & Matthew's (1979) work with asthmatics and the work of the Philadelphia group carried out with diabetics (Minuchin et al, 1978). A number of exemplary research projects typifying this approach in the field of child abuse are described in Cicchetti & Carlson (1989).

4. There is more than one form of power. Both Haley and Bateson lump all forms of power together. Analyses of the construct of power in the field of social psychology indicate that this is an oversimplification (Smith & Peterson, 1988, pg. 127). Distinctions may be made between sources of power and their mode of operation. For example, in the previous section of this paper it was noted that an individual's power to influence others may be based upon enduring aspects of his or her physical, psychological, or social context. French & Raven (1959) argue that social power may be subclassified into five categories: reward power, coercive power, legitimate power, expert power and referent power.

Symptoms and resistance to treatment probably arise as a result of coercive power struggles. Effective therapeutic influence, on the other hand, probably involves reward, legitimate, expert or referent power or some mix of these. Both of these assertions are partially supported by research. For example, two distinct lines of inquiry have shown that the exercise of coercive power is associated with symptom maintenance. First, Patterson has demonstrated a clear link between the development of aggressive behaviour in young boys and coercive parent-child interaction (Patterson & Chamberlain, 1988). Second, in families where one member has a diagnosis of schizophrenia, high levels of expressed emotion (EE) particularly negative criticism shown by parents or partner, has been shown to lead to relapse (Falloon, 1985). Coercive power struggles have also been shown to characterize the interactions of families where physical child abuse or spouse abuse occurs (Goldstein et al., 1985; Neidig & Friedman, 1984).

Research on the social psychology of individual counselling has identified two major sources of therapist power: credibility and attractiveness (Strong and Claiborn, 1982). Therapist credibility is conveyed by reputation, credentials, responsive yet confident style and perceived trustworthiness. Therapist attractiveness is conveyed in part, through non-verbal behaviour such as smiling, eye contact, forward posture, and responsive accepting gestures. These sources of therapist power, i.e. credibility and attractiveness, are distinct from coercive power. They probably entail legitimate, expert or referent types of power contained in French and Raven's typology.

5. Power may be exerted co-operatively or competitively. In both the human and the animal kingdoms relationships may evolve through episodes of co-operativness and competitiveness (Gilbert, 1988). At any point, the presence of co-operation or competitiveness may be acknowledged or denied.

From Haley's perspective symptom development within a family system occurs when the relationship is covertly competitive but where it is defined overtly as co-operative and where there is no opportunity to leave the relationship (Haley, 1963). When a client-system requests treatment, Haley assumes that while overtly the client-system is defining the therapist-client relationship co-operatively, covertly the relationship is competitive. In response, Haley argues that therapists must view the therapeutic relationship as essentially competitive.

Bateson, on the other hand, argues that the therapeutic relationship is essentially co-operative. The therapist and client embark upon an exploration of the place of the client difficulties within the clients ecosystem (Keeney, 1983, p129-134.) Bateson (1972) wrote "A human being in relation with another has very limited control over what happens in that relationship. He is a part of a two person unit, and the control which any part can have over any whole is strictly limited...We social scientists would do well to hold back our eagerness to control that world which we so imperfectly understand (p.267-269)".

My view is that any therapeutic system will contain a complex mix of competitive and co-operative relationships between the various different members which changes over time. Monitoring the patterning of these relationships and one's own place within the pattern is one of the consultant's key responsibilities. This issue will be discussed further below.

6. Mutuality of influence does not imply equality of power.
Bateson (1972) asserted that unilateral power was a myth. He argued that.. "a human governor in a social system..is controlled by information from the system and must adapt his own actions to it" (Bateson, 1972, p. 316). All human interactions are at least bi-directional. When, in keeping with this theme, he revised the double-bind theory from a lineal victim-victimizer formulation to a bi-directional formulation, he swept the violence of more powerful family members towards weaker members under the carpet for 25 years (Bateson, 1976; Dell, 1989).

A central problem with Bateson's position is the assumption that mutual influence implies 'a mutual amount of influence'. There is no doubt that in any social influence situation both parties are influenced by each other. However, often one party is influenced more than the other. For example, wives are more often seriously physically injured by their husbands than visa versa (Neidig & Friedman, 1984). Children are more often abused by their parents than visa versa (Goldstein et al, 1985).

7. People and social systems develop over time so circularity is a poor metaphor for patterns of mutual influence. Bateson argued that social and mental process were complex, and that simple lineal models of causality were insufficient to capture the richness of social interaction. He said: "Mental processes require circular or more complex chains of determination" (1979, p.92).

Unfortunately this insight has led our field to be dominated for some time by the notion of circular causality as a useful model for describing patterns of mutual influence. In Figure 3.1 an example of a pattern of mutual influence is presented. What follows is an analysis of it in terms of circular causality. Within a circular causality model, these types of patterns of social interaction are analysed by classifying events that are functionally equivalent (within fairly broad limits) together. So events A1 and A2 are classified as events in Class A. B1. and B2 are classified as events in class B and so forth. Thus, once all events have been coded, it could be said that events in class A lead to events in class B. These lead to events in class C. These lead to events in class D, and these lead back to events in class A in a circular fashion.

This type of analysis has a number of implications. First, events which are functionally equivalent but significantly different in intensity become classified together. So the important differences between verbal abuse (C1) and physical abuse (C2) are obscured.

Figure 3.1. An escalating repetitive sequence of interaction

a criticism by a husband (event A1 at time 1.1)

is followed by

a retort by a wife (event B1 at time 1.2)

is followed by

the husband being verbally abusive (Event C1 at time 1.3)

and then

the wife withdraws emotionally hurt (Event D1 at time 1.4)

Some time later....

a criticism by a husband (event A2 at time 2.1)

is followed by

a retort by a wife (event B2 at time 2.2)

is followed by

the husband being physically abusive (Event C2 at time 2.3)

And then

the wife withdraws bleeding (Event D2 at time 2.4)

Second, the individuals who carry out the actions in each episode of the cycle are assumed to remain in some sense equivalent to the individuals they were when the cycle occurred previously. This type of assumption fails to account for the significant internal psychological changes which occur in both the victim and the perpetrator over the course of repeated abuse. These changes may exacerbate the amount of power used by participants in the pattern of interaction. Thus, the frequency and intensity of the abuse may change over time.

Third, the analysis removes the time dimension from a description of the evolution of this escalating spiral of violence and in doing so makes an ethical judgement of the situation difficult (Fish, 1990). Without a time dimension it is plausible to say that the wife's withdrawal (Event Class D) causes the husband's criticism (Event class A). (This problem is exacerbated by Bateson's rejection of the notion of power inequality, since both husband and wife would be viewed as equally powerful).

Bateson's metaphor of circular causality (as it has been popularised within the family therapy culture) entails difficulties for the researcher, the clinician and jurisprudence. From a research perspective, it precludes the study of the development of social systems and the incorporation of the wealth of knowledge available from the field of developmental psychology into systems consultation (Stratton, 1988). It is difficult to see how the study of predisposing, precipitating or protective factors, in the development of psychological problems, can be incorporated into a framework which collapses events across time and endorses the idea of circular causality. Only symptom maintaining factors could be studied within this framework.

From a clinical viewpoint, the devaluing of historical etiological factors can lead to treatment guided by unrealistic expectations. The notion of circular causality offers little guidance to the clinician on goal setting. It offers no clear way of planning movement towards goals and away from dysfunctional patterns of social interaction. In practice the skilfully deployed social power and influence of the therapist helps the family-therapist system avoid becoming stuck in homeostatic problem maintaining interactions. The skilful therapist, through the judicious use of influence, helps the system evolve to a new level of operation where problem resolution/growth/structural realignment is possible. The unskilled therapist fails to facilitate this evolution (Wynne 1986, 1988).

From the point of view of jurisprudence, the concept of circular causality precludes the notions of both accountability for criminal action.

Finally, in the political sphere a failure to acknowledge the role of history in the evolution of injustice (such as racism; sexism; child & spouse abuse) is naive.

Models of systems consultation which allow the time dimension to be incorporated into the description patterned social interaction avoid many of the difficulties entailed by the metaphor of circular causality.

CLINICAL AND ETHICAL IMPLICATIONS

A number of implications for systemic consultation in general and clinical practice in family therapy in particular are entailed by the propositions set out above. Three are of particular importance. First, evaluate problem-systems with the power structure and the systems potential for evolution in mind. Second, evaluate your own position in the system. Third, decide how your capacity to influence the system might best be deployed given your assessment of the system and your position within it. Each of these points deserves elaboration.

(1) Evaluate the power structure and evolution potential of problem systems. First, include the spiral patterns of interaction in which members of problem-system are engaged. For example, assess patterns of interaction where parents and children become more and more abusive towards each other and thereby place the children in danger. Also assess patterns of interaction where members of the problem system become more and more co-operative and less and less competitive.

Second, assess the relatively enduring features of problem-system members' physical, psychological and social contexts which have implications for their capacity to influence others within the problem-system. This may include physical size, gender, age, personality and intelligence.

Third, evaluate the constraints and affordances entailed by the patterns of interaction and enduring features of the physical, psychological and social contexts in which members of the problem system find themselves. This will throw light on the differences between the amount of power and influence wielded by different system members. Thus, particularly vulnerable system members may readily be identified.

Fourth, identify the types of social power that characterize the patterns of interaction between problem-system members. For example, reference may be made to co-operative or competitive relationships or to patterns of interaction which entail reward power, coercive power, legitimate power, expert power and competitive power.

(2) Evaluate your own position in the system. First, assess your relationship with each member of the problem-system in terms of its potential for co-operation or competition. Second, evaluate these relationships in the light of your relationships with members of the organization within which you work. Depending upon your work context this may include relationships with your team, your manager, your insurance company or the state (if you work within a profession which is statutorily empowered).

Pitfalls associated with this process are described elsewhere (Carr, In Press).

(3) **Decide how you wish to deploy your influence.** In the light of your assessment of the power structure and evolution potential of a system and the potential for developing co-operative relationships with its members, the therapist may deploy influence in a variety of ways. Three are of particular relevance here.

First, the therapist may decide against deploying influence herself. For example, a psychologist referred a patient apparently presenting with chronic anxiety to a physician for assessment and treatment of thyrotoxicosis, a condition which resembles chronic anxiety in its presentation.

Second, the therapist may use statutory power to influence the client. For example, a psychiatrist employed as an approved doctor by the NHS involuntarily detained a suicidal patient under the Mental Health Act.

Third, therapists may use their power to influence the client within the context of a therapeutic relationship. de Shazer (1988) argues that it is useful to distinguish between clients who wish to engage in visiting, complaining or customer relationships with the therapist. The mode of influence used by the therapist must be matched to the type of relationship the client wishes to have with the therapist. Visitors are largely influenced to change by compliments. Complainers respond to non-behavioural tasks, but not to behavioural prescriptions. Customers accept direct suggestions to change their behaviour.

FINAL COMMENT ON NEUTRALITY AND POWER
The position concerning the use of power by therapists taken in this essay requires that the clinician adopt a neutral position while assessing problem-systems. However therapists are bound to then make a series of judgements which will guide later action. This action will rarely if ever be 'neutral'. It will always involve influencing some members of the problem-system more or less than others. Thus, neutrality applies to the therapist perception of the problem system, not to his or her action within it.

REFERENCES
Bateson, G. (1972). Conscious purpose versus nature. In G. Bateson (Ed.),*Steps to and Ecology of Mind*. New York: Ballantine.

Bateson, G. (1972). *Steps to an Ecology of Mind*. New York. Ballantine.

Bateson, G., Weakland, J. & Haley, J. (1976). Comments on Haley's "History". In C. Sluzki & D. Ransom (Eds.) *Double Bind: Foundation of the Communicational Approach to the Family*. New York: Grune & Stratton.

Berman, J. and Norton, N. (1985). Does professional training make a therapist more effective. *Psychological Bulletin,* 98, 401-407.

Carr, A. (1990). Failure in family therapy: A catalogue of engagement mistakes. *Journal of Family Therapy, 12,* 371-386,

Cicchetti, D. & Carlson, V. (Eds.) (1989). *Child Maltreatment: Theory and Research on the Causes and Consequences of Child Abuse and Neglect.* Cambridge: Cambridge University Press.

Cronan, V. (1990). *Toward an explanation of how the Milan Method works.* Workshop given under auspices of KCC at Norwich.

Cronan, V. & Pearse, W. (1985). Towards an explanation of how the Milan Method works: An invitation to a systemic epistemology and the evolution of family systems. In D. Campbell & R. Draper (Eds.), *Applications of Systemic Family Therapy.* London: Grune & Stratton.

Dell, P (1989) Violence and the systemic view: The Problem of Power. *Family Process*, 28, 1-14.

de Shazer, S. (1988). *Clues: Investigating Solutions in Brief Family Therapy.* New York: Norton.

Falloon, I. (1985). *Family Management of Schizophrenia. A Study of Clinical, Social, Family and Economic Benefits.* Baltimore: Johns Hopkins University Press.

Fish, V. (1990). Introducing causality and power into family therapy: A correction to the systemic paradigm. *Family Process,* 16, 21-37.

French, J. & Raven, B. (1959). The bases of social power. In D. Cartwright (Ed.) *Studies in Social Power.* Ann Arbour, MI: Institute for Social Research, University of Michigan.

Gilbert, P. (1989). *Human Nature and Suffering.* London. Lawrence Erlbaum.

Goldstein, A., Keller, H. & Erne, D. (1985). *Changing the Abusive Parent.* Champaign, Ill: Research Press.

Haley, J. (1963). *Strategies of Psychotherapy.* New York. Grune & Stratton.

Haley, J. (1985). *Problem Solving Therapy.* San Francisco. Jossey Bass.

Haley, J. (1976b). Development of a theory: A history of a Research Project. In C. Sluzki & D. Ransom (Eds.), *Double Bind: Foundation of the Communicational Approach to the Family.* New York: Grune & Stratton.

Heatherington, L. (In Press). Control, controllingness and family therapy. *Journal of Family Psychology.*

Hoffman, L. (1985). Beyond power and control. *Family Systems Medicine,* 3, 381-396.

Hoffman, L. (1990). Constructing Realities: An art of lenses. Family *Process,* 29, 1-12.

Boscolo, L., Cecchin, G., Hoffman, L., & Penn, P. (1987). *Milan Systemic Family Therapy: Conversations in Theory and practice.* New York: Basic Books.

Leyland, M. (1988). An introduction to some of the ideas of Humberto Maturana. *Journal of Systems Consultation,* 10, 357-374.

Keeney, B. (1983). *Aesthetics of Change.* New York: Guilford.

Lask, B. & Matthew, D. (1979). A controlled trial of family psychotherapy. *Archives of Disease in Childhood,* 54, 116-119.

MacKinnion, L and Millar, D (1987). The new epistemology and the Milan Approach: Feminist and sociopolitical considerations. *Journal of Marital and Family Therapy,* 13, 139-155.

Maturana, H. (1978). Biology of language: The epistemology of reality. In G. Miller & E Lennneberg (Eds.), *Psychology and Biology of language and*

thought. New York: Academic Press.
Minuchin, S., Rosman, B. & Baker, L. (1978). *Psychosomatic Families.* Cambridge, MA. Harvard University Press.
Neidig, P. & Friedman, D. (1984). *Spouse Abuse: A Treatment Programme for Couples.* Champaign Ill: Research Press Company.
Patterson, G. & Chamberlain, P. (1988). Treatment process: A problem at three levels. In L. Wynne. (ed.), *The state of the Art in systems consultation Research: Controversies and Recommendations.* New York: Family Process Press.
Selvini-Palazzoli, M. (1986). Towards a general model of psychotic family games. *Journal of Marital and Family Therapy,* 12, 339-349.
Simon, R. (1982). Haley, Part 11. *The Family Therapy Networker* 6 (6): 32-33, 35-36,49.
Smith, P. & Peterson, M. (1988). *Leadership, Organizations and Culture.* London, Sage.
Stratton, P. (1988). Spirals and circles: potential contribution of developmental psychology to family therapy. *Journal of Family Therapy,* 10, 207-231.
Strong, S. & Claiborn, C. (1982). Change through Interaction: Social *Psychological Processes of Counselling and Psychotherapy.* New York: Wiley.
Will, D. (1989). Feminism, child sexual abuse and the (long overdue) demise of systems mysticism. *Context,* 1, 12-15.
Wynne, L. (1988). Editors comments. In L. Wynne. (Ed.), *The state of the Art in family therapy Research: Controversies and Recommendations.* New York: Family Process Press.
Wynne, L. (1986). Structure and lineality in family therapy. In H. Fishman and B. Rosman (Eds.) *Evolving Models of Family Change. A Volume in Honour of Salvador Minuchin.* New York: Guilford Press.

CHAPTER 4

COUNTERTRANSFERENCE REACTIONS TO FAMILIES WHERE CHILD ABUSE HAS OCCURRED

ABSTRACT
In this paper five countertransference reactions, which may be experienced by workers on child abuse management teams, are described. Karpman's Drama Triangle is used as a framework within which to define these reactions. The reactions are: (1) rescuing the child; (2) rescuing the parents; (3) rescuing the mother and child while persecuting the father, (4) rescuing the father; and (5) persecuting the family.

INTRODUCTION
Even well-seasoned clinical teams are challenged by the assessment and treatment of families where physical or sexual child abuse has occurred (e.g. Dale et al, 1986a; Furniss, 1983; Giaretto, l982; Irving et al., 1988; Sgroi, 1982). Some of the difficulties which occur in the management of these cases stem from the strong personal emotional responses which these families evoke in team members. In particular, these emotional reactions may interfere with the capacity for collective balanced decision-making about child protection. Throughout this paper such reactions shall be referred to as CTRs, an abbreviation for countertransference reaction (Freud, 1955). In this paper I am using the term CTR to refer to a process, which occurs outside a clinician's awareness, where an intense emotional reaction is elicited by certain characteristics of a family being treated but is fuelled by significant prior experiences.

Figure 4.1. Karpman's triangle

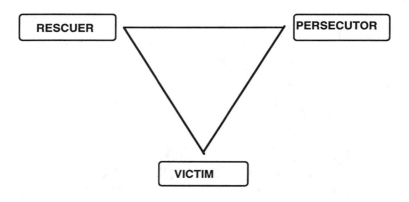

The destructive impact of these personal emotional reactions upon team functioning may be neutralized. This may be achieved by first accepting that such CTRs are inevitable. An important second step is to develop a conceptual framework within which to comprehend these strong emotional reactions. Once team members have acknowledged and come to terms with their CTR's, they often view them as an important source of information about the family being treated (Box et al., 1981; Skynner, 1981).

In the next section a classification of CTRs based on Karpman's (1968) Drama Triangle will be presented. The Drama Triangle is set out in Figure 4.1. The Victim role is characterized by helplessness; the Persecutor role, by aggressiveness; and the Rescuer role, by help fullness. In the basic drama a rescuer assists a victim to escape from a persecutor. In more complex dramas individuals switch roles at critical points. For example, a helpful rescuer may become an aggressive persecutor if the victim does not capitalize upon the rescuer s help to escape the aggression of the original persecutor.

FIVE COUNTERTRANSFERENCE REACTIONS

Five CTRs which occur in clinical teams who work with families where child abuse has occurred will be described below. the victim role is seen to be occupied by the child in the first CTR, the parents in the second, the mother and child in the third, the father in the fourth and the family in the fifth.

Figure 4.2. Rescuing the child

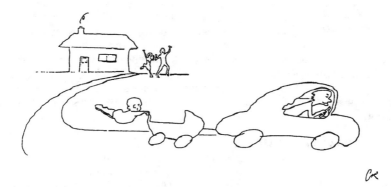

The details of these CTR's are based on observations made while working with the Child Abuse Team at Thurlow House and informal discussions with members of similar teams.

RESCUING THE CHILD

Here the worker in the position of rescuer, views the abused child as a victim of the persecuting parents and all who advocate on their behalf. This CTR is common in cases where a non-accidental injury has occurred. It is characterized by an intense emotional desire to protect the child. It may be accompanied by an additional desire to persecute the parents. The child is experienced as someone who would gladly be forever separated from the parents. The parents are experienced as 'sick' or 'bad' and therefore undeserving of the child. Evidence which points to parental competence and the child's desire to be with the parents is minimized, denied or discounted. The worker finds it difficult to empathize with the parents or members of the extended family who wish to see the reunification of the family. Workers with this CTR become involved in angry disagreements with team members who point to factors which suggest that family rehabilitation is possible.

This CTR is most likely to occur in workers who have, in the past, erroneously assessed a family as safe, and where a child in that family has been subsequently abused. In such instances the family currently being assessed is identified with the family where a failure in child protection has occurred. Guilt and anger associated with the previous failure is the primary source of the CTR.

Young workers who are struggling to achieve a personal sense of autonomy from their families of origin are also likely to experience this. CTR. In older workers too, where the issue of differentiation from the family of origin remains unresolved or has been reactivated by a personal crisis or involvement in personal therapy, this CTR may occur. In each of these cases, the worker identifies with the abused child, and much of the emotion felt about the parent's of the family being assessed has its roots in the worker's feelings about his or her own parents. Finally this CTR may occur in workers who have themselves been victims of child abuse.

RESCUING THE PARENTS.
When this CTR occurs, the worker, in the position of rescuer, construes the parents as victims of a hostile social environment and a punitive child protection system. This CTR is common in cases where a non-accidental injury has occurred. The worker experiences a strong desire to support the parents and ensure that they retain custody of the abused child. An intense sense of outrage at social circumstances such as unemployment, poor housing or social isolation which places stress upon the parents is felt. Anger towards extended family members and help-giving agencies who are unsympathetic to the parents plight is also experienced. Evidence which points to parental incompetence, and factors which suggest that the child is at risk when living with the parents is minimized, denied or discounted. Within the team, the worker may accuse colleagues of 'playing it safe'. That is, they may be seen as taking children into care inappropriately, so as to avoid the possibility of censure from senior management, should child abuse occur within a family on their caseload. Workers with this CTR may become engaged in heated arguments where they define current child protection laws and practices as an intrusive involvement of the state in family life. In a team, when one or more workers experience a strong desire to rescue the parents, a polarization occurs and at least one other team member experiences a desire to rescue the child.

Workers who have insecurities about their adequacy as parents and their capacity to meet their own children's need for nurturance and safety may be prone to experiencing this CTR. The CTR arises partly through identifying closely with the parents of the abused child. Workers may unconsciously believe that if they can demonstrate the competence of the parents in the family being assessed, in a magical way their own competence as parents will be vindicated.

Figure 4.3. Rescuing the parents

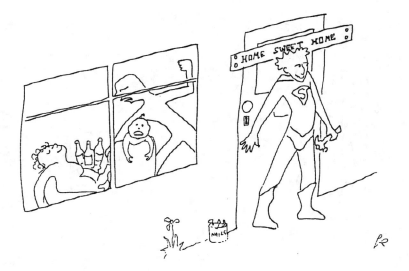

RESCUING THE MOTHER AND CHILD AND PERSECUTING THE FATHER

Here, the worker in the position of rescuer, sees the mother and child as helpless victims of a persecuting father. The main way the mother and child can be rescued, from the worker's viewpoint, is by persecuting the father. The worker experiences extreme anger towards the father and a strong sense of sympathy for the mother and child. This type of reaction is common in teams working with families where sexual abuse has occurred (e.g. Dale et al., 1986b). The worker experiencing the CTR denies or discounts evidence which points to the collusive role of the mother in failing to protect the abused child from the father. Feelings of loyalty (albeit mixed with anger) of the mother, child or siblings for the father are also discounted. Anger is felt towards team members who bring such evidence to the attention of the worker. Anger is also felt towards team members who sympathize with the father or advocate rehabilitating the family as a unit. The parallel between child sexual abuse and rape, and the necessity for treating the child abuser as a rapist, are points frequently made by workers experiencing this CTR.

Figure 4.4. Rescuing the mother and child and persecuting the father

Male workers who have difficulty accepting their own sexual or aggressive desires and fantasies may experience this CTR. Unacceptable aspects of themselves are projected onto the father of the abused child. The legitimate anger felt towards the father becomes mixed with anger that the worker harbours towards himself for having unacceptable desires. Female workers may identify with the mother as another woman who has been oppresses by a man. Through this identification the worker brings emotional energy associated with her own experiences of male oppression to bear on the father of the abused child.

Figure 4.5. Rescuing the father

RESCUING THE FATHER.

I have only come across this CTR in cases of sexual abuse and will therefore describe the reaction as it relates to this type of child abuse alone. When this CTR occurs the worker in the role of rescuer sees the father as a victim of a cold and distant wife and a seductive daughter. The worker feels a strong sympathy for the father, who is seen as lonely and unloved. Anger towards the wife is felt for not meeting the father's needs. Anger is also felt towards the child for being seductive. The child protection system, which is perceived as being unsympathetic to the father's lonely and painful position, is also a focus for the worker's anger. The defenceless position of the child, the duty of the father to protect his child, the father's abuse of parental power and the father's responsibility for his own sexual desires and the quality of his marriage are denied, distorted or discounted. Team members who point to these issues and oppose reunification of the family are met with anger from the worker experiencing this CTR. In a team where one or more workers have a strong desire to rescue the father, a polarization usually occurs between them and other team members who wish to rescue the mother and child and persecute the father.

Male workers, who themselves feel isolated and misunderstood are prone to identify with abusing fathers and so experience this CTR. This CTR appears to be rare in women.

PERSECUTING THE FAMILY

This is a more complex CTR. It usually evolves through three stages before an endpoint is reached where the whole family is experienced as a victim which is being rescued by other team members. The worker experiencing this CTR feels an intense emotional desire to punish the family by withdrawing from the team or sabotaging their work. In the first stage, the worker develops one of the four CTR's described above, while working with the family or one of its subsystems. The family or the subsystem of the family fails to respond to the worker's attempt to rehabilitate them. In the second stage, the ineffectiveness of the worker's interventions give rise to a sense of impotence. The family is experienced as a persecutor who threatens the identity of the worker as a helping professional. Thus the worker experiences him or herself as a victim. The other team members may be viewed as potential rescuers for the worker. The third stage usually occurs when the worker does not receive support from the team. An intense desire to punish the family by withdrawing from the case or sabotaging the work of the other team members occurs. This CTR is a hallmark of professional burn-out (Armstrong, 1981). When workers persecute families, predisposing factors associated with at least one of the four CTR's outlined in previous sections of this paper are usually present. However, these must be coupled with a low level of team support (or professional supervision) for the CTR described in this section to occur.

Low levels of team support arise for both organizational and personal reasons. At an organizational level, high case loads and a model of professional practice which encourages workers to manage families single handed contribute to feelings of isolation. Personal factors may also keep workers stuck in unsupported and isolated positions. For example, workers may need to give abundant care and attention to their clients so that the clients will repay them with gratitude and so meet the workers' unfulfilled desire for (parental) approval. A reluctance to ask for team support may also stem from workers' fears that requests for team work, or team work itself, may lead to colleagues viewing them as weak or incompetent. Workers may fantasize that such views will culminate in painful rejection or criticism.

Figure 4.6. Persecuting the family

DISCUSSION

CTR's are patterns of emotions and behaviour which have their roots in previous significant relationships. CTRs initially occur outside awareness. If they go undetected they may influence, in a dramatic way, assessment and decision making about families where child abuse has occurred. Within child abuse teams, when one member experiences a CTR, another member usually experiences a complementary CTR. For example, if one worker begins to rescue a child, another will try to rescue the parents. A similar process holds true for inter-agency working. If CTR's remain outside awareness, such polarization will continue until inter-worker or inter-agency cooperation becomes impossible. Divisions within families come to be mirrored in teams and agency groups. Poor problem solving and decision making about child safety and growth, which are the defining characteristics of our clients, become attributes of our child protection and family rehabilitation system. Ultimately it is the families we serve who suffer.

CTR's, in my view, cannot be avoided. However, extreme polarization can be curtailed if teams and agency groups devise strategies for bringing CTRs to their awareness. Once in awareness, valid information contained in various team members' CTRs may be distinguished from workers' personal contributions to CTR processes. This valid information may be usefully incorporated into the team's evaluation of the family being treated. Electing a team member for each case who agrees to take a consultant role and monitor team dynamics is one strategy for facilitating this process.

For team members to trust each other enough to allow team dynamics to become a focus in case management, a high level of team cohesiveness is necessary. One way to foster team cohesiveness is for a team to spend whole days together on a quarterly or biannual basis to review difficulties and develop ways of overcoming these in the future. This process may be greatly facilitated by an external group consultant. An attempt has been made within this paper to address both intrapsychic and interpersonal processes which occur when teams work with families where child abuse has occurred.

The primary intrapsychic process used to account for CTR's here has been identification. The concept of triangulation, as set out by Karpman (1966), has been employed to explain the patterns of interaction which emerge when workers develop differing CTR's in their management of these cases. Within the structural, strategic and systemic family therapy literature, analyses of the problems addressed in this paper have focused largely on the interpersonal domain, with little reference being made to intrapsychic processes.

Haley's (1967) seminal paper on the perverse triad has had a marked influence on the way in which many family therapists conceptualize countertransference phenomena. In Haley's 'perverse triad' a covert coalition exists between a parent and child against the other parent. Many theorists have recognized that this pattern of relationships between two parents and a child may be mirrored in the relationships which develop between two workers (or agencies) and the family. The Milan Group have described a triangular process involving the family, the team and the referring agent (Selvini Palazzoli, 1980). More recently this analysis has been extended to cover multiagency families, e.g. Imber Coopersmith (1985). Within the child abuse literature, Furniss (1983) has described the patterns of triangulation which occur in cases when the primary intervention is to remove and prosecute the father or alternatively remove and protect the child. In all of these analyses, which build on Haley's notion of the 'perverse triad', the feelings which bind one worker into a covert coalition with the family and the other worker into a complementary polarized position are the countertransference reactions described in this paper.

CTRs within child abuse teams and their effects on assessment and decision-making have not been systematically studied. This paper offers a framework for much needed empirical research in this area.

REFERENCES
Armstrong, K. (1981). Burnout. *Caring*, 2, 7-11

Box, S., Copley, B., Magagna, J. & Moustaki, E. (1981). *Psychotherapy with Families: An Analytical Approach.* London: Routledge & Kegan Paul.

Dale, P., Davies, M., Morrison, T. & Waters, J. (1986a). *Dangerous Families.* London: Tavistock.

Dale, P., Davies, M., Morrison, T. & Waters, J. (I 986b) The towers of silence: Creative and destructive issues for teams dealing with child sexual abuse. *Journal of Family Therapy*, 8, 1-33.

Freud, S. (1955) The dynamics of Transference. *In Standard Edition. Complete Psychological Works of Sigmund Freud (Vol . 12).* London: Hogarth Press.

Furniss, T. (1983). Mutual influence and interlocking professional family process in the treatment of child sexual abuse and incest. *Child Abuse and Neglect*, 7, 207-223.

Giaretto, H,. (1982). *Integrated Treatment of Child Sexual Abuse.* Palo Alto: CA, Science and Behaviour.

Haley, J. (1967). Towards a theory of pathological Systems. In G. Zuk and I. Boszormenyi Nagi (eds) *Family Therapy and Disturbed Families.* Palo Alto, CA: Science and Behaviour.

Karpman, S. (1968). Fairy tales and script drama analysis. *Transactional Analysis Bulletin*, 7 (26), 39-44.

Imber-Coopersmith, E. (1985). Families and Multiple Helpers: A systemic perspective. In: D. Campbell and R. Draper (Eds.), *Applications of Systemic Family Therapy.* London: Grune and Stratton.

Irving, N., Carr, A., Gawlinski, G., & MacDonnell, D. (1988).Thurlow House Child Abuse Programme: Residential family evaluation. *British Journal of Occupational Therapy*, 51, 116-119.

Selvini-Palazzoli, M. (1985). The problem of the sibling as the referring person. *Journal of Marital and Family Therapy*, 6, 3-9.

Sgroi, S. (1982). *Handbook of Clinical Intervention in Child Sexual Abuse.* Lexington, MA: Lexington Books.

Skynner, R. (1981). An open-systems, group-analytic approach to family therapy. In A. Gurman & D. Kniskern. (eds.), *Handbook of Family Therapy.* New York: Bruner Mazel.

CHAPTER 5

THURLOW HOUSE ASSESSMENT PROGRAMME FOR FAMILIES WITH PHYSICALLY ABUSED CHILDREN

ABSTRACT
A comprehensive assessment programme for families where physical child abuse has occurred is described in this paper. The programme is informed by a multifactorial understanding of child abuse. Programme staff are members of a multidisciplinary team based in a Department of Child and Family Psychiatry. The main function of the programme is to provide a sound basis for long term-planning in cases of non-accidental injury.

INTRODUCTION
Child care inquiry reports and the recent DHSS guidelines highlight the complex problems faced in the management of families where children have been physically abused. (DHSS, 1986; DHSS, 1982; Beal et al., 1985). They also draw attention to potential pitfalls professionals can make when dealing with these cases.

Eight distinct steps may be identified in the management of cases of child abuse:
1. detection;
2. crisis intervention;
3. first case conference leading to an interim plan;

This paper was jointly written with George Gawlinski, Dermot MacDonnell and Nick Irving.

4. execution of interim plan;
5. comprehensive assessment leading to a long term plan;
6. second case conference;
7. execution of long term plan;
8. periodic review

Errors in the handling of child abuse cases may be viewed as arising from failure to deal competently with each stage (e.g. poor crisis intervention) or omitting one or more steps completely (e.g. comprehensive assessment with an eye to long term planning).

The Thurlow House Assessment Programme for Families with Physically Abused Children evolved as a service to help avoid some of these pitfalls ,particularly those associated with long term planning. The programme was developed by the authors, who constitute the senior members of a multi-disciplinary team. The team is based in the Department of Child and Family Psychiatry of the West Norfolk and Wisbech Health Authority. The programme has been running now for four years. The purpose of the programme is to reach an independent opinion on whether it would be safe to return the child to the care of the parents, and if so, the specific conditions under which this should occur. Referrals are typically accepted from case conferences when there is difficulty making such decisions.

Referrals into the programme are accepted after the case has been conferenced and an interim plan developed and implemented. Such a plan usually involves the offending adult facing charges in court and the child being placed with foster parents under a care order. Thus entry into the programme may occur as late as three to nine months following the non-accidental injury (NAI) incident.

Within the programme the full range of factors which may have contributed to the occurrence of the NAI are assessed with a view to formulating a comprehensive hypothesis to explain how the incident occurred. In the light of this hypothesis, potential targets for change are sought. Where realistic targets for change can be identified, appropriate rehabilitative interventions are specified. Where such targets cannot be identified, access recommendations are made. Recommendations on monitoring and periodic review are made in each case. The comprehensive nature of the assessment allows the team to set out in broad strokes a five year plan (alongside specific immediate courses of action). A member of the programme staff attends the second case conference, responds to comments on the report, clarifies recommendations, and offers his or her services as a consultant at periodic review meetings.

Figure 5.1. Factors to consider in the assessment of families where a non-accidental injury has occurred.

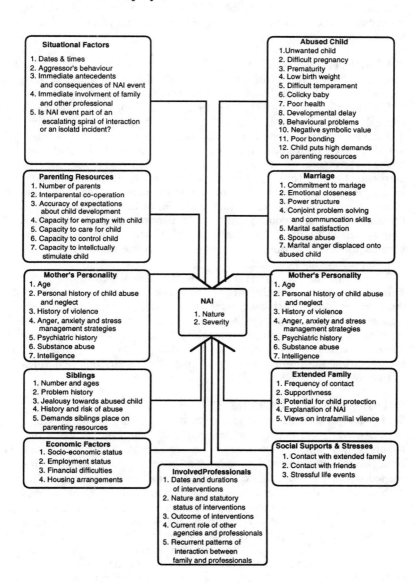

Situational Factors
1. Dates & times
2. Aggressor's behaviour
3. Immediate antecedents and consequences of NAI event
4. Immediate involvment of family and other professional
5. Is NAI event part of an escalating spiral of interaction or an isolatd incident?

Abused Child
1. Unwanted child
2. Difficult pregnancy
3. Prematurity
4. Low birth weight
5. Difficult temperament
6. Colicky baby
7. Poor health
8. Developmental delay
9. Behavioural problems
10. Negative symbolic value
11. Poor bonding
12. Child puts high demands on parenting resources

Parenting Resources
1. Number of parents
2. Interparental co-operation
3. Accuracy of expectations about child development
4. Capacity to empathy with child
5. Capacity to care for child
6. Capacity to control child
7. Capacity to intellctually stimulate child

Marriage
1. Commitment to mariage
2. Emotional closeness
3. Power structure
4. Conjoint problem solving and communcation skills
5. Marital satisfaction
6. Spouse abuse
7. Marital anger displaced onto abused child

Mother's Personality
1. Age
2. Personal history of child abuse and neglect
3. History of violence
4. Anger, anxiety and stress management strategies
5. Psychiatric history
6. Substance abuse
7. Intelligence

NAI
1. Nature
2. Severity

Mother's Personality
1. Age
2. Personal history of child abuse and neglect
3. History of violence
4. Anger, anxiety and stress management strategies
5. Psychiatric history
6. Substance abuse
7. Intelligence

Siblings
1. Number and ages
2. Problem history
3. Jealousy towards abused child
4. History and risk of abuse
5. Demands siblings place on parenting resources

Extended Family
1. Frequency of contact
2. Supportivness
3. Potential for child protection
4. Explanation of NAI
5. Views on intrafamilial vilence

Economic Factors
1. Socio-economic status
2. Employment status
3. Financial difficulties
4. Housing arrangements

Social Supports & Stresses
1. Contact with extended family
2. Contact with friends
3. Stressful life events

InvolvedProfessionals
1. Dates and durations of interventions
2. Nature and statutory status of interventions
3. Outcome of interventions
4. Current role of other agencies and professionals
5. Recurrent patterns of interaction between family and professionals

In this paper the conceptual model which underpins our approach to the assessment of families with physically abused children will first be outlined. A description of the clinical and administrative procedures which constitute the assessment programme itself will then be presented.

THE MULTI-FACTORIAL MODEL

Evidence from a variety of sources suggests that child abuse is most fruitfully conceptualised as a multi-dimensional phenomenon (Belsky, 1980; Friedman et al., 1981; Lee, 1978; Garbarino, 1977; Mrazek & Mrazek, 1985; Parke & Collmer, 1975; Rosenberg & Reppucci, 1983).There is now some consensus within the literature as to which variables are important to consider in the etiology of physical child abuse. These are presented in Figure 5.1. However, controversy surrounds the way (or ways) in which these variables interact to cause non-accidental injuries. For this reason, at the outset of the evaluation of any given case, we simply assume that all of the variables listed in Figure 5.1 may have contributed to the occurrence of the NAI. This is represented in Figure 5.1 by linking, with unidirectional arrows, the various potential contributing factors to the NAI itself. Thus Figure 5.1 is a simple forcefield diagram.

This diagram offers a framework within which to categorise information gained from the various evaluation procedures described in the next section. In each case, once the relevant information has been gathered and located within the simple forcefield diagram, the team develops a specific hypothesis to explain the unique way in which the variables contained in Figure 5.1 interacted to lead to the occurrence of the non-accidental injury. Such hypotheses are usually quite complex (Calam & Franchi, 1987, p.187).

PROGRAMME STRUCTURE

We have experimented with a variety of staffing arrangements and team structures. For the purpose of this paper we shall mention the one which is most likely to be used for the foreseeable future. In a given case, two team members take Ion keyworker roles for the parents of the abused child. They develop close relationships with the parent, liaise with other involved agencies, collect background information, and solicit specialist evaluations from other team members as required. The keyworkers ensure that all meetings are scheduled and the final assessment report is completed within three months of the first day of the contracting interview. The core keyworker team are offered consultancy and supervision on request from a team chairperson. At this stage in the team's development, a number of members can competently take on this difficult role. However, in the early stages of the project the team social worker was primarily responsible for fulfilling this function.

A chronologically ordered list of the clinical procedures which comprise the programme is set out in Table 5.1. Detailed   comments on these procedures will now be presented.

Table 5.1. Components of the Thurlow House Assessment Programme for Families with Physically Abused Children

---

1. Contracting interviews with referring agent, family and
   foster family
2. Initial psychiatric evaluation
3. Client centred interview with parents
4. Marital interviews
5. Family of origin interviews
6. Foster parent interviews
7. Parent child interaction observational sessions
8. Records review and interviews with involved
   professionals
9. Psychometric evaluation
10. Residential review and planning conference
11. Residential family evaluation
12. Second psychiatric evaluation
13. Formulation conference
14. Report writing
15. Feedback session
16. Case conference

CONTRACTING INTERVIEWS

Separate contracting interviews are held with the area social worker responsible for the case, the parents of the abused child and the foster parents. Usually these occur one after the other on the same day and are followed by a joint session in which appointment schedules, access arrangements and transportation arrangements are clarified.

In the referrer's contracting interview, team members meet with the area social worker responsible for the case. Details of the programme are outlined and the responsibilities of the team and the area social worker for the duration of the assessment are specified. One point in particular, which is clarified at this meeting, is worth mentioning. The area social worker retains statutory responsibility for the child's protection throughout the assessment programme with the exception of the residential period during which the team social worker has this responsibility.

An important feature of the contracting interview with the family is underlining the participative nature of the assessment process. Much of the proceedings through which the parents will have gone until then will have been highly child centred. The team emphasises to the parents that the assessment programme offers them a chance to put their view on record, to be understood and supported. They are informed that they each will be allocated a key worker whose primary responsibility it is to ensure that this happens. It is also pointed out that throughout the process of assessment they will have a high level of access to their child so that their relationship with their child has a chance to grow and develop. The parents are told that if the assessment shows that they can understand their difficulties and begin to take steps to make changes in their lives which would prevent the recurrence of child abuse then the team will recommend that their child will be returned home under specific conditions. Failure to show insight and the capacity for constructive change, they are told, will lead to a recommendation that the child remain living separately from them. We point out to the parents that they cannot demonstrate insight and the capacity for change by turning up for scheduled assessment procedures and simply going through the motions.

In the contracting interview with the foster parents, details of access visits are clarified and the importance of these being very frequent despite the difficulties this may cause is emphasised. The team point out to the foster parent the important role that they will play in the assessment in offering direct observational data on the child and descriptions of the parent-child interactions on access visits.

PSYCHIATRIC EVALUATION
A psychiatric evaluation (comprising one or more interviews) is conducted following the contracting interview and also after the residential family assessment. Thus, the psychiatrist meets the family at the beginning and towards then end of the programme. He is, therefore, in a position to comment on significant changes in functioning displayed by the family over the course of the assessment. This, of course, is in addition to his comments, as a specialist, on the psychiatric and neurological status of each family member.

CLIENT CENTRED INTERVIEWS
Each parent is allocated a key worker from the team who conducts a series of client centred interviews with them. The purpose of the client centred interviews is to give each parent an opportunity to feel that their side of the story has been heard and understood and to clarify their individual perspectives on the NAI. In the sessions clients clarify their view of the marriage and their views of themselves as parents. The way

in which each parent sees their family of origin is explored. An inventory of current and past family stresses is also compiled by each parent. Genogram construction is a method we commonly use to aid this information gathering and relationship building process. (McGoldrick and Gerson, 1985). A genogram is a family tree annotated with significant information about family members. Genograms are useful for identifying patterns of family relationships both within a given generation and those that repeat across generations. This assessment method is particularly apt, since child abuse is a phenomenon that often occurs across a number of generations within the same family (e.g. Belsky, 1980).

In these sessions the therapeutic emphasis is on support rather than confrontation. Each parent's capacity to participate in, and benefit from, supportive client centred counselling is assessed during these interviews.

MARITAL ASSESSMENT

Once keyworkers have formed therapeutic alliances with the parents, the marital assessment is conducted. Both keyworkers meet conjointly with both parents for one or more interviews to assess the interactional characteristics of the marriage. The following are the major features of the marriage to which the assessors direct their attention: the couple's level of commitment to sustaining the marital relationship; the extent to which the partners can meet each other's needs for nurturance and emotional support; the power structure of the marriage; the couple's capacity for co-operative problem solving and clear communication; the way in which child care tasks such as nurturing and setting limits on the children are divided up and the impact this has on the couple's marital relationship; the major sources of marital satisfaction and dissatisfaction; and the presence of violent spouse abuse.

Information about these aspects of the marriage are obtained both by having the couple talk about them and by observing the couple interacting in the marital interview situations. Discrepancies between *what they do* and *what they say they do* are noted but not often commented upon. This information is presented at the pre-residential conference and may be used in a confrontative manner during the residential period. Although marital interviews may become highly emotionally charged events, by and large the keyworkers aim to keep them at a low key level with the focus being on insight rather than change.

FAMILY OF ORIGIN INTERVIEWS

The abused child's grandparents (i.e. the parents' families of origin) are interviewed by the keyworkers to assess their view of the facts surrounding the non-accidental injury and to check on the historical accuracy of the social histories that have been taken in the client centred interviews. In addition, the way in which violence, anger, drug abuse, psychiatric problems and life stresses were dealt within each of the parent's families of origin is established. The grandparents are also assessed as child care role models for the parents of the abused child.

In cases where there is a possibility that the child might be placed with the grandparents as part of the recommended treatment programme, the grandparents' capacity to meet the child's needs in this situation are assessed through interviewing and grandparent-child interaction observational sessions.

PARENT-CHILD INTERACTION OBSERVATION SESSIONS
The team's health visitor attends selected access visits at the foster parents' home and observes the abused child interacting with his parents. Deficits in child management skills are noted and the parents are coached in more appropriate child management strategies. Their capacity to respond to this coaching is also assessed .These sessions are conducted in a matter-of-fact way without recourse to elaborate teaching aids.

FOSTER PARENT INTERVIEWS
The key workers obtain the foster parents' observations of the abused child's behaviour and the developmental appropriateness of the child's responses to nurturance and structure in these interviews. The foster parents' observations of the child's behaviour during access visits are also noted and any change in this behaviour over time. The match or fit between the foster family and the abused child is noted and the suitability of the foster home as a long term placement is assessed.

INTERVIEWS WITH OTHER PROFESSIONALS AND RECORD REVIEW
Available documentation from social services, the general practitioner (GP), the paediatrician, health visitor, home help and other involved agencies are obtained and reviewed. Following the record review, involved professionals are contacted and interviewed if keyworkers deem it necessary.

PSYCHOMETRIC ASSESSMENT
The team's psychologist uses psychometric assessment procedures to furnish standardised information on the abilities and personalities of family members and on certain aspects of family functioning such as marital satisfaction (Snyder, 1981) or family stress (McCubbin et al., 1982).

THE RESIDENTIAL ASSESSMENT PERIOD
Prior to the residential assessment period, the team meet to pool their information and come up with a preliminary hypothesis. This hypothesis is a tentative explanation as to why the NAI occurred when it did.

The residential assessment period lasts 26 hours from 10.00 am on the morning of the first day until noon on the second day. It is attended by both parents and all of the children including the abused child. The assessment is conducted by a senior occupational therapist with specialised training in psychotherapy. A child keyworker and the team social worker attend this assessment period also. A self-catering cottage is rented as a venue for this part of the programme.

The goals of the residential assessment are to check out the psychodynamic validity of the team's hypothesis about family functioning and to assess the parents' capacity to make constructive personal and interactional changes through engaging in emotionally intensive insight oriented psychotherapy. We have given a detailed account of residential family assessment in a previous publication (Irving et al., 1988).

FORMULATION CONFERENCE
All team members meet for a formulation conference after the residential assessment period . The conference, for which an entire working day is scheduled, is usually held in a room equipped with a whiteboard large enough to contain a summary of all available assessment information. The goals of the conference are to condense the information that has been gathered and locate it within the forcefield model set out in Figure 5.1, to synthesise this information into a comprehensive hypothesis, and to outline a series of recommendations and a practical plan of action which follows from the hypothesis.

Two features of the information brought by the team to the conference deserve mention. First, all team members have some knowledge of all aspects of the family. Thus most facts may be double checked. This ensures that the hypothesis is based on fairly reliable information. Second, each team member has a particular circumscribed area in which his or her knowledge is authoritative. This authority is acknowledged by the team, the case conference and, indeed, the courts. Thus, the information on which the hypothesis is based is not only reliable, but also authoritative.

At the hypothesis formation stage, initially all team members brainstorm a variety of partial hypotheses. Then one member attempts to synthesise these into a unified comprehensive explanation. This is altered and refined by other team members.

A hypothesis is a brief explanation, based on information contained in the forcefield diagram, which shows how the family and the wider social network within which it is embedded functions, and how this relates to the occurrence of the NAI. A hypothesis has the following characteristics:

1. it is stated in specific rather than vague terms;
2. the statements within the hypothesis are logically connected;
3. it is comprehensive and so takes account of most available significant information;
4. it contains statements about predisposing and precipitating factors
5. it identifies factors which continue to place the family at risk for further child abuse such as *vicious cycles* of social interaction
6. it points to a clear action plan and also suggests courses of action that should be avoided. (We have previously presented a full account of this approach to hypothesis construction in Carr, 1987).

Once the hypothesis has been formulated, a set of recommendations which follows from it are listed and prioritised. First, a statement must be made as to whether the family and its network display sufficient flexibility for change to permit the child to be returned to the care of the parents. If it is decided that this can occur, the conditions under which this would be possible must be set out. The practical steps that need to be taken for these conditions to be met must be clarified .This is the action plan. It contains details of resource allocation and the role of our team in the future rehabilitation of the family. In practice we have found that primary care services (in the form of support, monitoring, and child management training) are best provided by community based workers such as the area social worker, the health visitor, the GP, Home Start workers, or volunteer counsellors. Members of our team may provide a backup consultative service to these workers, and if necessary specialist primary care services such as individual psychotherapy or family therapy.

If the assessment reveals that the child cannot safely be returned to its parents' care, then the plan of action must specify placement arrangements, monitoring and intervention services for the child and the services to be offered to the parents to help them to cope with the loss of their child and related problems.

The conference is facilitated by a designated chairperson. This is an exacting role, requiring the following skills and attributes. Team members must trust the chairperson and respect his or her judgement. That is, a team must invest the chairperson with authority. The chairperson must be able to elicit and condense each team member's contribution and locate it within the forcefield diagram. He or she must

also be able to orchestrate the creative powers of the team during the hypothesis formation stage of the conference. When the team have listed tentative recommendations and plans, the chairperson must be able to assess each team member's commitment to them. He or she must be prepared to delay closure, if one or more team members have lingering doubts about some aspect of the hypothesis and recommendations. The chairperson must facilitate the team member's exploration of these doubts so that eventually a consensual team opinion
may be reached. However, he or she must also be able to recognise when a consensual team position is unobtainable, and advise that the dissenting team member's view be recorded as such in the final report.

Throughout the conference, when differences of opinion occur between team members, the chairperson must be able to determine the extent to which the disagreement is based upon differences in professional assessment or differences in personal countertransference reactions. Ideally the chairperson should have a low level of direct contact with the family so that he or she is to some degree protected from countertransference issues. Thus the chairperson is in a position to help other staff to deal with these issues, particularly the keyworkers who have been intensively involved with the family. (We have described these countertransference problems fully in Carr,1989).

FEEDBACK TO THE FAMILY AND THE CASE CONFERENCE

The keyworkers and the chairperson meet with the family a few days before the NAI case conference and present to them in a detailed way the hypothesis, the evidence on which it is based, the recommendations and the action plan. The keyworkers allow the parents an appropriate amount of time and space to emotionally process the results of the assessment. For example, if the recommendation is that the child remain in care, feedback may be given in a day long session, so as to provide the parents time to understand and react to the loss of their child.

One keyworker then writes up a report to be presented to the case conference. This report contains:
1. a list of members of the assessment team;
2. a list of the assessment procedures, the dates on which they were conducted and the staff members responsible;
3. a statement of the circumstances leading to the referral;
4. a clear narrative statement of the information obtained under the headings specified in the forcefield diagram;
5. the completed forcefield diagram;
6. the hypothesis in narrative and diagrammatic form (if clarity warrants this)

7. the recommendations and the proposed action plan;
8. the family's reaction to the feedback.
    Fuller specialist reports such as those from the psychiatrist, psychologist, and psychotherapist may be appended to the team's composite report along with those of other involved professionals, e.g. the radiologist or paediatrician.
    This report is presented at the case conference by one or more team members. Conference members are invited to explore the accuracy of the facts at which the hypothesis is based, the plausibility of the hypothesis and the viability of the recommendations. In all cases we have assessed in this manner, the conference has accepted the core of our report and recommendations.

CLOSING COMMENTS

The assessment programme described in this paper is expensive. An average of 159 man hours of professional time are required per case. When the cost of this professional time investment and administrative overheads are combined, the total cost per family assessment is about £4,000. However, a reading of the inquiry reports suggests that at least in some cases where recommendations about childcare; are bought more cheaply and based on a cursory rather than an intensive assessment, the consequences can be very expensive (Beal et al., 1985; DHSS,1983)
    We do not believe that a comprehensive assessment as complex as that described here is necessary in every case of non-accidental injury. However, we do believe that this type of assessment service can be invaluable to case conferences where there is difficulty making decisions about long term planning for specific cases. In our district, which has a population of 47,600 children under the age of 16, about 18 cases of physical child abuse (as distinct from other forms of abuse) are identified annually. Only four families (or 25 per cent of all registered physically abused cases) are referred to us per year for this type of extensive assessment.

REFERENCES

Beale, J., Blom-Cooper, L., Brown, B., Marshall, P. & Mason, M. (1985). *A Child in Trust: A Report of the Panel of Inquiry into the Circumstances Surrounding the Death of Jasmine Beckford.* Middlesex: London Borough of Brent.
Belsky, J. (1980). Child maltreatment: An ecological integration. *American Psychologist*, 35, 20-335.
Calam, R. & Franchi, C. (1987). *Child Abuse and its Consequences: Observational Approaches.* Cambridge: Cambridge University Press.
Carr, A. (1987). *Constructing Hypotheses to Guide Systems Interventions.* Workshop presented at the Association for Family Therapy Training Conference, York.

Carr, A. (1989). Countertransference reactions to families where child abuse has occurred. *Journal of Family Therapy*, 11, 87-98.

DHSS (1982). *Child Abuse: A Study of Inquiry Reports: 1973-1981.* London HMSO.

DHSS (1986). *Child Abuse: Working Together for the Protection of Children.* London: Draft Circular.

Friedman, R. M., Sandler, J., Hernandez, M. & Wolfe, D. A. (1981). Child Abuse. In E. Mash & L. Terdal (eds.), *Behavioural Assessment of Childhood Disorders.* London: Guilford Press.

Garbarino, J. (1977). The human ecology of child maltreatment: A conceptual model for research. *Journal of Marriage and the Family*, 39, 721-726.

Irving, N., Carr, A., Gawlinski, G. & MacDonnell, D. (1988). Thurlow House Child Abuse Programme: residential family evaluation. *British Journal of Occupational Therapy*, 51, 116 119.

McCubbin, H. I., Patterson, J. M .& Wilson . (1982). Family inventory of life events and changes (FILE). In D. H . Olsen et al. (eds.), *Family Inventories.* St. Paul, MN: University of Minnesota Family Social Science Department.

McGoldrick, M. and Gerson, R. (1985). *Genograms in Family Assessment.* New York: Norton.

Mrazek, D. and Mrazek, P. (1985). Child maltreatment. In M . Rutter & L. Hersov (Eds.) *Child and Adolescent Psychiatry: Modern Approaches* (Second Edition). Oxford: Blackwell.

Parke, R. & Collmer, C. (1975). Child abuse: An interdisciplinary review. In E. Hetherington. (ed.), *Review of Child Development Research* (Volume 5,) Chicago: University of Chicago Press.

Rosenberg, M. & Reppucci, N. (1983). Child abuse: A review with special focus on an ecological approach in rural communities. In A. Childs & . B. Melton (eds.), *Rural Psychology.* New York: Plenum Press.

Snyder, D. (1981). *Marital Satisfaction Inventory.* Los Angeles, CA: Western Psychological Press.

SECTION 2

CLINICAL TECHNIQUES

There are ten chapters in this second section which is concerned with techniques of clinical practice. Detailed case treatment studies of relatively focal problems, which nonetheless have been found to be fairly resistant to routine treatment approaches, are presented in Chapter 6 (Concurrent individual and family therapy in a case of elective mutism) and Chapter 7 (Anorexia Nervosa: The treatment of a male case with combined behavioural and family therapy). In both cases, ways in which individual and family therapy may be combined are described and detailed evidence of treatment efficacy is provided. The team at Thurlow House and the Paediatric Department of the Queen Elisabeth Hospital, King's Lynn were centrally involved in the management of both cases and indeed the series of other similar cases of which they are two exemplars.

While the cases described in Chapters 6 and 7 concern relatively focal problems, a multidisciplinary approach to the assessment and management of complex multiproblem cases involving adolescents is presented in Chapter 8 (Thurlow House Adolescent Assessment Programme). The approach to practice is family based, but encompasses interventions at both the individual level and at the level of the wider social systems within which families are embedded. It was this work which informed the chapters on individual consultations and network meetings included in the *Positive Practice* textbook (Carr, 1995).

With systemic practice, we found that some families drop out of treatment or fail to respond to interventions that for theoretical or empirical reasons would otherwise be expected to be effective. Our analysis of the way in which engagement difficulties lead to such problems is described in Chapter 9 (Failure in family therapy: A catalogue of engagement mistakes). This approach to network analysis laid the groundwork for the approach to planning an intake interview described in the 1995 *Positive Practice* textbook (Carr, 1995).

While failures in family therapy may be reduced through managing the engagement process more thoughtfully; careful formulation, clear goal setting, a sensitive approach to giving explicit directives to clients, a planful way of managing mid-therapy resistance, and the inclusion of children more fully in the therapeutic process may also enhance the effectiveness of treatment. Our approach to these issues are described in detail in Chapters 10 (A formulation model for use in family therapy); Chapter 11 (Systemic consultation and goal setting); Chapter 12 (Giving directives effectively: The implications of research on compliance with doctor's orders for family therapy); Chapter 16 (Resistance, dilemmas and crises in family therapy: A framework for positive practice) and Chapter 13 (Involving children in family therapy and systemic consultation). More extensive accounts of these issues are given here than in the 1995 *Positive Practice* textbook (Carr, 1995).

Some of our work over the years has involved teamwork and some has been conducted on a solo basis. Both solo and team based practice pose challenges some of which are addressed in Chapters 14 (Three techniques for the solo-family therapist) and 15 (Carrying parcels and making puddings: Two co-operative styles).

REFERENCES
Carr, A. (1995). *Positive Practice: A Step-By-Step Guide to Family Therapy.* Reading: Harwood.

CHAPTER 6

CONCURRENT INDIVIDUAL AND FAMILY THERAPY IN A CASE OF ELECTIVE MUTISM

ABSTRACT
In this paper, following a literature review, a family containing a child who had been electively mute for four years is described. A concurrent programme of individual and family therapy and the systemic hypothesis which guided these interventions is then presented in detail. Behavioural and psychometric data are presented to illustrate the dramatic improvement which the identified patient showed over the course of treatment. Finally, the probable mechanisms underpinning the child's improvement, and how these differed from our initial expectations, are discussed.

DEFINITION AND INCIDENCE
Elective mutism, a condition first described by Tramer in 1934, is characterized by a refusal to speak to anyone except a small group of intimate relatives or peers for a substantial period of time, e.g. six months. The condition is also known as selective mutism. Persistent elective mutism is rare and estimates of incidence range from 0.3-0.8 per 1000 (Brown & Lloyd, 1975; Fundudis et al., 1979). The condition usually develops between the ages of three and five years but is typically noted when the child first enters school and refuses to speak with teachers or classmates (Elson et al., 1965).

This paper was jointly written with Shahin Afnan.

Unlike other language disorders, elective mutism is slightly more common in girls than in boys (Kolvin & Fundudis, 1981; Wilkins, 1985).

Elective mutism should be distinguished from mutism secondary to conditions such as mental retardation, developmental language delay, hearing loss, psychosis or hysterical aphonia (Cantwell and Baker, 1985). A distinction should also be made between elective mutism and low-frequency or reluctant speech (Sanok and Ascione, 1979). The condition holds many features in common with other emotional disorders of childhood, but is distinguished from them by a variety of features also. For example, speech difficulties and maternal overprotection are more common among elective mutes (Wilkins, 1985)

ETIOLOGICAL THEORIES
Theories concerning the etiology and maintenance of elective mutism may be loosely classified as family-oriented, psychodynamic or behavioural. What follows is our synthesis of the more important ideas in each of these conceptual domains. Review papers by Cunningham et al. (1984) and Hesselman (1983) may be consulted for a more detailed appraisal of the theoretical literature and extensive bibliographies .

According to family-oriented theories, the elective mute's family is characterized by mother/child enmeshment, a peripheral and passive father, and the presence of one or more shy family members. The identified patient's symptoms are precipitated or exacerbated when a family with this structure is faced with the developmental task of allowing the child to move out of the home and attend school. This transition in the family life-cycle may be more disruptive if the family is physically, socially or culturally isolated, since the extrafamilial environment is viewed as threatening by the family as a whole. The core symptom of the identified patient may be seen as serving a variety of functions within the family. For example, it may allow the parents indirectly to express their aggression or anxiety about their isolated position within the community. Mutism may also indicate that the family have a secret which they do not wish to divulge, e.g. sexual abuse.

A variety of psychodynamic formulations have been suggested, many of which attribute a cardinal role to the elective mute's attempts to deal with aggressive impulses. For example, elective mutism has been interpreted as an inhibited or denied oral aggression, or anal retentiveness (i.e. a form of passive aggression) .

Hypotheses offered by behavioural theorists tend to focus on reinforcement contingencies which maintain the symptomatic mute behaviour. For example, refusal to speak may lead to anxiety reduction in children who suffer from social anxiety. Where children have conduct disorders, elective mutism may be viewed as a strategy the child uses to manipulate the environment in a coercive fashion to obtain secondary gains.

TREATMENT AND PROGNOSIS

The prognosis for elective mutes is poor. In a retrospective five- to ten-year follow-up study of treated cases, only 46% showed improvement (Kolvin and Fundudis, 1981). The condition has proven resistant to traditional individually oriented behavioural and psychodynamic interventions (Kratochwill et al., 1979). Direct attempts to coerce the child to speak are ineffective. A gradual and supported progression from non-verbal to verbal play characterizes most individually oriented treatments.

Of the systems-based behavioural interventions that have been developed, stimulus fading coupled with reinforcement is currently the most effective treatment for elective mutism (Sanok and Ascione, 1979; Cunningham et al., 1984). The term *stimulus fading* refers to the role of the child's mother and family on the one hand, and his teacher and school on the other as discriminative stimuli for mutism and speech, respectively. The child attends school with a member of the family to whom he or she will talk. Within the school (usually in an empty room), the child and family member talk together. By arrangement, the class teacher gradually approaches the child and family member as they converse. Once this has been achieved without the child becoming silent, the teacher begins to contribute to the conversation, and the family member reduces his or her participation. Peers may be introduced into the conversation group at this point. The family member then gradually withdraws from the school, and the conversation group is gradually moved into a normal classroom situation. Throughout the programme, the parent and teacher reinforce the child's successive approximations to normal conversational behaviour. A programme such as this is usually conducted over a number of sessions (ranging from twelve to 180), although one-day marathons have been reported (Reid et al., 1967) .

There are few reports in the literature describing the progress of the concurrent family and individually based interventions with elective mutes (Rosenberg and Linbald, 1978). In the case described below, a family therapy format was used to implement a variant of the stimulus fading plus reinforcement programme. Concurrently, the child attended individual play therapy sessions in which successive approximations to normal play involving verbalization were rewarded and individuation was facilitated.

CASE EXAMPLE
Background information.
        The identified patient. Jenny Conn, a six-and-a-half-year-old girl was referred to our clinic by her general practitioner. She had a four-year history of elective mutism, the onset of which coincided with the birth of her younger brother. Her refusal to speak was first noted at that time by the teachers at the playschool which she was attending and indeed, her mutism was confined to this playschool environment. At the age of three-and-a-half, she got lost in a large shopping centre in a neighbouring town, and since then had displayed a strong fear of being left alone with strangers, a reluctance to venture far from the house alone and a marked reduction in the number of people with whom she was willing to talk. At the age of five, she refused to talk to her next door neighbour after the neighbour gave birth to another child. When we first met the Conns, Jenny had been attending primary school for two years and had never spoken in that environment. On the child behaviour checklist (Achenbach and Edelbrock, 1983) which was completed by both parents, Jenny obtained an internalizing T score of 59 and an externalizing T score of 67. These psychometric results indicated that in addition to the central symptom of mutism, Jenny also displayed a large number of conduct problems (in comparison with age-matched peers). She had a history of nocturnal enuresis which was resolved without treatment when she was four years of age.
        The family. The family comprised Mr and Mrs Conn (neither of whom had previously been married), Eileen (thirteen years), Jenny (six-and- a-half years) and John (five years). Neither parent had a psychiatric history, although both reported personal life events which had significance for Jenny's condition. Throughout Mr Conn's youth and until the early years of his married life, he had a fear of eating meals outside the home. To this day, he still gets *twinges* in his stomach when eating at a restaurant. He presented as a shy but congenial man in contrast to his outgoing and talkative wife. Mrs Conn had a history of miscarriages, one prior to Eileen's birth and another (involving twin girls) before Jenny was born.
        There was no evidence of marital discord, problems with Jenny's siblings or significant grandparental involvement in the presenting problem. On the McMaster family assessment device (Miller et al., 1985), the parent's scores did not suggest the presence of serious family pathology. The family structure was clearly one of an enmeshed mother-daughter dyad with a less involved (though by no means peripheral) father.
        Social interaction surrounding the symptom. Part of the

delay in the referral reaching our clinic may be attributed to two factors. First, the family and school waited a year for Jenny to grow out of her mutism before taking any action. Secondly, on her own initiative, Mrs Conn in conjunction with the teacher, devised and implemented a stimulus fading programme during Jenny's second year at school. At the stage where Jenny would read to her mother and the teacher at school in the same room, Mrs Conn (without Jenny's consent or knowledge) sneaked home. When Jenny noticed this, she clammed up again and suffered a complete relapse.

At the time of referral, Jenny's school, family and peer group had all accepted her elective mutism and developed ways of accommodating it. For example, her parents would tape-record her reading at home and bring this to school so that the school could provide Jenny with reading material to match her ability. Her peers at school would communicate with her in sign language or by passing notes.

Hypothesis. The following predisposing factors were identified as setting the scene for the development of Jenny's symptoms. First, because Mrs Conn had her second miscarriage before Jenny's birth, she welcomed Jenny (a child she thought she might never have) with great warmth and developed a deep and involved relationship with her. Second, because of his own difficulties about eating in public, Mr Conn was predisposed to be accommodating to similar symptoms such as elective mutism in his daughter. Third, Mr Conn provided his daughter with a model for *shy behaviour*. Fourth, Mr Conn's neurotic traits may have been inherited by his daughter.

The birth of a sibling and of a neighbour's child, the incident on the shopping trip and school entry were the main precipitating and exacerbating factors.

The symptom was maintained over time because it probably served a variety of functions for Jenny and her family. Initially, it may have been a way for Jenny to express anger at those who attempted to usurp her position as *the baby* of her social network (e.g. her playschool teachers and next door neighbour) without suffering reprisals. Following the shopping incident, it may have helped Jenny to reduce anxiety associated with separation and entry into new social situations. However, from the point of view of treatment planning we assumed that the central function of the symptom was to provide Mrs Conn with a way of legitimizing her overinvolved relationship with Jenny after the birth of her son.

The symptom was also maintained by the way in which the school had accommodated it. Initially, the school placed few demands for speech on Jenny because they believed that she would spontaneously recover. Later, they accepted the intractability of the

disorder when the mother's stimulus fading programme, which seemed
eminently plausible, was ineffective. The school saw Jenny's mutism as
an expression of illness rather than disobedience and their response was
to socialize her into an invalid rôle.

FAMILY THERAPY

Session 1. In an initial evaluation and contracting interview
attended by the entire nuclear family and conducted by both of us, the
background information (set out above) was obtained and the
hypothesis drawn up. We thought that a treatment programme aimed
directly at symptom removal would be met with little resistance,
provided a way could be found to allow Mrs Conn to channel into it her
high level of concern for her daughter (Alexander and Parsons, 1982).
However, the programme would also have to provide Jenny and her
mother with legitimate opportunities for separation. Our overriding
treatment strategy was to offer Mrs Conn a chance to successfully rerun
her stimulus fading programme (with back-up from us), but to ensure
that concurrently Jenny attended play therapy sessions without her
mother.

After the break, during which the hypothesis and treatment
plan were developed, we told the family that we were impressed by the
severity and duration of the symptoms. Mother and father looked
relieved at this statement. We said that we wondered what would have
happened if Mrs Conn's programme had been carried out more slowly,
and the parents replied that it probably would have worked. We
acknowledged this and offered to help Mr and Mrs Conn plan such a
programme in a slow and careful manner over four sessions. The family
accepted this treatment offer. We said that only the parents need attend
these meetings.

We then pointed out that unless we had a fair understanding of
Jenny herself, and her view of the world, we would have no basis for
developing alternative solutions if the stimulus fading programme
failed. The parents agreed with this wholeheartedly. Individual play
therapy sessions for Jenny (with S.A.) were then suggested as a way of
achieving this goal. With some anxiety, the family agreed to this. S.A.
said that she would also attend the family therapy sessions and feedback
in broad terms useful information arising from the individual sessions,
but she emphasized that the blow-by-blow details of these meetings
would remain a confidential matter between Jenny and herself.

The parents consented to having the play therapy sessions
videotaped. Data sampled from these videos and the details of the
individual sessions are described in later sections of this paper.

Session 2. The second family session was held after a three-
week interval. Jenny had just completed her first two play therapy

sessions that week. The parents mentioned that Jenny was frightened to attend the sessions and that she had fantasized that S.A. might harm her in some way. During the three-week interval, Jenny had been even more withdrawn at school. Mrs Conn had taken a job as lunch time assistant at the school and was spending her morning in Jenny's classroom working informally as a teacher's aid. Our instinct was to confront Mrs Conn's further overinvolvement with Jenny, but in keeping with our view that this would elicit resistance we informed Mrs Conn that we fully approved of her decision and that her special role within the school would be valuable in solving her daughter's problem. In keeping with the contract, we devoted the session to planning a stimulus fading programme. The final version of the programme contained the following elements.

(1) In Jenny's presence, the parents were to avoid attributing Jenny's mutism to fear or malice. Rather, they were to attribute it to a lack of readiness. For example, they should avoid saying *Jenny doesn't speak because she's scared* or *She doesn't speak to get special attention, the little brat.* Rather, they should say *She is not ready to speak at school yet.*

(2) Mrs Conn was to describe the stimulus fading plus reinforcement procedures (set out in points (3) and (4) below) to Jenny as the best way to help her. Mrs Conn was to decline to help her daughter until she clearly indicated that she was ready. The failure of Mrs Conn's previous attempt to help her daughter using a stimulus programme was to be highlighted to Jenny by her mother as the main danger of starting the programme before Jenny was ready.

(3) Mrs Conn was to arrange a series of stimulus fading sessions with the school teacher in which Jenny was to read, while the distance between herself and her mother was increased, and that between herself and the teacher was decreased. The steps in the programme were to be decided by Mrs Conn, but Jenny was to be given control over when they occurred and the speed of the overall programme.

(4) Mr Conn was to set up a star chart reinforcement programme at home. Each day Jenny spoke at school she was to receive a star from her father when he came in from work in the evening, and five stars (even if they were not consecutive) could be cashed in for a treat. Mr Conn was encouraged to draw up a reinforcement menu of treats for Jenny with her help.

In developing this programme, the parents were encouraged to outline the best they could come up with. We then offered broad modifications, e.g. points (1), (2) and (4), and encouraged them to operationalize these. A participative rather than prescriptive approach to programme construction was used so that the family could ultimately take responsibility for Jenny *cure*, should the programme be successful. The proposed programme provided and opportunity for Mrs Conn to constructively channel her overinvolvement, without excluding her husband.

    Session 3. An interval of two weeks elapsed between this and the preceding session. Jenny had attended five individual sessions in all at this point, but she had screamed throughout each of them. The parents had outlined the programme to Jenny with one modification. Mrs Conn had told Jenny that she could earn stars by both speaking within the context of a stimulus fading procedure at school and by not screaming at the clinic when she attended individual sessions.

    On the day following this, Jenny spontaneously whispered to her mother in school and obtained a star. The next day, the teacher directly asked Jenny to read (outside the context of the agreed stimulus fading programme) but Jenny was unable to do so. Mrs Conn told Jenny's teacher and the class that she could not read aloud yet because she was not ready. Mrs Conn admitted that this reframing took considerable pressure off both herself and Jenny.

    Because of the constant screaming during the individual sessions, S.A. invited Mrs Conn to participate in session 5 and to note its effect on Jenny's behaviour within the play therapy situation (see below). The day following this session, Mrs Conn was playing a game of *I spy* with the children at school and asked the children what they could spy beginning with *M*. Jenny said *Mum*. All Jenny's classmates responded to this, her first word in school, by engaging her in conversation, to such a degree that Mrs Conn had to ask them to stop. Jenny still did not converse with the teacher. That night, while Jenny was being bathed by her mother, she said, *The old Jenny has gone away now and good riddance to her. The new Jenny is going to speak to everyone at school.* Jenny then asked if she had to continue coming to individual sessions at the clinic, which her mother took to mean that she wanted to terminate individual treatment. The next day, Jenny spoke to the next door neighbour, with whom she had not conversed since the birth of her baby a few months previously.

    In keeping with their previous attempt to solve the problem, the parents were showing evidence of wanting to rush the treatment process. Mrs Conn had stuck to points (1), (2) and (4) of the agreed programme, but had decided of her own accord to change the stimulus fading element once Jenny showed signs of spontaneous speech in school. She also wanted to stop the individual sessions.

    The interventions described below may appear paradoxical. In fact, they were intended to be straightforward directives aimed at slowing up the process of problem-solving so as to avoid mistakes. We took such an approach because the Conns were a family who rushed at problem-solving but accommodated well to a directive therapeutic style (de Shazer, 1 982) .

(1) We expressed concern at the speed of Jenny's improvement and advised that the family prepare itself for a relapse. We pointed to the dangers of demoralization which can result from falsely based optimism. We described in detail a number of families with whom we had worked and highlighted the pattern of gains and setbacks which symptoms and habits follow before a long-lasting change can be reached.

(2) When Jenny relapsed in school, we advised Mrs Conn to tell the other children that she needed a rest because she was not used to talking a lot and had become exhausted.

(3) We highlighted the importance of the individual session as a format that could be used for understanding Jenny herself, and that such an understanding would be crucial to the correct management of relapses.

(4) We advised Mrs Conn to have a dialogue with the teacher in Jenny's presence about the importance of not requiring Jenny to do oral classwork until she was ready. We said that a reinforcement menu, separate from that used at home, should also be discussed and drawn up in Jenny's presence.

Session 4. This session occurred a week after session 3. The family took on board our views concerning relapses and completed the tasks we set them in the previous session. Mrs Conn never formally constructed and executed the stimulus fading procedure as planned. Rather, she followed Jenny's lead by rewarding her for spontaneous speaking in school, and Jenny spontaneously enlarged the number and type of people with whom she talked and the distance that her mother was from her while this occurred. At this point, she was talking to all the members of her class and to teachers in the school. The school said that her speech could best be described as baby talk. Jenny had participated in a school play, albeit in a non-speaking part, and had gone horse riding for the first time. Mrs Conn had reduced the time she spent in Jenny's class to thirty minutes per day. We congratulated the family on their excellent progress and gave them full credit for the gains made.

Jenny continued to attend individual play therapy sessions, had stopped screaming in them and had progressed from non verbal to verbal play. Her mother continued to express anxiety about the necessity for Jenny's attendance at the individual sessions and would frequently try to spend time with S.A. before and after these meetings discussing her concerns about Jenny.

We closed the session by framing Jenny's reluctance to speak as a way of slowing down the process of separating out from the nuclear family and growing up. The parents spontaneously added that her conduct problems, which were now resolving, were really immature behaviour. We took this to indicate that the family accepted our reframing of Jenny's symptoms. In the light of this reframing, Jenny's attendance at the individual sessions was described as a forum within which Jenny could learn to be comfortable with an adult outside the bounds of her nuclear family. We acknowledged that Mrs Conn's unscheduled conversations with S.A. were an expression of her wish to help us understand her daughter. S.A. confessed that she often forgot some of what Mrs Conn said and would prefer if she kept her observations in a diary and brought them to future family therapy sessions for review. We also pointed out that the urgency with which she typically gave these to S.A. before and after the individual sessions might give Jenny the erroneous idea that her mother did not view the play therapy sessions as safe. Mrs Conn confessed that she talked to S.A. to reduce her own anxiety and said that she would try to use a diary as suggested for this purpose instead. We agreed to meet two months later.

Session 5. The parents reported that Jenny was now speaking fluently in all social situations. Her conduct problems had also reduced markedly. Jenny continued to go horse riding and had begun swimming. Mrs Conn had withdrawn from Jenny's class completely. Credit for change was once again given to the family.

The parents noted that Jenny still showed a fear of tackling new and challenging situations. S.A. confirmed that this had also been observed in individual sessions.

We put it to the family that this situation might resolve spontaneously but that Jenny's social development could be facilitated by her continued attendance for individual therapy. We referred to Mrs Conn's admission to experiencing anxiety when her daughter was separated from her and offered her an opportunity for individual therapy with another therapist to deal with this issue. The family accepted the offers of individual therapy for Jenny, individual work for Mrs Conn and attendance at a follow up appointment in three months.

Session 6. The parents reported that Jenny's progress had continued. She was no longer electively mute. Her T score on the internalizing scale of the child behaviour check list had dropped from 59 to 45. On the externalizing scale, her T score was now 58, whereas it had been 67. These changes reflected the clinically significant improvement which Jenny displayed. Jenny was now attending swimming, horse riding and had just been sworn in to the Brownies that week in front of a large group of children and parents! This was her crowning glory.

At the contracting interview with the individual therapist Mrs Conn decided not to pursue the individual therapy option for herself and also decided it was time for Jenny to terminate individual therapy. The parents said that Jenny found conversation intrinsically reinforcing and that her self-confidence would improve as her speech allowed her to make more and better friendships. Seeing this happen, Mrs Conn said, would lessen her own anxiety about Jenny's well-being. Mr Conn acknowledged that when Jenny changed class, she might relapse. He said that he thought they could probably handle such relapses, but would contact us if they met with difficulties beyond their competence. n a telephone conversation five months after this final session, Mrs Conn reported that the gains Jenny made had been maintained.

INDIVIDUAL CHILD-CENTRED THERAPY
These sessions took place in a well-equipped play room. They were spaced between three and ten days apart, with the exception of a three-week break at Christmas.

Sessions 1-4. Throughout these sessions which comprised the first stage of the individual work, Jenny displayed a high level of anxiety and did not speak. In sessions I and 2, she would stand next to the door rigid with her hands in her pockets or over her mouth and scream. In sessions 3 and 4, she drew a series of pictures of people. Initially, her productions were age-appropriate, but as she progressed through the sequence, the figures became more distorted and features were added (e.g. a face with three eyes) or omitted (e.g. a body without a head). In these sessions, she also drew a series of repetitious simple patterns. Her art work was quite messy and her behaviour during it was clumsy.

The main therapeutic intervention during these sessions was to acknowledge Jenny's distress, but to communicate that the play therapy room was a safe place (Axline, 1947).

Sessions 5-8. Because of the level of anxiety displayed by Jenny during the preceding sessions, her mother was invited to session 5 to reassure Jenny. The session also provided a forum within which to directly observe mother-daughter interaction.

S.A. asked Mrs Conn and Jenny to play together while she observed. The overriding conclusion afforded by this exercise was that Mrs Conn typically treats Jenny as if she were a two-year-old. Mrs Conn initiated and led the play rather than following; she stayed overly close to Jenny; she overpraised accomplishments and frequently spoke for Jenny. On the positive side, the deep affection between Jenny and her mum was clearly obvious in the session.

Over the next three sessions, Jenny displayed decreasing levels of anxiety and anger at her mother's absence from the play room. Her tearfulness diminished.

Figure 6.1. Time spent talking and screaming over the course of treatment

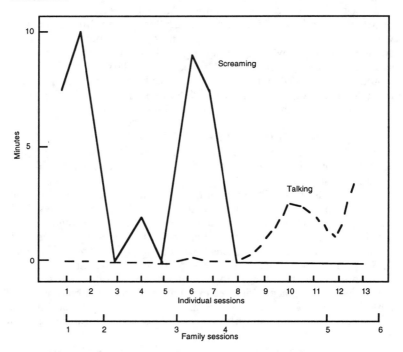

At the end of session 6, she spoke her first word in individual therapy, *Mummy*. (It is noteworthy that this was the first word she spoke aloud within the school context on the following day (see family session 3).) By session 8, she was speaking a few sentences within each therapy period. She began to ask S.A. for things to play with but made no attempt to involve her in her games. At this stage, Jenny also became more mobile and exploratory.

In addition to reflection and reassurance, reinforcement for all vocalization approximating speech, and for all self-initiated constructive play activities, was the main therapeutic intervention during this phase of therapy (Ross, 1974).

Sessions 9-13. In the final five sessions, Jenny conversed more and more freely with S.A. Her grammar and pronunciation were age-appropriate, but the intonation she used was immature, so that her speech sounded like baby talk. Her exploratory behaviour expanded and she was able to walk about in the clinic corridors, although she was clearly afraid of strangers. Her clumsiness did not improve. Jenny's play was confined to drawing, painting and on one occasion she made some snowmen outside. She never initiated imaginative play involving role-playing with S.A. or dolls and puppets, although such toys were quite readily accessible to her within the play room. She was reluctant to try out unfamiliar activities. She showed little curiosity about the therapist herself and did not display any evidence that she had developed an attachment to her.

Three significant aspects of Jenny's world view were identified during this phase of therapy. First, she believed that her mother really wanted her to stay mute so that she could come to school and speak for her. Second, Jenny saw herself as inadequate and incompetent, and it was these beliefs that prevented her from engaging in challenging and unfamiliar activities. She said that she had developed this belief by observing her mother's reactions to her. Third, she was unable to recognize and distinguish the feelings of sadness and anger in herself and others, although she could identify happiness and fear.

Throughout this phase, a non-directive and reflective therapeutic style was used. Structured social reinforcement for speech was no longer used.

The amount of time Jenny spent (a) screaming and (b) talking was measured for the last ten minute segment of each videotaped play therapy session. These behavioural data are presented in Figure 6.1 to illustrate quantitatively the change in Jenny's symptoms over the course of therapy.

DISCUSSION

This case illustrates the way in which individual and family based treatment *tactics* may be effectively integrated into a unified treatment plan guided by a systemic hypothesis.

In retrospect, we have conceptualized the therapy in the following way. First, we developed a trusting relationship with the family to reduce their resistance to directive treatment by being non-blaming and by acknowledging the legitimacy of the mother's overinvolvement. Second, we defined the problem as difficult and only possibly solvable so that (a) they would agree to let Jenny attend individual sessions; (b) they would not try to rush for a solution and so exacerbate the problem as they had done in the past; (c) they would not feel that they were inadequate for failing to solve the problem previously; and (d) they would not be demoralized if no change occurred early on in the programme. Third, we reframed the problem in developmental terms and gave the parents a solution (stimulus fading and reinforcement) to explain to their daughter. When Mrs Conn told Jenny the plan, she probably communicated to her daughter that she no longer needed Jenny to behave in an immature way. Then, suddenly rather than gradually Jenny began to speak in school. This pattern of change suggests that the initiation of a behavioural stimulus fading programme led to a change in Jenny's perception of her relationship with her mother. An explanation based on classical conditioning would seem inadequate here. Fourth, the first four individual play therapy sessions amounted to a flooding procedure where both Jenny and her mother were exposed for long durations to the feared stimulus of separation, and ultimately this led to some reduction in their anxiety levels. Fifth, during the second phase of play therapy, both within these sessions and at school, Jenny received social reinforcement for speech. It was not long before she learned that speech is intrinsically rewarding and so a self-reinforcing cycle developed. Sixth, during the third phase of individual therapy core elements of Jenny's world view were disclosed and a focus for longer-term individual work identified. At the same time, Mrs Conn recognized that personal issues which fuelled her overinvolvement with Jenny might need to be addressed. However, in the light of Jenny's symptomatic improvement on the one hand, and Mrs Conn's view of individual therapy as threatening on the other, she ultimately declined offers of individual therapy for Jenny and herself.

Compared with cases reported in the literature, ours was a particularly severe one, given that the mutism formed part of a constellation of behavioural problems which had persisted for four years. Eighteen sessions conducted over a period of seven months were necessary to treat this case, and substantial symptomatic improvement occurred after seven of these. These observations suggest that concurrent individual and family therapy is a powerful brief treatment modality for this disorder, deserving controlled evaluation.

REFERENCES

Achenbach, T. & Edelbrock, C. (1983). *Manual for the Child Behavior Checklist and Revised Child Behavior Profile.* Burlington, VT: University of Vermont Department or Psychiatry.

Alexander, J. & Parsons, B. (1982). *Functional Family Therapy.* Monterey, CA: Brooks-Cole.

Axline, V. (1947). *Play Therapy.* New York: Ballantine.

Brown, J. & Lloyd, H. (1975). A controlled study of children not speaking at school. *Journal of the Association of Workers with Maladjusted Children,* 10, 49-63.

Cantwell, D. & Baker, L. (1985). Speech and language: developmental disorders. In M. Rutter and L. Hersov (eds). *Child and Adolescent Psychiatry: Modern Approaches* (2nd edition). Oxford: Blackwell.

Cunningham, C., Cataldo, M., Mallion, C. & Keyes,J. (1984). A review and controlled single case evaluation of behavioural approaches to the management of elective mutism. *Child and Family Behavior Therapy,* 5, 25-49.

de Shazer, S. (1982). *Patterns of Brief Family Therapy.* New York: Guilford.

Elson, A., Pearson, C., Jones, C. & Schumacher, E. (1965). Follow up study o childhood elective mutism. *Archives of General Psychiatry*, 13, 182-187.

Fundudis, T., Kolvin, I. & Garside, R. (1979). *Speech Retarded and Deaf Children: Their Psychological Development.* London: Academic Press.

Hesselman, S. (1983). Elective mutism in children 1877-1981: a literary summary. *Acta Paedopsychiatry*, 49, 297-310.

Kolvin, I. & Fundudis, T. (1981). Elective mute children: psychological development and background factors. *Journal of Child Psychology and Psychiatry*, 22, 219 232.

Kratochwill, T., Brody, G. & Piersel, W. (1979) Elective mutism in children. In A. Kazdin and B. Lahey (eds.), *Advances in Clinical Child Psychology* (Vol 2.) New York: Plenum.

Miller, I., Epstein, N., Bishop, D. & Keitner, G. (1985) The McMaster family assessment device: reliability and validity. *Journal of Marital and Family Therapy*, 11, 345-356.

Reid, J., Hawkins, N., Keutzer, C., McNeal, S., Phelps, R., Reid, K. & Mees, H. (1967). A marathon behaviour modification of an electively mute child. *Journal of Child Psychology and Psychiatry*, 8, 27-30.

Rosenberg, J. & Lindbald, M. (1978). Behaviour therapy in a family context: Treating elective mutism. *Family Process*, 17, 77-82.

Ross, A. (1974). *Psychological Disorders of Children: A Behavioural Approach to Theory Research and Practice.* New York: McGraw-Hill.

Sanok, R. & Ascione F. (1979). Behavioural interventions for childhood elective mutism. *Child Behavior Therapy*, 1, 49-68.

Tramer, M. (1934) Electiver mutismus bei Kinder. *Zeitschrft fur Kinderpsychiatrie*, I9, 49- 87

Wilkins, R. (1985). A comparison of elective mutism and emotional disorders in children. *British Journal of Psychiatry*, 146, 198-203.

CHAPTER 7

ANOREXIA NERVOSA: THE TREATMENT OF A MALE CASE WITH COMBINED BEHAVIOURAL AND FAMILY THERAPY

ABSTRACT
The successful treatment of a case of anorexia nervosa in a 14-year-old boy is described in this paper. The treatment comprised an initial month long hospital-based behavioural weight gain programme. Concurrently a family evaluation was conducted. Family therapy, involving the parents only, was conducted over a subsequent four month period. The management or a relapse four months after the termination of treatment is described and information obtained at 9 and 16 month follow up is presented.

INTRODUCTION
Anorexia nervosa occurs most commonly in young adult females and this population has been well-described (Garfinkel & Garner, 1982). Only recently have studies of younger anorexics (Jacobs & Isaacs, 1986; Fosson et al., 1987; Bryant-Waugh et al., 1988) and males (Beaumont et al., 1972) with this eating disorder been reported. The proportion of boys with anorexia is higher in the early teens than among young adults. (Fosson et al., 1987). Younger anorexics show more pre-morbid feeding difficulties and behavioural problems than their older counterparts and there is also a higher incidence of feeding difficulties among their relatives (Jacobs & Isaacs, 1986).

This paper was jointly written with Shahin Afnan and Dermot MacDonnell

Major clinical features and associated family difficulties vary little with the age and sex of the anorexic family member. Most anorexics have a fear of obesity, refuse to maintain a normal body weight, and have a disturbed body image. Often secondary hormonal and psychological characteristics resulting from starvation may develop. Difficulty in the establishment of personal autonomy is a central concern for many anorexics (Bruch, 1973; Garner & Bemis, 1982). A high degree of interdependence among family members, mutual overprotectiveness, poor conflict resolution and rigid patterns of interaction and communication difficulties are among the main features commonly noted in families with an anorexic member (Minuchin et al., 1978; Selvini-Palazzoli, 1974;Fosson et al., 1987).

The treatment of families with anorexic members using both structural (Minuchin et al., 1978) and systemic (Selvini-Palazzoli, 1974) family therapy has been well-described. The therapy outcome literature suggests that family therapy may be the treatment of choice for this disorder, particularly in younger cases (Russell et al., 1987) . Despite this, a literature review revealed no full length case study describing a complete course of family therapy with a young male anorexic. The present paper aims to fill this gap in the literature.

CASE STUDY
Circumstances of referral
In May 1986, Phil, aged 14, was assessed by his Family Doctor. His height and weight were at the third centile. Since Christmas 1985 he had lost 19 kg. The weight loss began when Phil was mocked at school for being overweight (54 kgs).
Although 14, he had a bone age of 10 years. His family doctor referred him to the Paediatric Department of our District General Hospital.

The paediatric examination and laboratory investigations revealed no abnormalities. Psychiatric evaluation confirmed a diagnosis of anorexia nervosa and excluded bulimia. Phil showed the following characteristics: 35% weight loss, meticulous dieting, excessive exercise, guilt and depression associated with eating. He expressed a fear of becoming fat again and being mocked at school. There was no evidence of bingeing, vomiting or laxative use.

Phil was treated with a standard management programme. This involved monthly outpatient contact where he would be weighed and the parents instructed on the management of their son's diet and exercise. Hospitalization occurred when significant weight loss was noted. Phil was admitted to the Paediatric Ward for four days in mid-July when he showed a weight loss of 2 kg. He was treated with chlorpromazine, 25 mg bd and Imipramine, 50 mg nocte. The Chlorpromazine was given as sedation to reduce activity and facilitate weight gain during hospitalization. Phil was placed on antidepressant medication during the period of hospitalization and the trial continued for six weeks following discharge.

Figure 7.1. Phil's average monthly weight between December 1985 and February 1988.

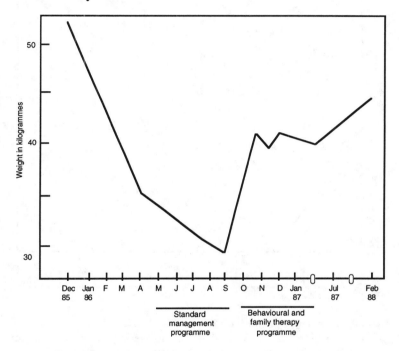

Between May and September Phil lost about 5 kg (see Figure 7.1). He was hospitalized for the second time on September 28th for a month-long weight gain programme. He was confined to bed under sedation and deprived of normal ward privileges. He was placed once again on antidepressants.

Two days after he was admitted to hospital the Paediatrician referred the case to us. He asked that we develop and implement a ward based behavioural weight gain programme which would allow Phil to earn back his privileges and come off sedation, if we agreed that this was an appropriate method for increasing his weight. In addition, a family evaluation was requested, since the Paediatrician suspected that certain family process might be involved in maintaining Philip's eating disorder.

Figure 7. 2. Phil's weight for the month prior to the individual hospital based behavioural programme and for the month during which the programme occurred .

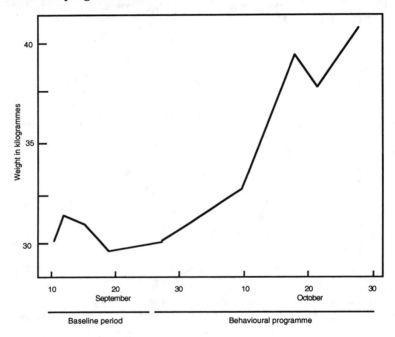

Behavioural weight gain programme

Before describing the family evaluation and therapy, a brief outline of the weight gain programme will be given. At the start of the programme Phil was confined to bed on 25 mg of Chlorpromazine. His wash basin was covered and sealed and the lower halves of his windows were secured. He was required to use a bed pan for urination and defecation. A target weight of 40 kg, a target diet of three meals per day, and a target three-daily-weight-increment of 300gr. were set by the team. Phil was given freedom to work out with the dietician, the precise contents of the three daily meals. We negotiated a contract with Phil which defined how privileges would be returned for achieving eating and weight targets. The parents consented to the programme. The nursing staff were briefed as to the importance of consistency in the implementation of such programmes.

Four main types of problems arose during the implementation of the programme. First, Phil tried to artificially innate his weight by retaining faeces or urine. Second, he tried to accelerate weight gain by bingeing on Mars Bars and Complan drink. Third, he tried to misrepresent his weight by manipulating the scales. Fourth, he used arguments about the details of the programme to split the treatment team. The first three difficulties were dealt with by renegotiating the contract with him directly. The fourth difficulty was managed by training the nursing staff in how to monitor Phil's behaviour and dispense privileges in a benevolent but authoritative way.

A graph of Phil's body weight over the month prior to hospitalization and the month he spent on the weight gain programme is presented in Figure 7. 2.

Family evaluation

Family session 1, 9.10.86: Three family evaluation sessions were held while Phil was in hospital. The first was attended by Phil and his parents. Initially the parent's feelings about the evaluation process were explored. They felt guilty, helpless and ashamed for failing to carry out the previous treatment team's instructions and causing their son's further deterioration. They were apprehensive about the proposed evaluation, since it might point to other areas in which they had failed as parents. In view of their self-deprecatory position we defined the family evaluation as a way of assessing how the parents might best help their child avoid relapsing when he returned home.

We then explored explanations different family members had of Phil's anorexia and the solutions entailed by each of these explanations. Four main problem explanations emerged from this discussion.

Mother attributed Phil's food refusal to depression and construed the boy's vulnerability to depression as a characteristic inherited from his paternal grandmother. Poor peer-relationships, in her view, had precipitated his present episode of depression. The treatment advocated by his mother for his depressive state. Talking to Phil about his troubles in a supportive manner was the primary treatment advocated by his mother for his depressive state. When the depression lifted, she expected the eating problem to cease. Mother extended a great deal of energy trying to talk to her son about his depression.

Father, in contrast, described Phil a s innately stubborn, like his paternal grandfather. The depression, described by his wife, potentiated Phil's pre-morbid stubbornness. It was the stubbornness that caused him to refuse to eat when asked. To overcome the stubbornness it was necessary to engage Phil in enjoyable activities. Once active and happy, the stubbornness would recede and Phil would eat again.

Father had bought Phil a hunting gun and an elaborate set of tools in an attempt to engage him in shooting and woodwork, but to no avail.

Both parents agreed that the paternal grandfather saw Phil as disobedient. If he were smacked, according to this theory, he would soon begin eating again. The theory had not been tested because Mother saw Phil as too depressed to be smacked.

A final explanation offered by the family was that Phil's behaviour was reinforced by the attention it brought him. If this were the case the solution would be to ignore him. The parents had tried this occasionally, between bouts of talking him out of his depression and actively encouraging him away from his stubbornness.

The parents noted a number of negative effects of Phil's anorexia on family life. First, family mealtimes and outings, once the cornerstone of family life, were now dreaded by all family members. Inevitably, a battle between Phil and his parents would occur on these occasions. Second, Mother's self-esteem as a parent had dropped markedly. Cooking family meals used to give her a sense of pride and satisfaction. Now she dreaded cooking because it reminded her of the rows with Phil. Third, Father worried a great deal more than he used to, because of the way he saw Phil affecting his wife's self-esteem. Finally, both parents now focused all their energy on Phil's anorexia and had little time left for themselves or their marriage.

Despite the severity of Phil's condition and its profound impact on family life, he denied or minimized his symptoms and the parents denied or minimized the family difficulties. The family displayed a number of other characteristics which have been attributed to families with an anorexic child, i.e. enmeshment, overprotectiveness and a spirit of self-sacrifice, rigidity, poor problem-solving, poor conflict resolution and overvaluation of academic achievement (Selvini-Palazzoli, 1974; Minuchin et al., 1978; Garfinkel and Garner, 1982).

We ended the session by affirming the severity of Phil's condition but noting the family's willingness to help in finding a useful solution.

Family session 2, 13.10.86: Only the parents attended this meeting. Phil refused to come on the grounds that his only problem was getting his weight up so the team would let him leave hospital.

The session was used to draw a genogram, take a family history and clarify Phil's developmental history. With respect to the nuclear family, it was noted that Phil had only one sibling, a 15-year-old sister, Sue. She was described as a model child, just like Phil used to be. In looking to the future both parents said that Sue would have little difficulty achieving independence but that Phil was a home-bird and would have difficulties separating from the family when the time came.

The parents contrasted Phil's paternal and maternal grandparents in the following way. The paternal grandparents lived some way from the family home and had little contact. The maternal grandparents lived nearby and had daily contact. Within the paternal family of origin relationships were emotionally distant. Within the maternal family of origin emotionally close relationships were highly valued and very common among all family members. The paternal family were described as strict; the maternal family as lax. The paternal family solved problems by taking action. The maternal family solved problems by talking. These contrasting features of the two families made it clear why the parents had outlined such contrasting explanations of Phil's difficulties in the previous session.

A number of important items concerning the maternal family of origin were noted. The maternal grandmother had been depressed all her daughter's life. Mother had helped her mother with the depression by talking to her for hours on end about her problems. In I 983 the maternal grandfather had become senile. Caring for him, had helped the maternal grandmother with her depression. One of the first signs of the maternal grandfather's senility was food refusal. Phil was the maternal grandmother's favourite grandchild. She was a great cook and used to show her love for Phil by cooking special dishes for him.

The child's developmental history revealed that Phil had been born by caesarean section and was a poor sleeper for his first 18 months. While his psychological development had been normal, he was always small for his age. These factors led mother to view Phil as vulnerable and in need of protection. Like the maternal grandmother who had no sons, Phil's mother prized him as the first male child of the family in two generations. The result was the development of a highly enmeshed, overprotective relationship.

Father worked night-shifts during much of Phil's life. This resulted in him becoming gradually more peripheral to the exclusive mother-son relationship in particular, and family life in general, over the years. In primary school Phil had been a model child showing good adjustment both inside and outside the classroom. In his first two years in secondary school, his teachers began to acknowledge that he had outstanding abilities. However, this got him a poor name among some school bullies who mocked him for being *brainy and fat*. It was their jibes that had precipitated his first bout of dieting.

He began to diet sensibly at first. Then he went to stay with a German family for a couple of weeks. The family placed little emphasis on food. Both of the parents worked full time and left Phil and their son to prepare their own meals. The boys had a disagreement and Phil became quite homesick and would ring his mother daily. It was at this point that he began to diet in an extreme way. He continued to lose weight steadily from that point onwards.

Table 7.1. Formulation outlining factors contributing to the genesis and maintenance of Phil's anorexia nervosa

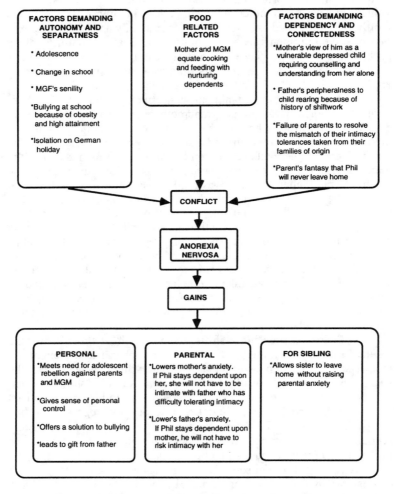

Formulation: A formulation, based on the assessment described above, is presented in Table 7.1. The formulation indicates that Phil was caught between two sets of demands: one for autonomy and the other for dependence. Coming from a family where food symbolized dependent nurturance, restrictive eating offered him a solution to his dilemma. It provided him with an arena for adolescent rebellion. It allowed him to take control of his life and reap a variety of personal gains. I t also enabled him to reduce anxiety his mother might have about him growing up and leaving her. This anxiety was founded in his mother's view of him as a vulnerable child. Once he stayed anorexic he would not have to leave home. His illness also took pressure off his father to be close to his mother. Father had a low tolerance for intimacy because of the emotional distances which characterized the relationships in his own family of origin. Finally Phil's symptoms ensured that his sister, Sue, could safely leave home.

This formulation draws on explanations of anorexia offered by systems theory (Selvini-Palazzoli, 1974; Minuchin, 1978) behavioural psycho-logy (Kellerman, 1977; Garner & Bemis, 1982) and ego psychology (Bruch, 1973).

Strategies and goals: Our overriding strategy was to try to change Phil's perception of his parents as demanding that he stay dependent. If he could see them as accepting the inevitability of his autonomy, then his conflict would be resolved and the anorexia would no longer be necessary. A number of subgoals were identified within the context of this overall strategy: (I) to help Phil to see his parents as a united couple who could survive without him; (2) to decrease the enmeshment between Phil and his mother; (3) to move the focus of parent-child exchanges away from food and onto normal adolescent issues such as limits, relationships, achievements and pastimes; (4) to coach the parents in managing normal parent-adolescent conflict and (5) to encourage Phil to engage in normal peer relationships, leisure activity and academic pursuits.

Family session 3, 24.10.86: Both parents and both children attended this session on the ward. Phil had reached his target weight and the team had agreed to discharge him after the session. We presented the formulation and empathized with each family member's role in this way of framing the problem. We then suggested the following tasks which would alter family life so as to minimize the probability of Phil relapsing. First, Phil and his parents should avoid talking about food and dieting. Second, we acknowledged that Phil may have got the mistaken idea that his mother needed to talk to him a lot for personal reasons, whereas the truth was that she did not. She only did this, we said, to try to get him out of his depression. We suggested he make a sign for his room which said *Mum can look after herself.* Third, we acknowledged that mother would find it difficult to avoid talking to Phil about food and his depression because of her habit of regularly doing so. We advised that she take some time each evening when she could share her anxieties about Phil with her husband. Finally, we advised that Phil be responsible at home for his own eating behaviour and weight. A separate and private arrangement would be made by the team with Phil to come to the clinic to have his weight checked. Consequences for weight loss would be worked out privately between Phil and the team. After some clarification the family agreed to do these tasks and the parents accepted an offer of a follow-up appointment in a few days.

Treatment Programme

Crisis phone call, 29.10.86: The day before this crisis call we phoned Phil to give him details about having his weight checked at the clinic. Father, who made the crisis call, said that after the phone conversation, Phil became moody and annoyed. He said his illness was over and he wanted no more contact with the hospital. The next morning he became openly defiant and ran into town before finishing breakfast. The parents chased him in the car. From time to time Phil would make himself visible to them and then duck back into hiding. In the end they gave up the chase. Both parents were very upset.

Father then went on to deny the validity of the family evaluation, question the value of family therapy and frame Phil's eating difficulties as an individual problem. He said *We don't need marriage guidance, which is what you're offering. Our son is mentally ill and needs expert help in a special unit!*

A number of issues were probably leading father to reframe Phil's eating difficulties as an individual problem. Father's involvement in a game of cat and mouse with Phil in full view of the neighbours had left him feeling humiliated and angry. In his anger he could only define his son's behaviour in one of two extreme ways: as *bad* or *mad*. If Phil's behaviour was *bad,* he was completely responsible for it and therefore had managed to make a fool of his father. This position was unacceptable because it violated father's self-image as a competent and respected parent. Also, if Phil were *bad* he would have to be punished. Mother would have objected to her husband doing so and he feared involving himself in disagreements with her because the couple were poor at conflict resolution. So, instead father saw his son as *mad* and therefore not responsible for his behaviour. If his son were *mad* he could only be *cured* by experts. Thus, father was absolved the responsibility of dealing with his son's relatively normal rebellious adolescent behaviour.

Rather than become embroiled in debates about individual and family models of anorexia nervosa we offered father the following *expert advice.* He and his wife should go home and stop chasing Phil. If after 12 hours (8.00 pm) Phil failed to appear, then the police should be informed and a proper search conducted. Father agreed to bring Phil to the session that was scheduled for the parents for two days time.

Family session 4, 31.10.86. We believed that Father in particular had found the first crisis very threatening and required a lot of support if he were to continue being involved in family treatment. However, he resented being given such support in front of his son. Also, as we found out in session 1, his view of his son's difficulties was quite different from that of his wife. We guessed that he would be reluctant to expose his feelings about their differences in her presence. In the light of these considerations we decided to see the family members for separate interviews initially, and then for a conjoint family meeting. SA interviewed mother. AC interviewed father and subsequently Phil.

Father began by acknowledging that our advice on how to handle Phil's runaway escape had been useful. He said that Phil came home for lunch at 2.30 and spent much of the rest of the day alone in his room. We admired his courage in following such difficult advice.

Father revealed his 'true theory' about Phil's eating disorder. Ever since Phil had been a toddler he had engaged his mother in battles. Various arenas were used. For example Phil might express an extreme view to his mother about a television programme and goad her into arguing the opposite position. His food refusal was another one of these battles. Inevitably Phil beat his mother in all of these battles and she would withdraw feeling sad and dejected. When father saw his wife in this state he would feel both angry at Phil and sad that his wife had been viciously hurt by Phil. He said he felt powerless to stop them having these battles. His wife always fell into the traps that Phil set and she disapproved of father chastizing Phil about these matters. Father desperately wanted the battles between Phil and his wife to stop.

Information from the interview with mother revealed that she felt inadequate, especially when Sue, her daughter, looked after Phil by cleaning his room or making him meals. She was unaware why she became involved in battles with Phil. However her reluctance to punish him for them stemmed from a fear she had that he might try to kill himself. This fear arose from experiences with her own depressed mother who had made suicidal threats and gestures when she was a child. Phil said that the battles always ended in his mother withdrawing and so were a way of getting some breathing space away from her. He said he wanted his parents to back off and give him some room to grow. In the family meeting which followed the individual interviews we relayed this information to the three family members. All of them looked relieved. Little discussion or clarification was required.

The following homework arrangements were made. Mother agreed to try to cut down on her contact with Phil. Father agreed to be completely responsible for child care for those times in the next week when he was not at work. Phil agreed to be more assertive about his privacy.

The parents agreed to attend four further sessions. Phil declined an offer of concurrent individual work. He reluctantly agreed to continue to attend the clinic for weight checks.

Family session 5, 6.11.86: The parents reported that a second crisis had occurred. Phil had refused to eat supper and father had physically chastized him. Phil, in response, locked himself in his room until the next day. Mother supported her husband wholeheartedly and called the family doctor who visited and gave father some sleeping medication. Thus, the crisis led to a weakening of the cross-generational coalition between mother and son and a strengthening of the parental alliance. The next day the parents made arrangements for Sue to stay with an aunt for a couple of weeks until the end of her school examinations. They did not want their difficulties with Phil to interfere with her academic achievement.

After the crisis, Phil insisted that other family members respect his privacy and not enter his bedroom uninvited. He also joined an amateur dramatics group.

The parents were congratulated on the way they handled the crisis. We predicted three or four more crises would occur over the next six months and that they needed to have a plan prepared for handling them. We advised that in each crisis, one parent take responsibility for dealing directly with Phil and the other be available afterwards to support the parent who had dealt with the crisis. We suggested that they alternate roles from one crisis to the next. We ended the session by facilitating the parent's rehearsal of dealing with Phil after he had stolen some money and run away for a few days. We asked them to phone for an appointment after the next crisis.

Family session 6, 26.11.86: The session opened with the parents account of the third (and final) crisis. It began when Phil received a letter from the team containing a list of dates on which he had to attend the clinic to be weighed. He had been missing almost every second weight check appointment. The letter stated that he needed to complete a sequence of four weekly weight checks successfully before their frequency could change to once a fortnight. After four of these, he then needed to be weighed once a month for two months.

Having read the letter he ripped it up, in anger, and bolted out of the house. As in the case of the first crisis, the parents chased him by car but decided to terminate the search after an hour. In the afternoon he instructed them, by phone, to bring his sports gear to a designated spot in town. He wished to attend a body building club which he had recently joined. They collected him at the agreed meeting place and by force, brought him home where father once again physically chastized him. Mother supported her husband and called the family doctor who came and spent an hour talking to Phil. The doctor supported the parent's for *taking a firm stand* with Phil.

Father said that he felt he needed some way of asserting his parental authority without smacking his son. We invited the parents to draw up a list of alternatives and decide on which of these they would feel comfortable using. They found the task quite difficult because the main options involved withdrawing privileges from Phil. This seemed cruel to them. They settled on sending him to his room with holding back pocket money as a backup.

The parents had difficulty connecting the three crises with Phil's original symptoms. Once again, we presented our formulation and described anorexia nervosa as an adolescent's battle for independence with food as the battle arena. Since Phil could no longer fight with his parents about food, because this issue was now dealt with directly by the team, his battle for independence had to find expression elsewhere. We described his running away as a request for more freedom and his locking himself in his room as a request for more privacy. We defined both, as normal adolescent behaviour which could best be dealt with if the parents and son could find a way to openly negotiate about these matters.

Family session 7, 16.12.86: The parents gave the following account of their son's social adjustment for the three-week interval which had elapsed since the previous session. Phil continued to attend amateur dramatics and the body building club. At school he was top of the class and captain of the school quiz team. He had been involved in one altercation with a bully and he stuck up for himself, something he had never done at secondary school. He had gone to his first disco and had met his first girlfriend who he had now been seeing daily for two weeks.

We congratulated the parents on the work they had done to help Phil achieve this new independence. We cautioned against relapses at times of stress. They told us that they would handle such relapses by allowing Phil privacy and avoiding battles over food. Because we had never fully dealt with Mother's fantasies about her son's potential for suicide, we assured her that if she ever had evidence that he might injure himself, we would admit him to the paediatrics ward immediately and without question. She was confident that her fears were really unfounded. In view of Phil's improvement the antidepressant medication was gradually withdrawn after this session.

Family session 8, 16.3.87: This final session was attended by the parents only. Phil's excellent social adjustment continued. He had withstood three sizeable life stresses without relapsing. First, at Christmas his maternal grandfather had died. Second, he had gone to Germany for a two-week holiday similar to the one which precipitated the onset of anorexia nervosa. Third, he had ended his first romance which lasted for a couple of months. Both parents commented that they found themselves spending a lot of time alone together. They were enjoying watching their children become independent and took vicarious pleasure from the children's social and academic conquests. However they also missed the enmeshment and home-centredness of pre-adolescent family life. The team initially thought that Father, in particular, would find this *forced intimacy* quite threatening. These fears were unfounded. The couple's marital satisfaction had increased over the course of treatment.

Crisis phonecall, 3.7.87: Four months later Mother phoned to say that her husband had been forced by his employer to change jobs. His new job was of a lower status and so he had suffered a major loss of self-esteem. Phil had responded with moodiness and food refusal which had lasted 48 hours. Mother was sure he was going to relapse and she was in a state of panic.   After clarifying the facts and empathizing with mother's position, the following interpretation was offered. We suggested that Phil felt responsible for cheering up his father, but powerless to do so except by becoming ill again. This would force father to overcome his depression and involve himself in the care of his son. If mother attempted to talk her son out of his present state she would in fact be re-establishing the original pattern of family interaction. We cautioned against this approach. If, however, she demonstrated to her son through her actions, that she could support father through this crisis and that his help was unnecessary, then he would probably not relapse. We advised her to set *private time* aside for herself and her husband which they should spend away from both the house and the children. During these periods she should be maximally supportive of her husband. The children should be informed that the parents are having *private time* together, but the details should be kept a secret from them.

Mother thanked us for the advice and said that she would contact us only if the intervention was ineffective. She also asked that we keep the conversation confidential from her husband.

Follow-up phonecall, 10.12.87: When we called the family about five months later Father said that he had settled into his new job and was feeling a lot better. He mentioned Phil's brief relapse but said that he was now fully recovered and was planning to go away to college in the near future. Father was unaware of our telephone conversation in July with his wife but offered the following spontaneous comment which suggested hat Mother had complied with the directives that had been given during the crisis telephone call: *I couldn't have made it without my wife. I got really down but she used to make me go out with her and pulled me out of it.*

Phil was last weighed at the clinic in February 1988 and had attained a weight of 45.4 kg (see Figure 7.1.).

DISCUSSION

That factors other than the therapy described in this paper may have been central to ameliorating Phil's eating disorder seems unlikely. Figures 7. I and 7.2 show that during the standard management programme, Phil's weight decreased whereas from the onset of behavioural and family therapy programme his weight increased markedly.

A family's capacity to weather crises without symptom recurrence is one criterion for successful therapy. By this standard, the therapy described here was effective (since Father's demotion four months after the termination of therapy was a major family crisis. Structural changes within the family were associated with this improvement in family functioning. Over the course of therapy, the intergenerational boundaries became more clearly defined and the parental alliance strengthened. Alongside the improvement in family functioning and the change in structure, Phil resolved his developmental conflict in that he achieved a marked degree of autonomy and was able to contemplate leaving home.

The treatment described in this paper has a number of features which might fruitfully guide the management of cases where young adolescents present with physical complaints other than anorexia nervosa. These include: (1) close co-operation between the paediatrician and the family therapy team; (2) behavioural and/or medical treatment of symptoms on an inpatient basis and concurrent family evaluation; (3) the development of a comprehensive formulation which can be presented to the family as a rationale for homework tasks given just before the adolescent is discharged from hospital. The tasks should facilitate the establishment of a strong intergenerational boundary between the adolescent and the parents; (4) separate sessions (or therapists) should be allocated to the adolescent and the parents as a way of modelling and reinforcing the intergenerational boundary; (5) the symptom should be monitored by the adolescent's therapist and discussion about the symptom between the adolescent and the parents should be prohibited; (6) the parents should be advised that they will be supported by the team when they become involved in inevitable battles with their adolescent about freedom and privacy; (7) when crises occur, the parents' therapists should provide immediate support for them and use these occasions to teach parent/adolescent negotiation and limit setting skills; (8) cases should be followed up until the family have successfully dealt with a major family stress and demonstrated the capacity to cope without a serious relapse.

102   *Family Therapy and Systemic Practice*

REFERENCES
Beaumont, P., Beardwood, C. & Russell, G. (1972). The occurrence of the syndrome of anorexia nervosa in male subjects. *Psychological Medicine*, 2, 216-231.
Bruch, H. (1973). *Eating Disorders.* New York: Basic Books
Bryant-Waugh, R. Knibbs, J., Fosson, N., Kaminski, Z. & Lask, B. (1988). Long term follow up of patients with early onset anorexia nervosa. *Archives of Disease in Childhood,* 63, 5-9.
Fosson, N., Knibbs, J., Bryant-Waugh, R. & Lask, B. (1987). Early onset anorexia. *Archives of Disease in Childhood,* 62, 114-118.
Garfinkle, P. & Garner, D. (1982). *Anorexia Nervosa: A Multidimensional Perspective.* New York: Brunner/Mazel.
Garner, D. & Bemis, K. (1982). A cognitive behavioural approach to anorexia nervosa. *Cognitive Therapy and Research,* 6, 123-150.
Jacobs, B. & Isaacs, S. (1986). Pre-pubertal anorexia nervosa: A retrospective controlled study. *Journal of Child Psychology and Psychiatry,* 27, 237-250.
Kellerman, J. (1977). Anorexia nervosa: The efficacy f behaviour therapy. *Journal of Behaviour Therapy and Experimental Psychiatry,* 8, 387-390.
Minuchin, S. Rosman, B., & Baker, L. (1978). *Psychosomatic Families: Anorexia Nervosa in Context.* Cambridge: Harvard University Press.
Russell, G., Szmukler, G., Dare, C., & Eisler, I. (1987). An evaluation of family therapy in anorexia nervosa and bulimia nervosa. *Archives of General Psychiatry,* 44, 1047-1056.
Selvin-Palazzoli, M. (1974). *Self-starvation.* London: Chaucer.

CHAPTER 8

THURLOW HOUSE ADOLESCENT ASSESSMENT PROGRAMME

ABSTRACT
A comprehensive community based assessment programme for multiproblem adolescents is described in this paper. The assessment programme is guided by a multidimensional understanding of adolescent difficulties and is staffed by a multidisciplinary team. The programme is jointly funded and staffed by the Health Authority and Social Services.

INTRODUCTION
A substantial body of evidence suggests that 12-13 per cent of adolescents display behavioural problems salient enough to bring them to the attention of psychiatric or social service agencies (Rutter et al., 1976). A sizeable minority of these youngsters present with multiple problems or come from multiproblem families. Matching available resources within a given area to the needs of this subgroup of troubled teenagers in a co-ordinated manner has been identified as a core problem by the Health Advisory Service (1986). In this paper we describe a community based adolescent assessment programme for dealing with this problem in the West Norfolk Health District.

The conceptual framework which underpins our approach to assessing adolescents will first be presented.

This paper was jointly written with George Gawlinski, Dermot MacDonnell, Nick Irving and Shiela Docking

A description of the clinical and administrative procedures which constitute the programme   itself will then be outlined.A useful assessment framework helps a worker to define a youngster's problems from multiple perspectives and to evaluate the full range of factors which have led to the development and maintenance of the identified difficulties (Rutter, 1979; Achenbach, 1985). Furthermore, a useful assessment model directs the worker's attention to resources which may be used in solving the presenting problems. The model on which our programme is based is informed by these considerations and is presented in Figure 8.1. Details of the categories contained within the model will now be outlined.

PROBLEM DEFINITION
Adolescents' difficulties are often situation specific. For example, a teenager of separated parents may present difficulties at his mother's house and at school, but not at father's house or in the clinic. For this reason our model includes categories where youngsters' problems are defined from their own viewpoints and also from those of significant members of their social networks who necessarily come into contact with the youngster in different social contexts. Where adolescents are involved in complex networks containing foster parents, multiple agencies and the judicial system, problem definitions from these sources are placed under the *professional problem definition* category.

PREDISPOSING FACTORS
Enduring psychological traits, somatic factors and developmental stresses are often involved in predisposing youngsters to developing problems during their teenage years. A few examples of each will be given.
Temperament and intelligence are among the more important enduring psychological characteristics which have implications for adjustment. If a child's temperament does not *fit* with his or her parents expectations, a destructive pattern of social interaction involving the child and the parents may evolve. The child, and possibly the parent, may subsequently develop adjustment difficulties (e.g Garrison & Earls, 1987). Similarly a child's educational placement may not *fit* with his or her intelligence and constellation of aptitudes and abilities. The child, the school staff and the child's fellow pupils may become involved in unproductive patterns of interaction. This may lead to the child being reported by school staff as having school based achievement or behaviour problems (e.g., Rutter, 1985).
Congenital difficulties and genetically inherited predispositions to various illnesses are commonly identified somatic features which

may predispose children to develop psycho-social difficulties during their adolescent years.

A variety of developmental stresses may be associated with poor adjustment in adolescence. These may be categorised as entrances, exits, changes, illnesses and abuse (e.g Johnson, 1987; Wolfe, 1987). Entrances are events which involve new members joining the child's network, such as when a parent remarries or a sibling is born. Exits occur when the child is separated for a significant period from an important member of his or her network. An older sibling leaving home, or a death n the family are both exit events. Some events involve both entrances and exits, e.g., going into foster care. A predisposition to developing difficulties in adolescence may arise as a result of major changes in routine early in the child's life. Multiple changes in residence or school are good examples of such changes in routine. Illnesses which disrupt a child's life to a marked degree or are interpreted by the child as highly threatening may predispose a youngster to developing behavioural problems. Finally, a variety of abusive or neglectful experiences may predispose a child to develop later adjustment difficulties. Physical abuse, sexual abuse and failure of parents or parent surrogates to adequately meet the child's needs for care, control and intellectual stimulation fall into this category.

PRECIPITATING FACTORS
Problems in the second decade of life may be precipitated by the onset of adolescence itself, or by other stresses in the teenager's life (e.g., Johnson, 1987). Precipitants of adolescent difficulties often involve members of the adolescent's social network. This network may include the youngster's immediate and extended family, school personnel, the peer group, organisers of recreational activities and involved helping agencies and professionals. Precipitating factors may usefully be categorised (like predisposing developmental stresses) as entrances, exits, changes, illness and abuse

MAINTAINING FACTORS
Teenagers with persistent- and multiple difficulties have often become involved in recurrent patterns of social interaction with members of their network. These recursive vicious cycles may maintain the youngsters' persistent problems (e.g Imber-Coopersmith, 1985).

Such interpersonal processes often are associated with dysfunctional intrapsychic processes. The adolescent may hold a world view which impairs his or her overall adjustment That is, basic beliefs and expectations about the self and others may lead to behaviour and emotions which in turn confirm the teenager's dysfunctional world view (e.g Beitman, 1987). Examples of both types of maintaining factors are presented in a later section of this paper.

Figure 8.1. Predisposing, precipitating and maintaining factors to consider in the assessment of multiproblem adolescents.

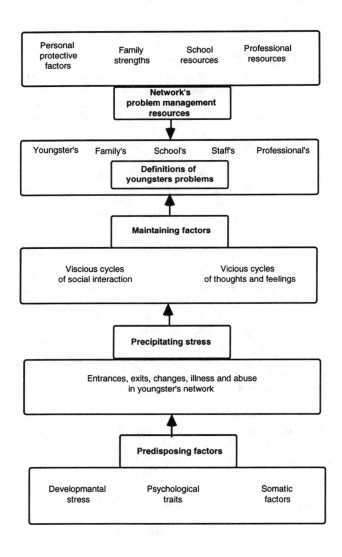

PROBLEM MANAGEMENT RESOURCES

Problem management resources are those factors which are preventing a problem from becoming a lot worse, or which might fruitfully be used in devising a solution to a youngster's difficulties.

High intelligence, well developed skills which lead reliably to experiences of mastery, and a likeable temperament are among the more important personal protective factors to consider in adolescent assessment (e.g., Anthony & Cohler, 1987).

Within the family, the school and the professional network individuals who are willing and able to contribute to meeting the youngster's needs for care, control and appropriate intellectual stimulation may be viewed as problem management resources. In concrete terms, such individuals may provide youngsters with a special relationship, therapy, skills training, a residential educational placement, foster care, or statutory child protection monitoring.

CLINICAL PRACTICE WITHIN THE ASSESSMENT PROGRAMME

The programme was developed between 1984 and 1988 by a multidisciplinary team based in an outpatient Department of Child and Family Psychiatry. The team comprises both senior and junior members of the following disciplines: social work, psychology, psychiatry, and occupational therapy. Members of all disciplines with the exception of social work are National Health Service employees. Social workers are, of course, employees of Social Services. Thurlow House, where the programme is conducted, is a free-standing building in its own grounds about two miles from our district general hospital. Social Services' Family Centre, Hamilton House, is next door. A number of social work staff from the programme are based in that building. Also, the Family Centre contributes sport equipment and the use of their minibus to the programme. Staff devote one day per week to the programme, an outline of which is presented in Table 8.1. The programme takes 13 weeks to complete. It is run three times a year: January-April, April-July, and September-December. These times coincide roughly with school terms. The average number of cases referred to the programme is 16 per term or 48 per annum. In our district there are about 15,000 children between the ages of 11 and 16, so about three per 1000 participate in the programme. Details of the programme components listed in Table 8.1 will now be presented.

INITIAL PSYCHIATRIC EVALUATION

The majority of referrals to the programme come from general practitioners, area social workers, paediatricians, educational psychologists, education and welfare officers and teachers. The initial psychiatric interview provides a preliminary evaluation of each case and screens out youngsters with focal difficulties of low severity.

Table 8.1. Adolescent assessment programme schedule

	Timing	Programme component
	Following referral	**Initial psychiatric evaluation**
Day 1	Morning: Afternoon:	Intake meeting Arrange contracting interviews
Day 2	Morning: Afternoon:	Contracting interviews Arrange contract with school and involved professionals
Day 3	Morning: Afternoon:	Plan schedule for first two child centred days Family interviews
Day 4	All day:	First child centred assessment day
Day 5	All day:	Second child centred assessment day
Day 6	All day:	Interviews with family, school and other involved professionals
	After school contact	**Psychoeducational evaluation if necessary**
Day 7	Morning: Afternoon:	Plan residential child centred assessment period Family interviews
Day 8 & 9	All day and night :	Residential child centred assessment period
Day 10	All day:	First review and formulation meeting
Day 11	All day:	Second review and formulation meeting
Day 12	All day:	Write reports
Day 13	All day:	Feedback interviews
	Close of programme	**Second psychiatric consultation**

These cases require less intensive assessment and so are managed in other ways. Here is a typical example:

> Tom, a 12 year old boy, was refereed because his attainments, since he had moved to secondary school, were below the expectations of his parents and teachers. The central issue was

whether Tom's underachievement was a reflection of adjustment difficulties associated with the transition to secondary school or due to the presence of a specific learning difficulty which had gone undetected during the boy's primary schooling. The case was referred to the staff psychologist for psycho-educational evaluation and plans were made to discuss the results of this evaluation with the parents and the school staff.

Only multiproblem youngsters, teenagers from multiproblem families and those who have had a multiplacement experience are included in the programme. Where immediate crisis intervention is required, appropriate arrangements are made. Our policy is to provide, where possible, crisis intervention consultancy to community based professionals responsible for these cases. Concurrently these cases are placed on the waiting list for the programme which will provide a thorough assessment and recommendations for long term management.

Cindy was referred urgently by the community psychiatric nurse (CPN). This 15 year old girl was the daughter of a woman with a 12 year history of psychiatric treatment for a depressive illness. Cindy had presented with a long list of home and school based conduct problems which had escalated considerably in the three months prior to the referral. This escalation coincided with her father, a long distance lorry driver, spending more time away from home. The CPN was particularly concerned about the girl's violence towards her depressed mother. The violence occurred within the context of a clear pattern of interaction. When Mr Cox had been away from home for more than three days, Mrs Cox would begin to complain about him to her daughter and then berate herself for being critical of her husband. Cindy and her mother would then become involved in an angry escalating row about Mr Cox which occasionally culminated in Cindy hitting her mother. We offered the CPN and the family the following crisis intervention. First, we advised Mrs Cox to phone the CPN at set times when her husband was away and to *sound off about him*. Cindy was advised to go to her room or to visit a friend if she found herself becoming involved in discussions with her mother about father's absence. Father was to spend set periods of special time with mother and daughter separately when he arrived home. These periods were to be spent in mutually satisfying activities. He might take Mrs Cox out to dinner and take Cindy for a walk by the sea. The CPN was invited to meet periodically with a staff member at our clinic to discuss any hiccups in this crisis intervention and to obtain support in dealing with this difficult case.

REFERRAL MEETING

On the first day of the programme, staff meet and review referrals from the waiting list. If there are more than ten referrals, the programme is run as two separate but concurrent projects. This is a common occurrence. Group membership is kept to a maximum of nine per project for a number of reasons. First, on the child centred assessment days described below, the requisite tasks cannot be carried out effectively in larger groups. Second, we try to keep staff teams for each project group to a maximum of five and allocate two cases only per key worker. Larger staff groups, in our experience, work less efficiently and cohesively. If staff members carry more than three cases, the quality of the work with the family, school and other network members may suffer because the worker feels overloaded.

Referrals to the programme are divided into two project groups in such a way that each group is balanced for age, sex, primary presenting difficulties, and compatibility with staff team members' skills and areas of expertise. This *balancing* process is difficult to describe succinctly. However, a few examples will be given to illustrate the process. We try to avoid groups which would contain one child who is clearly different than other group members such as placing a girl in an all-male group; placing a 16 year old in a group of 11 and 12 year olds; or placing a child from an intact family in a group of multiplacement children. We try to ensure that children with psychosomatic difficulties are placed in a group with those staff members who are skilled in the management of children with such difficulties, or that bereaved children are placed in that group where staff are experienced in grief work.

The composition of each project's staff team is also decided in the referral meeting. Four main considerations determine team membership. First, staff should feel that they are personally compatible. Second, each project team should contain a mix of women and men, representatives of different disciplines and members with different areas of expertise and levels of clinical experience. Third, teams should remain fairly stable over time so that they can develop a team identity and cohesion. However, staff members should also have some opportunity to explore different co-working arrangements. Ideally, each project team comprises three core members who stay together for at least three terms, and two members who vary from programme to programme within that year. Fourth, each team should contain a group leader and a group consultant. The group leader chairs planning meetings and accepts overall responsibility for ensuring that the child-centred assessment days run smoothly. The group consultant has four

main responsibilities:
i. conducting an emotionally intense piece of group work on the evening of the third child centred assessment day;
ii. chairing the review and formulation meetings;
iii. 'filling in' for any team member who cannot meet part of their key worker responsibilities due to unforeseen circumstances;
iv. offering supervision on case management or staff difficulties which arise over the course of the programme.

The group consultant is the only team member who has no keyworker responsibilities. Thus the position of consultant is one of relative objectivity with respect to the clients who participate in the programme.

CONTRACTING INTERVIEWS

The initial job of the keyworker is to conduct a contracting interview with the adolescent, the caregivers, and those legally responsible for the youngster. The cardinal function of the contracting interview is to set the foundations for building a trusting working alliance with the parents or legally responsible caregivers of the referred youngster. If at the end of the contracting interview, the seeds of this alliance have not been planted, then the parents or carers may have difficulties fully exploiting the benefits of the programme in helping them to deal with their youngster's difficulties.

Because forming this alliance is critical, workers must adopt a non-judgmental, empathic style which communicates to the carers that they are concerned and trustworthy. The worker's style must also be characterised by a professional curiosity which communicates to the carers that the worker is competent to conduct a thorough assessment.

During this contact, the presenting problems are clarified. Previous attempts which the youngster and the family have made at solving these and related problems are explored. An inventory of other involved professionals is also obtained.

The keyworker summarises this information for the family highlighting the complexity of the youngster's difficulties and the inappropriateness of further attempts at active problem-solving which is not guided by a comprehensive assessment. It is in this context that the structure of the programme is outlined. The following is an excerpt from the last ten minutes of a contracting interview which illustrates the process. The referring social worker, Brian, is present since he is legally responsible for Andrew, a multiproblem-multiplacement adolescent. The foster parents, the Hickeys, are present as the caregivers.

> *Worker (KW):* Let me go through the picture you've drawn so far. Andrew moved in with you five years ago when he was seven. The original plan was that he would stay with you for a

brief period and later move in with another foster family on a long term basis. In fact eh .. this didn't happen. Because of difficulties at the social service department, the placement dragged on.

Foster Father (FF): Yes, they were short staffed and short of foster families prepared to take long term kids ... Then our social worker left. mm.. It was a year before we were really .. allocated Brian ..m.. here.

KW: By this stage you were attached to Andrew and so agreed to make a commitment to have him live in your family permanently as a foster son, when Brian made this suggestion.

Foster Mother (FM): mmm ..

KW: You both put in Trojan work helping Andrew overcome a lot of bad habits and difficulties during his first four years at your house. You helped him stop wetting and soiling. You taught him how to control his temper and how to take a hug at the end of a big row rather than sulk for weeks ... Have I got that bit right?

FM and FF: Yes well .. you know . . it's eh .. You just do that for kids don't you. *KW:* I'm not sure. A lot of people would have given up on Andrew during those four years but you stuck with him and saw him through it. Andrew, were things OK up till last September and the way that I've described them or did you want to leave?

Andrew (A): Yes .. no I didn't want to leave

KW: In September, Andrew was bullied at school. Then he and another boy skived off once or twice a week. During one of these episodes, he stole a car and crashed it. The owners, were friends of yours Mr and Mrs Hickey and decided not to prosecute. However, Andrew would not discuss this whole business with you despite your patience with him.

FF: We tried everything but it was like ... (to wife). He had shut us out ..

KW: And I suspect, Andrew that you were feeling fairly guilty, although I'm not entirely sure about that ... and it was then that you ran away.

A: (head bowed) ...uhhh...

KW: Anyway, there are other possibilities and we don't have time to go into that here today but it sounds like you, Andrew, are finding yourself now in a difficult patch. You are not talking to your folks about it. From my viewpoint that's fair enough. Privacy is important. However, you, Mr and Mrs Hickey are in a bit of a scrape too, as I understand it, because you and Brian are wondering if this is a resolvable situation.

You are wondering if it was a mistake to take Andrew on as a foster son in a permanent way. You are wondering should he be placed elsewhere and want same way to decide about this. This is difficult because he will not speak to you.

FM: He used to tell us everything .. Well almost... He's never said much about .. you know..... when he lived with his parents ... and we wonder if something about that is bothering him.

KW: You have a good relationship with Andrew but in some way that is blocked at the moment and has been since about September when all this started. You are wondering if something in Andrew's past is creating this block ... hmm

FM: Yes, that's it.

KW: And the school ... the education and welfare officer ... both of these have concerns relating to Andrew's truancy. They may be pushing for Andrew to be placed in another school.

Social Worker: Yes, it was partially because of that, that and because of the foster placement issue that I made this referral.

KW: Brian, I know that you know our programme inside, but let me say a few words about it to you Mr and Mrs Hickey and to your Andrew.

At this point in a contracting interview, the keyworker then underlines a series of positive aspects of the programme. The viewpoints of all network members will be taken into account. The recommendations will be based on a good understanding of the presenting difficulties and the network's strengths and weaknesses. Participation is voluntary. Except where it would be injurious to a member of the network, confidentiality when requested is respected. From the youngster's viewpoint, the activities on the child centred days are fun and they are given an opportunity to be listened to in an adult way. Parents are given an opportunity to be understood and supported.

Negative features of the programme are also mentioned. It is a lengthy process and the family will have to endure their uncertainty about the right way to handle their difficulties for the duration of the programme. Parents are warned that the child centred assessment days may precipitate crises such as family rows, running away, aggression or self-injury. However, it is made clear that the keyworker will support the family through such crises if they occur. The possibilities that the programme will point to recommendations which the parents know are in the child's best interests but which they must reject is also pointed out.

If the family decide that they wish to contract into the programme the youngster and his parents or cares are given copies of Achenbach and Edelbrock's Child Behaviour Checklist (1983; 1986) to complete as homework. Permission to have the school and other involved professionals or family members complete copies of the checklist and furnish the keyworker with reports on the youngster's difficulties and related matters is also obtained. The information furnished by these comprehensive checklists allows youngsters' views of their own problem behaviours to be compared with observations made by teachers, parents and others in a highly structured way.

If no contract is established the family are offered a second psychiatric consultation before being returned to the referring agent.

PLANNING MEETINGS

In these meetings (which are held on days 3 and 7 of the programme) assessment exercises, activities and staff responsibilities for the child centred assessment days are clarified. Assessment exercises are referred to as *work*. These allow youngsters to gain an understanding of their difficulties. Activities are referred to as *play*. These enable the group to develop a sense of cohesion and identity. They also provide staff with an opportunity to observe the youngsters in free play in a peer group setting. A more detailed account of *work* will be given in the next section.

Resources necessary for the activities are arranged in the planning meeting. For example. Minibuses are booked and cash to cover costs of activities is obtained from our units Special Projects Fund. Horse riding, swimming, roller skating, bowling, beach walking and table tennis are among the activities we have used. Facilities for these activities often have to be booked in advance. For the residential child-centred assessment period (Days 8 and 9), self-catering accommodation must be booked and grocery shopping arrangements need to be made.

Planning meetings are also used for training students or volunteer counsellors on the team in skills necessary for contributing effectively to the assessment programme.

CHILD CENTRED ASSESSMENT

The child centred assessment period which spans four days has one core objective. We aim to develop a working alliance with the youngsters so that at the close of the programme they will feel able to participate effectively in the feedback meetings and any subsequent work which follows on from the programme. In working to this objective, we have two subgoals in mind. First, to help the youngsters develop a clear understanding of their difficulties and second to observe youngsters' behaviour directly. The schedule of *work* and *play* activities drawn up in the planning meeting is constructed with the core objective and subgoals in mind. While schedules vary from one programme to the next, certain core themes are invariably present.

The *work* sessions are paced and timed in a coherent sequence. Early work sessions focus mainly on helping youngsters clearly define the problem from their perspective. Concurrently, the team generates through *work* and *play* a group climate of trust, warmth, acceptance and safety. A variety of structured individual, dyadic and whole group assessment exercises are used. During such exercises the team coach youngsters in interpersonal problem solving skills if they show deficiencies in this area. Such skills include putting thoughts, feelings and observations into words accurately; checking that these have been understood; listening to feedback and incorporating feedback into their own view of the world. In doing this, the keyworker has to be sensitive to each youngster's pace. The following example illustrates some of these points.

On the morning of the first day of the group, the leader invited the youngsters to participate in the following exercises in pairs, with one keyworker per couple. First, they were asked to draw a life map of the past which documented significant positive and negative life experiences. Then they were invited to project this into the future they hoped for on the one hand and the future which they guessed would occur on the other. Paul, a 15 year old boy, noted that every two years or so his family moved house to a new RAF base because of his father's job. Paul could remember five such moves. After each move Paul would be sad, steal from his parents and fight with them. In the past and at present Paul believed that his parents saw his conduct problems as a sign that he was basically a bad son and a disappointment to them. Over the years, the period of adjustment following a move became briefer but the extent of the stealing became greater. Paul was referred to the programme after he had stolen some of his mother's very expensive jewellery. Looking into the future, Paul hoped his family could move back to Germany where his friends were, but guessed that they would probably settle in Norfolk for about four years and that he would finish secondary school here. Paul was then invited to summarise the key points in this account to his partner in the exercise. He refused point blank even with a bit of cajoling. The keyworker said that he was pleased that Paul could hold his ground, since this was a sign of maturity. He then involved the other member of the dyad, Dick, in recounting three amusing anecdotes from his life map. Paul then clammered to do likewise. One of the incidents he described occurred in Germany. Dick, asked him why he moved. In the natural flow of the conversation, Paul

recounted the salient points from his life map to Dick, the task
he had refused to engage in a few minutes earlier.

Only when a basic level of trust has developed and youngsters have
clearly defined their difficulties from their own perspective can they be
confronted with the views that significant members of their networks
hold of them. This usually occurs during the early work sessions of the
residential period (Days 8 and 9 in Table 8.1). By this time key
workers have collected and summarised relevant information from the
family, the school and involved professionals. The task then, is for each
teenager to integrate their own view of their difficulties with the views
that others have of them.

    Paul, mentioned in the last example, was given an opportunity
to compare his view of his difficulties with the following
information which was obtained during the family and school
interviews. His father said that he sometimes believed that
Paul's stealing was a malicious attempt to jeopardise his
position in the RAF by escalating the theft to a level where
police involvement would be necessary. However, at other
times, he agreed with his wife's position and saw the stealing
as Paul's way of looking for attention and contact. He had
doubts about this, however, since he was sure that Paul knew
the strength of the love he felt for him as his only son. Paul's
mother also sensed that the fighting and arguments in which
she and Paul engaged were largely an expression of his sadness
at having to leave his friends and change schools yet again.
This was a source of heartache for her because she cared for him
so much. The present and previous schools were in agreement
that Paul was of above average ability. His previous schools
all noted that an initial period of underachievement was
followed by a period of good performance. His present school
had been informed of this and so were expecting his work to
pick up over the next few months, but were prepared to allow
Paul some settling in   time. Paul was surprised by much of
this. He was unaware of how strongly his dad felt for him. He
never knew that his mum felt so bad about all the losses he
had endured. He was also relieved that the school knew what
he was capable of.

    Against this background, potential solutions to youngster's
difficulties may be explored. The role of the youngster and of significant
network members in these potential solutions are clarified. The pros
and cons of these various options may then be enumerated and the
youngster's preferred solution identified. Paul's worker explored various
options including:

i. family work which focused on mum, dad and Paul's understanding of

how the multiple moves had affected each of them;
ii. boarding school (for which an assisted place could easily be obtained through the RAF) which would protect Paul from having his study programme interrupted again;
iii. making plans to leave home at 16.

At the end of each child centred assessment day, staff meet to formally record observations of how each youngster has related to both peers and staff. Observations of problem behaviour are also noted.

Up to this point, the play activities (e.g. swimming, horse riding) have usually allowed the group to share a high level of positive feelings. However, the work sessions have characteristically been devoid of intense emotional expression. That is, the work has helped the youngsters obtain only intellectual appreciation of their difficulties.

On the evening of the residential period, the team consultant conducts a series of group exercises which allows youngsters an opportunity to access painful emotional material which underpins their problem behaviour. We refer to this as *touching the heart of the problem*. The following are the more important elements of this group work. Taking turns at speaking and active listening must be facilitated. Group members must be helped to give feedback to indicate that active listening has occurred. The consultant must create a climate where the youngsters feel that expressing hidden feelings or strong emotions will be accepted by the group. The way in which experiencing painful emotions, which underpin personal difficulties, can be useful in finding a way through such difficulties must be demonstrated. The group usually closes with a series of group games that encourage positive feelings and group cohesion.

> The group began with G showing the group a conch and telling the story of the role of the Conch in Golding's *Lord of the Flies*. The central idea is that only the person with the conch can speak. All others must listen. After the conch holder has spoken the group members have an opportunity to give feedback by saying *I believe you* or *I don't believe you* Group members each are given a chance to hold the conch and speak. Initially a round of speaking about trivial matters occurred. Later, the members were invited to talk about how something they believe leads to strong feelings which cause them to act in ways that get them into trouble. Two staff gave examples from their own experiences to model the process. When it came to Paul's turn (the lad mentioned in previous examples in this section), he expressed the anger he felt towards his father in particular for moving the family about and making him leave his friends and said this led to his fighting and stealing. When he connected with the anger he found that he was also angry

that his dad spent so much time at work and had little time for him. Finally, this anger gave way to the strong feelings of hurt and loss he felt at losing his friends and at becoming estranged from his father. He said he wanted to find a way to reconnect with his dad. He was facilitated through this process by GG.

After this piece of group work the youngsters retire and the consultant convenes a staff meeting. The meeting has two functions. First, for each case, new information arising from the *touching the heart of the problem* group is identified and recorded. Second, staff are given an opportunity to unwind. We have found that this period is important for facilitating team cohesion.

Throughout the child centred assessment period, team members have a commitment to adopting the *reasonable parent role* (Becker, 1964). This role involves relating to youngsters with warmth, communicating directly and clearly, giving age appropriate responsibilities, consequating acceptable and unacceptable actions consistently with praise or disapproval, and resolving conflicts through negotiation. Because we adopt this role, if youngsters want to opt out of any *work* or *play* activity they may do so and a compromise is negotiated with their keyworker. For example, some youngsters opt out of swimming but play table tennis instead. Others opt out of the *touching the heart of the matter* group but as an alternative, engage in less emotionally charged work with their keyworker.

At the end of the child centred assessment period (which is usually a fairly emotional event) key workers inform their clients that they will meet with them and their families to feedback the assessment results in the near future.

FAMILY ASSESSMENT
Between the child centred assessment days at Thurlow House and the residential assessment period, key workers conduct a family evaluation. This usually involves between one and three sessions. However, more sessions are often required. For example, it would be difficult to conduct a thorough family evaluation in three sessions if a youngster's parents were divorced and if he had lived in three different foster homes and with both sets of grandparents.

The family evaluation has one primary objective. It provides a forum within which the keyworker can deepen his or her working alliance with the significant members of the youngster's social network which began in the contracting interview. The development of this relationship is crucial. Whether the parents (or those responsible for the youngster) accept or reject the recommendations presented to them at the end of the programme will depend to a large extent upon the rapport the keyworker has developed with them.

This relationship with the youngster's family is developed within the context of evaluation exercises where the keyworker gathers information on family membership, development, structure and functioning. The genogram is one of the central methods we use for family evaluation (McGoldrick & Gerson, 1985). The keyworker facilitates the family's participation in drawing a family tree, spanning at least three generations. Nine levels of information are placed onto this framework:

i. individual demographic information: names, dates of birth and death, education and occupations;

ii. individual personal characteristics: developmental history, appearance, personality, interests and achievements, strengths, illnesses, problems and addictions;

iii. entrances to, and exits from family relationships: circumstances of birth, circumstances of death, stillbirths, adoptions, fosterings, homeleavings, marriages, divorces;

iv. parenting beliefs and skills: how nurturance is given; how discipline and control are exercised; how play and intellectual stimulation occur; how parenting tasks are divided between parents; parents' beliefs about how the presenting problems should be handled; parents' views on what the grandparents or significant others think is the solution to the presenting problem; whether intrafamilial child abuse has occurred; and how parents deal with sex and aggression;

v. marital relationships: duration and stability of present and previous marital or cohabiting relationships; how each partner manages closeness and emotional intimacy; roles and power structure of present and previous marital relationships;

vi. family factions and patterns of relationships: factions and patterns within current nuclear and extended family; patterns which recur from parents' treatment of one child to the next within the nuclear family; patterns which recur from generation to generation; patterns associated with birth order, age, sex or other personal characteristics;

vii. stage of lifecycle of nuclear family at present and adequacy of their management of main developmental tasks;

viii. extrafamilial social support: relationships of nuclear family and extended family to friends, schools, and other agencies;

ix. extrafamilial stress: physical stresses such as cramped housing conditions; financial stresses such as unemployment and poverty; social stresses such as living in a community with a high crime level; cultural stresses such as being a member of an ethnic minority group.

The following example illustrates how collecting information on parenting beliefs and skills and extrafamilial social support (levels iv and viii set out above) can be used in deepening the working alliance with a single parent. The keyworker uses empathy and warmth to connect with the mother and frames the questions about the extended family in a way that gives the mother access to family resources that have remained untapped. Karl Tomm has written extensively on this style of interviewing (Tomm, 1987).

Key Worker (KW): You've said that she won't do a thing you ask.

Mother (M): (With anger) That's right.

KW: (Curiously and with respect) If your mother or father were here what advice do you think that they would give you?

M: They're no help.

KW: At the moment they provide little support, I understand that. But when you were a youngster like Sam, if you behaved like she does what would your mum and dad have done.

M: Well mum would have screamed at me and dad would have took no notice. *KW:* You've tried both of those approaches with Sam and many others?

M: Yes. She won't listen to reason. She's a chip off the old block. She's going to make all the mistakes I did ... I can just see it.

KW: Could anyone help you see reason when you were her age? Was there anyone who knew how to get through to you?

M: (Switches from anger to thoughtful sorrow) Well there was Nan but she's dead now.

KW: (Smiling warmly) What was special about Nan.

M: (With warmth) Well she didn't bully you ... and you know ... you just did with her.

KW: She understood you?

M: Mmmmhh.

KW: She was on your side?

M: Yes, that's it. She was on my side and the others were against me.

KW: But at the moment, no one is on your side in helping you sort our Sam and from Sam's viewpoint no one is on her side.

M: I want to be, but it's just impossible to get there. Do you know what I mean.? She wants out. I can't cope with her. That's it.

KW: You want to be on her side. You guess that she wants you to be on her side. But that's hard to arrange, especially without Nan here to show us.

M: Yes. Nan would have sorted her out.

KW: Nan would have understood her and could have helped you do the same.
M: Yes. KW: Let's look at that ...

ASSESSMENT OF THE ROLE OF THE SCHOOL AND OTHER AGENCIES

The youngster's present and past schools and other agencies involved in helping the teenager or members of the family are contacted, and the views of such involved professionals are sought on the following issues: the way in which they came into contact with the family; whether their involvement is statutory or not; the type of help they have offered the family; the effectiveness of this family; whether their continued involvement is maintaining or relieving the presenting problems; helping resources that they could potentially offer the family; their investment in various possible types of solutions to the presenting difficulties. From the youngster's present and past schools information is sought on attendance, achievement, conduct. and peer relations.

Social Services, general practitioners, health visitors, the National Society for the Prevention of Cruelty to Children, the School Psychological Service, the Educational and Welfare Office, Departments of Paediatrics and Adult Psychiatry at our local district general hospital, and various voluntary agencies are among the more common agencies that have to be contacted. In cases where a youngster or member of the family has moved to our district from another, we trace records from previously involved agencies.

Whether contact with involved agencies is made by letter, phone or interview depends upon a large number of factors. However, if a keyworker has good reason to believe that an involved professional or agency could make a substantial contribution to the solution to the problem or could oppose a potentially fruitful solution, then face-to-face contact is made. We believe that such face-to-face contact, while time consuming in the short term, is essential if the worker is to develop a good working relationship with colleagues from other agencies. The following closing dialogue from a school visit illustrates this point.

Key Worker (KW): So Mary has been a poor attender for two years, has been involved in a lot of conduct problems, is a poor achiever, but leans on you for support when her mother is going through bad patches and she also has it in for three particular staff members who keep pressurizing you to expel her.
School Principal (SP): That's the way it is.
KW: You're a martyr (Laughing)Do you know that? I don't know how you've had the patience to hold on to her, especially with resourcing the way it is.

SP: It's a relief that someone else can see it as it is.
KW: When I've spoken to all involved and have some ideas on a way forward with this one can I get back to you then?
SP: Please do ...

PSYCHO-EDUCATIONAL EVALUATION

This evaluation is carried out if a youngster has academic difficulties which remain puzzling for parents and involved professionals. It is also conducted if there is doubt about the suitability of a youngster's current educational placement. This type of evaluation usually occurs after information from the youngster's schools and the School Psychological Service has been obtained. The assessment is normally carried out in a single two hour session. The Revised Wechsler Intelligence Scale for Children, the Revised Wide Range Achievement Test and the Neale Analysis of Reading Ability Test constitute the standard test battery.

Previously undiagnosed specific learning disabilities or mild mental handicap are the most common conditions which come to light from our psycho-educational evaluation.

REVIEW AND FORMULATION MEETINGS

These meetings are chaired by the team consultant and attended by all team members. Usually four cases are formulated by the team on each day. A room equipped with a whiteboard large enough to contain a summary of available information on one case is used for this part of the programme.

These meetings have two main functions. First, they provide a forum within which available information on each case may be integrated into a coherent formulation. Case management plans which follow from such formulations are then drawn up. Second, the meetings are used to train junior staff and students in formulation and case management planning skills.

For each case, the team consultant facilitates the keyworker in the presentation of the information that has been collected. He then summarises this and writes it up on the board. The principle headings under which information is summarised are:
i. circumstances of referral and presenting problems;
ii. child behaviour checklist scores;
iii. illegal behaviour;
iv. family structure and functioning;
v. developmental stresses;
vi. previous interventions and role of other professionals;
vii. school report;
viii. observations made on child centred assessment days;
ix. youngster's view of the problem;

x. psychoeducational evaluation.
This practice allows all staff to have access to the same information at the same time.

The keyworker then attempts to categorise this summary of the available information into the model outlined in Figure 8.1. Thus, certain pieces of information will be labelled as predisposing factors. Others will be recognised as precipitating, maintaining or protective factors. The consultant facilitates this process and where appropriate encourages input from other team members, but guards against it becoming a free-for-all discussion. The onus is on the keyworker to do the bulk of the work at this point. Once the information has been categorised within the model, the consultant facilitates the keyworker in the development of a comprehensive formulation which links the information in the model together in a coherent way. When the keyworker reaches the point where he or she is either satisfied with the formulation or stuck, other team members are invited to offer comments on the formulation. The consultant facilitates this process by encouraging creativity, lateral thinking and so forth, rather than being judgmental and critical. This process of team brainstorming is often appreciated by students. It provides an illustration of the value of multidisciplinary work.

After a period of brainstorming, the consultant summarises the various ideas that have been proposed and facilitates the keyworker in reaching a final formulation. A good formulation has five main characteristics:
i. It is specific rather than vague;
ii. All statements are logically and coherently connected;
iii. It is comprehensive so takes account of most of the available information;
iv. It points to clear practical recommendations the efficacy of which may be easily tested;
v. it points to case management options that should be avoided (Carr, 1987). Here is an example of a formulation (because of space limitation it is presented in narrative rather than diagrammatic form.)

> *Problem definition:* John is a 13 year old boy who presents with faecal soiling, stealing, social withdrawal and attainment and conduct problems at school.
> *Maintaining factors:* John steals and soils, and this usually occurs after one of three sorts of exchanges: when his mother (Brenda) tries to help him improve his conduct at home or with his attainments at school by giving him *a good talking to*; when he sees his stepfather (Bill) or mother praise his only brother (Mick) for his accomplishments; when his father (Frank) alters arrangements about access visits. After his

stealing or soiling is discovered, usually his mother tries her best to set him straight by giving him *a good talking to.* John then steals or soils again. Occasionally there may be a period of sulking during which John confines himself to his room and thinks about his difficulties or builds model aeroplanes. This is the cycle of interaction surrounding the problem. What follows are the vicious cycles of thoughts and feelings in which John, Brenda and Bill are ensnared.

When John is involved in any of the three trigger situations outlined above he (mistakenly) sees the actions of his mother, father and stepfather as proof that he is no good and that no one cares about him. He becomes sad but doubts that his mother or stepfather could comfort him. Then he becomes angry. He knows that he can not beat his parents or his brother in an open argument. He then finds himself stealing things from them or soiling and surmises that this is the way he expresses anger at them.

Brenda tries to help him overcome his problems by reprimanding him but finds herself becoming more angry with him than she intends. This anger is fuelled largely by guilt. She feels guilty because she believes that the divorce has caused John's difficulties; that she favours Mick over him; and that from time to time she displaces anger at Frank (about him changing access arrangements) onto John.

Bill has never become fully involved with John as a father figure. He does not discipline him nor does he take him on father-son outings. This is because he does not want to offend his wife. If he took a more active role in fathering the boy, Frank might criticize Brenda for letting him do so.

John is of borderline intelligence and attends a mainstream secondary school. He is in mixed ability classes for most of his subjects. This philosophy is adopted by the school so children with learning difficulties will not feel stigmatised. Unfortunately, the additional teaching resources necessary to effectively run mixed ability classes have not been made available to the school. John therefore receives only the same type of learning experiences as his more able peers and so sees himself failing in relation to them most of the time. This confirms his view of himself as *no-good.* This belief, which events at home and school reinforce, has eroded his motivation to try harder at school and has also made him frustrated. His low motivation and frustration find expression in poor application to academic tasks and disruptive behaviour in school. This has led his teachers to see him as delinquent or lazy rather than as a lad with learning difficulties who is demoralised.

Precipitating factors: John's stealing and soiling began four years ago when Frank and Brenda's marital difficulties became severe. After the separation and even after Bill moved in, the problems began to improve.

Three factors precipitated a recurrence of the home based problems and the beginning of the school based difficulties when was eleven and a half years old: the move to secondary school; decreased contact with his father after Frank moved to a new house 30 miles away; his brother's outstanding school achievement which resulted in Mick obtaining a scholarship to attend a private grammar school. This underlined the contrast between the two boys.

The present referral was precipitated by the failure of the parents to secure additional educational resources for John, following a section 5 assessment under the 1981 Education Act, and an episode where Brenda came close to physically abusing John when he defecated in her underwear drawer.

Predisposing factors: John has always had a special relationship with his father and this predisposed him to developing difficulties at the time of the separation when Frank left the household. From Brenda's perspective, John resembles Frank physically and so reminds her of him. This predisposes John to being scapegoated more than Mick, who does not resemble his father. John has always been of borderline intelligence and this predisposed him to having difficulties finding an appropriate education placement.

Protective factors: At a personal level John has the capacity to make and maintain supportive relationships with adults (e.g his father) and peers. He is also skilled in constructing model aeroplanes. This is his single area of technical or academic mastery.

At a family level, his stepfather is an untapped resource. If all family members' apprehensions about Bill becoming involved with John could be dealt with, he could offer John a supportive relationship within the household.

Within the educational context three protective factors are present.

i. The team, historically, has a good working relationship with John's school.

ii. Our unit's assessment may be used as a basis for appealing against the decision not to offer additional educational resources and requesting that a welfare or teaching assistant be made available to the school to help them meet John's needs.

iii. Our team has a good relationship with a school for mildly mentally handicapped youngsters to which John could be transferred if necessary.

At a professional level, the keyworker has developed good working relationships with all involved parties and is willing to be involved in further work with John's network.

Once the formulation has been drawn up, the keyworker proposes a series of management options which follow directly from it. The pros and cons of each option are then examined by the team. Finally, the most viable package of options is specified. Options which would maintain or exacerbate the presenting problems and which should be avoided are also noted. Responsibilities for carrying out the plan are then agreed upon.

Goals: In the example just presented we set the following goals: to disrupt the cycle of interaction underpinning his stealing and soiling which occurred at home; to disrupt the cycle of interaction surrounding his school based difficulties.

Recommendation 1: With respect to the first goal, a number of tactics were considered. The cycle could be interrupted by arranging for John to live elsewhere, e.g with his father, with another relative, in boarding school or in voluntary care. Work focused on helping John and Brenda develop a more positive relationship could occur concurrently and John could be reintegrated into the family at a later point. This is the sort of solution favoured by Brenda at the contracting interview. It would remove the opportunity for her to physically abuse her son. However, it had its difficulties. First, John might interpret his mother's desire that he leave as rejection rather than protection and so confirm his belief that he was *no good* . Second, for John to live with Bill or other relatives was not practical for a variety of reasons. Third, given the failure of the school to obtain additional teaching resources for John throughout the statementing procedure, it was unlikely that a boarding school placement could be obtained (on social grounds) by appeal. Even if a place could be obtained, between red tape and school holidays it would be nine months before John could begin.

An alternative set of tactics would be to invite Bill Frank and Brenda to agree that Brenda opt out of the cycle of interaction by handing over all parenting responsibilities to Bill and Frank, on a temporary basis. Bill and Frank could be encouraged to help John develop life skills necessary for adulthood as a way of raising John's self-esteem. For example, they could help John to find a way of using his model building skills to earn extra pocket money. They could also be coached in effective behavioural methods for dealing with encopresis and theft. Once this process had been set in motion, the focus could shift to enhancing John's relationship with his mother. Family work embodying this set of tactics was our recommended course of action.

Recommendation 2: On the educational side two tactics were considered. First, transfer John to a local day school for mildly mentally handicapped children. Second, feedback our formulation to John's teachers and discuss the implications of this for his management in his present school while concurrently appealing against the decision of the local education authority to deny John access to a teaching assistant to help him keep pace with his more able peers in mixed ability classes.

The transfer could be arranged immediately and such a placement would lead to fewer *failure experiences* for John. However, it could lead to him being stigmatised. The liaison work with his present school would only be effective if the appeal were to provide the school with a teaching assistant. The appeal would take at least three months and the outcome was uncertain. Our recommendation was that John, Brenda, Bill and Frank discuss these two options, visit the alternative school, consult with the Area Education Office and decide for themselves. The keyworker agreed to guide them through this process.

If the team have difficulty agreeing upon a formulation, a critical piece of information may not have been identified during the programme. The team must always keep this option open and be prepared to accept that further assessment may be required. In such cases the team can usually specify the area which should be addressed by subsequent investigations. For example, a critical member of the extended family may require interviewing or an ill parent's prognosis may need to be checked in person with an out-of-town specialist.

When student key workers are involved in the programme, the team usually chooses one case to be formulated in *slow motion* following step-by- step the guidelines set out in this section. Experienced keyworkers usually find that many cases can be formulated rapidly. Only about a third require lengthy deliberation. It is the consultant's responsibility to help the team decide upon which cases will require a lengthy review and which will be done more rapidly. This information allows the team to schedule the workload over the two whole days which are set aside for review and formulation.

REPORT WRITING

A team member other than the worker transcribes the summary of available information off the board onto a note pad for each case. The hypothesis and action plan are also transcribed. The keyworker uses this information as a basis for writing a comprehensive report which is placed on both the medical and social work files as a source document for future reference. A copy of this document is usually sent to the referring agent.

Sometimes additional reports have to be written. For example, where it is recommended that a child be taken into care, separate medical, social work and psychological reports may be required by the court. Where the Area Education Officer requests our opinion concerning a youngster's special educational needs, usually a brief resume of our position is all that is required.

FEEDBACK

The core of any feedback message contains our formulation or understanding of adolescent's difficulties and the management option which we think will serve the youngster's best interests.

Feedback is always given to the key people in the youngster's network. This invariably includes the adolescent, the people who hold parental rights, the people most concerned that the adolescent's problem behaviour is altered, and the referring agent. Others who may require feedback are: people who have held parental rights; actual or potential foster parents; members of the extended family; other members of the adolescent's household; other involved professionals and siblings.

Feedback is given for different reasons. If the sole purpose is to keep a person informed, then feedback may be effectively given by phone or letter. If, however, feedback involves offering a view on how a situation could fruitfully be changed, then feedback is best given at a meeting. If the proposed action plan involves co-ordinated decision making on the part of many members of the youngster's network, then we often convene a network meeting and offer feedback within this context.

If the keyworker has done the job effectively, the family interviews, the child centred assessment days, the school contacts and meetings with other professionals will have been used as a forum for developing good working relationships and fostering a climate of trust. However, we sometimes anticipate that some of the families referred to our programme will have difficulty accepting our feedback and so we plan to deliver feedback in a way which will minimise resistance (Anderson and Stewart, 1983). For example, we endeavour to present our formulation in a non-blaming way that is sensitive to every network member's good intentions. We encourage network members to discuss the pros and cons of various management options, including that favoured by our team.

Often it is useful for one or more team members to join the keyworker for the feedback meeting, e.g where a family is expected to be highly resistant; where specialist information has to be presented such as psychometric test results; or where family work is going to be offered as part of a case management package and the co-therapist has to be introduced to the family. Usually feedback meetings end with the adolescent and members of the network either accepting or rejecting our recommendations. At this point a second psychiatric consultation occurs.

FINAL PSYCHIATRIC CONSULTATION

One of us (DMcD) in the role of Clinical Director, meets with the youngster and the parents (or those with parental rights) to confirm the family's decision concerning the recommendations. On the rare occasions where recommendations are rejected the case is returned to the referring agent. Where the recommendations are accepted and these involve clinic staff, (eg. arranging a placement or offering counselling) a contract for this further work is made.

PROGRAMME ADMINISTRATION

Flexible and skilled administrative back-up is critical to the smooth running of the programme. Important administrative tasks include maintaining a waiting list, co-ordinating staff diaries, arranging appointments and hospital transport if necessary, booking community based activities, buying food and equipment, handling routine and crisis related phone calls, typing reports and correspondence, arranging feedback conferences and handling programme finances. These responsibilities are met by two sessional workers who are each employed three sessions a week for the 13 weeks of the programme. Our sessional workers were previously employed as an Education and Welfare Officer and as a Police Officer. Both have a facility for working with children and families and of course have a flair for administrative work. In addition to their administrative responsibilities, both join the clinical team on the child centred assessment days to help out with both *work* and *play* activities.

The development of a large enough petty cash float to meet the running costs of the child centred assessment days and to pay sessional workers deserves special mention. This amounts to £3,000 per year and is jointly funded by the Health Authority and Social Services.

FINAL COMMENTS
Our Heath Authority has no adolescent psychiatry inpatient unit. Our Social Services Department has no residential observational and assessment centre. Only three to four cases per annum are referred to such facilities outside our district. In view of this it is clear that the programme described in this paper in the majority of cases fulfils the function held by residential assessment units in other districts. This multidisciplinary and multidimensional approach to adolescent assessment can be replicated in other agency settings. For example, a social work child care team could organise and run this programme and co-opt the aid of a psychologist and psychiatrist on a sessional basis. We also believe that this approach to assessment can be useful with other populations, e.g. families where child abuse has occurred (Gawlinski et al., 1988).

REFERENCES
Achenbach, T. (1985). *Assessment and Taxonomy of Child and Adolescent Psychopathology.* Beverley Hills, CA: Sage
Achenbach, T. and Edelbrock, C. (1983). *Manual for the Child Behavior Checklist.* Burlington, VT: University of Vermont.
Achenbach, T. and Edelbrock, C. (1986). *Manual for the Teacher Report Form.* Burlington, VT: University of Vermont.
Achenbach, T. and Edelbrock, C. (1988). *Manual for the Youth Self-Report Form.* Burlington, VT: University of Vermont.
Anderson, C. & Stewart, S. (1983). *Mastering Resistance.* New York: Guilford.
Anthony, E. & Cohler, B (1987) .*The Invulnerable Child.* New York: Guilford.
Becker, W. (1964). Consequences of different kinds of parental discipline. In M. Hoffman & L. Hoffman (eds.). *Review of Child Development* (Vol. 1). New York: Russell Sage.
Beitman, B. (1987). *The Structure of Individual Psychotherapy.* New York: Guilford.
Carr, A. (1987). *Constructing Hypotheses to Guide Systems Interventions.* Workshop presented at the Association for Family Therapy National Training Conference, York.
Garrison, W. & Earls, F. (1987). *Temperament and Child Psychopathology.* Beverley Hills, CA: Sage.
Gawlinski, G., Carr, A., Irving, N., & MacDonnell, D. (1988). Thurlow House Assessment Programme for families with physical abused children. *Practice*, 2, 208-220.
Health Advisory Service (HAS) (1986). *Bridges over Troubled Waters.* A report for the NHS HAS on services for disturbed adolescents. London: DHSS.
Imber-Coopersmith, E. (1985). Families and multiple helpers: A systems perspective. In D. Campbell & R. Draper (eds.), *Applications of Systemic Family Therapy.* London: Grune Stratton.

Johnson, J. (1987). *Life Events as Stressors in Childhood and Adolescence.* Beverley Hills, CA: Sage.

McGolderick, M. & Gerson, R. (1985). *Genograms in Family Assessment.* New York: Norton.

Rutter, M. (1979). *Changing Youth in a Changing Society: Patterns of Adolescent Development and Disorder.* London: Nuffield Provincial Hospital Trust.

Rutter, M. (1985). Family and school influences: Meanings, mechanisms and implications. In R. Nichol (ed.), *Longitudinal Studies in Child Psychology and Psychiatry.* New York: Wiley.

Rutter, M., Graham, P., Chadwick, O., & Yule, W. (1976). Adolescent turmoil: Fact or Fiction. *Journal of Child Psychology and Psychiatry,* 17, 35-36.

Tomm, K. (1987). Interventive interviewing.1. Strategizing as a fourth guideline for the therapist. *Family Process,* 26, 3-14.

Wolfe, D. (1987). *Child Abuse: Implications for Development and Psychopathology.* Beverley Hills: Sage.

CHAPTER 9

FAILURE IN FAMILY THERAPY: A CATALOGUE OF ENGAGEMENT MISTAKES

ABSTRACT
Eleven key positions within the social system which evolves around a presenting problem are set out. A catalogue of common mistakes which arise from failing to distinguish between these elements and take account of their significance during the engagement process is presented, along with specific suggestions for avoiding these clinical errors.

INTRODUCTION
In a quarter to a third of cases, family therapy leads to little improvement in the presenting problem. In about a tenth of all cases the presenting problem becomes worse during the course of therapy (Gurman, Kniskern and Pinsof, 1988). Analyses of treatment failures have pointed to a wide variety of factors which may contribute to unsuccessful therapy (Coleman, 1985; Foa & Ellemkamp, 1983; Mays & Franks, 1985). Engagement difficulties loom large in these analyses.

The central thesis of this paper is that a failure to distinguish between important elements of the overall problem-system[1] may lead the therapist to engage with members of the problem system in ways that inhibit problem resolution. A catalogue of such engagement mistakes drawn from my own practice over the past 10 years and from the family therapy literature will be presented below. First, however, definitions of the 11 key positions within the problem-system will be given.

ELEVEN ELEMENTS OF PROBLEM SYSTEMS

While some of the elements defined below are well recognized, others are less frequently labelled in an explicit manner. The definitions are presented to enhance the clarity of the engagement mistakes listed in the subsequent section.

1. The Problem Person is identified by the customer as the individual with difficulties requiring professional help. There may be more than one such person in a problem system.

2. The Customer is the member of the problem system most eager that the referral be made so that treatment for the problem person may be secured (Fisch et al., 1982).

3. The Emotionally Attached Caregiver is the person who offers the problem person the greatest emotional support and nurturance. Close positive attachments tend to protect people from mental and physical breakdown (Barrera, 1988; Quinton & Rutter, 1988). Emotionally attached caregivers may therefore be viewed as a significant therapeutic resource.

4. Persons Legally Responsible for the Problem Person are vital members of the problem system since the problem person may not enter into a therapeutic contract without their consent.

5. System Members who Promote Stuckness are those who, by their actions or influence, prevent the resolution of the presenting problem. Usually, the homeostatic influence that these people exert is unintentional. System members who promote stuckness may be members of the problem person's family, peer group, school, work situation or professional helping network. Introjects and family ghosts may also be identified as members of this subsystem.

6. System Members who Promote Change are those members of the problem system whose energy may readily be deployed so as to resolve the presenting problem. This subsystem may include the therapist and the therapeutic resources to which she has access. It may also include individuals from those areas of the problem person's life listed in the previous paragraph.

7. The Referring Agent is that pivotal member of the problem system who connects the therapist, the team and the agency to the extant problem system.

8. The Therapist is that person who must engage with the problem system and intervene in it in a way that allows its members to find alternative and effective methods for dealing with the presenting problem.

9. The Team is that group of people which helps the therapist form hypotheses and decide about intervention strategies. The team also helps the therapist monitor her pattern of engagement with the problem system. The role of the team may also be filled by a supervisor or a co-therapist. Techniques which may be used by solo-therapists whose team offers indirect rather than live supervision have been described elsewhere (Carr, 1986).

10. The Agency is the context within which the therapist and the team offer their therapeutic services. Agencies employ therapists and teams and provide them with managerial and administrative support and control.

11. Agents of Social Control are system members who exert actual or potential statutory power over the problem person or members of her family. They are representatives of the State empowered to intervene in clients' lives without consent, for the common good. Social workers, psychiatrists and probation officers commonly find themselves in this role.

From this list of definitions, it is clear that in any problem system one person may carry out the function of more than one element. For example, in a self-referred single parent family the mother may be one of the problem people, the customer, the person legally responsible for the problem person and the referring agent.

A CATALOGUE OF ENGAGEMENT MISTAKES

1. Assuming that the nuclear family of the problem person is the unit of treatment. This faulty assumption stems from the notion that a dysfunctional family structure is the primary cause of the problem person's difficulties, which in turn reinforce the dysfunctional family structure. This view neither fits with the results of empirical studies of risk factors in various disorders (Rutter and Garmezy, 1983) nor is it clinically useful in many cases (Wynne et al., 1987) . The common practice in family therapy of arbitrarily drawing a boundary around the nuclear family is a similar error to at made by psychotherapists who routinely draw a boundary around the individual. Most of the engagement mistakes described below derive from the mistaken assumption that the family is the unit of treatment

An alternative position for the clinician is that the occurrence of a problem (for whatever reason) may lead various people to come together in an attempt to solve it (Goolishian & Winderman, 1988). This group may include members of nuclear, extended, step, adoptive and foster families. It may include peers and colleagues from work settings, and members of religious, recreational and other community-based organizations. It may also include a variety of statutory and non-statutory professionals such as physicians, social workers, probation officers, health visitors, dieticians etc. Occasionally, this group of people becomes organized into a problem system which is ineffectual in solving the presenting difficulties. The therapist is invited by the customer to join this system and to attempt to participate in it in a way that leads to problem resolution.

For the therapist to be of assistance to the problem system, she must engage the minimum sufficient network and establish a therapeutic contract (Skynner, 1968). This network always includes the problem person, the person legally responsible for the problem person and the customer. The contract must include the possibility that other members of the problem system beyond the minimum sufficient network be included in the therapy process. The contract may be written or verbal implicit or explicit.

2. Assuming that the person legally responsible for the problem person is the customer, when the referring agent is customer. This mistake usually occurs in cases where the problem-person presents with 'social control' problems such as conduct problems in children or addictive behaviour in adults (e.g., Carl & Jurkovic, 1983).

Example 1. A school principal referred a boy and his family for therapy, via the GP, because of the boy's school-based conduct problems. The family did not attend the intake interview. A phone call to the GP revealed that the parents felt antagonistic towards the school and were ambivalent about our unit which they viewed as aligned with the school. Here, the school was the customer.

Example 2. A probation officer referred a problem drinker and his cohabitee for marital therapy. The therapy was requested with a view to helping the husband gain control of his drinking problem. Initially the couple appeared to be committed to therapy however, after a few sessions, it became clear that they were only *going through the motions* to appease the probation officer. Here the probation officer was the customer.

To avoid this error it is useful to clarify by phone if the referring agent is the customer. If this is the case, the referring agent may be asked to be responsible for the family's attendance at the intake interview and to attend this meeting themselves. The focus of such meetings is to help the person legally responsible for the problem person and the referring agent clarify the pro's and con's of the problem and the person and the person legally   responsible for the problem person committing themselves to a therapeutic contract.

3. Assuming that the problem person's emotionally attached caregiver is the customer when the referring agent is the customer. This mistake usually occurs in cases where attachment difficulties between parents and children or husbands and wives are the central presenting problem.

> **Example 1.** A Social Worker referred a young single mother and her 2-year-old daughter for therapy. The Social Worker described the mother and child as having *poor bonding*. The mother often left the child to cry for periods of up to an hour and frequently felt as if the baby were trying intentionally to annoy her. The mother said that she wanted help with finding a way to deal with her child's crying. She also agreed to explore ways in which she could increase the social support available to her as an isolated single parent. However, her attendance at therapy was erratic and she rarely completed homework assignments. I invited her and the referring social worker to a meeting to explore reasons for the therapeutic failure. It transpired that the mother believed that the social worker had decided to take the child into care. The referral had been an attempt on the social worker's part, she believed, to prove that she could not be helped. No matter how hard she tried to benefit from the therapy, she believed that ultimately the social worker would take her baby into care. Therefore, she put little effort into the venture. The social worker was, in this case, the customer.

> Subsequently, the Social Worker attended a series of sessions in which she stated explicitly, in behavioural terms, the expectations held by her department of competent parents. This convinced the mother that her parenting was indeed competent. I then offered a contract to the mother for therapy that would focus on *enriching* her relationship with her child, since the social worker's criteria had demonstrated that remedial therapy was not required.

> **Example 2.** A concerned husband (the emotionally attached care giver) and his depressed wife were referred for marital therapy by their GP. Initially the husband behaved as if he

were the customer. The therapy went well at first but later floundered when the husband's attendance became erratic. A phone call to the GP revealed that he had been advising the couple for months to engage in marital therapy although the husband had always opposed this. The husband believed that only medication could solve his wife's difficulties. Thus,   in this case the GP was the customer.

The GP and I met the couple and negotiated a compromise whereby a trial of antidepressant medication would be given in conjunction with a series of marital therapy sessions.

In cases such as these, the referring agent and the therapist must meet the problem person and the emotionally attached caregiver to negotiate a mutually acceptable set of therapeutic goals and methods. In this contract the commitment of the emotionally attached caregiver to the therapeutic process must be made explicit. Outlining the significance of enriched emotional attachments for the mental and physical well-being of children and spouses is a useful tactic to use in these interviews serving to raise the motivation of attached caregivers. Often emotionally attached caregivers have become demoralized by the time they are referred for therapy. They feel angry and may mistreat the problem person. These experiences may lead them to blame themselves for th problem person's difficulties. Reminding them that they are a vital therapeutic resource may go some way towards removing this sense of demoralization .

4. Assuming that the referring agent has a positive alliance with all family members. If the referring agent has a very strong alliance with one or two subsystems of the overall problem-system and neutral or negative alliances with others, the therapist may be sucked into a particular role in the family drama which renders her impotent. Usually this role is one that was previously occupied by the referring agent. Selvini Palazzoli (1980) and her colleagues have described this problem in cases where the referring agent is a close friend of one family member. Physicians (either GPs or specialists) who have been treating one family member for years, counsellors who are very supportive of the mother in the family and social workers who act as middlemen between the patient and the parents, are the three main categories of referring agent identified by the Milan group in their study of this problem. The referring agent's relationship with the family progresses from one of apparent co-operation to a state where little progress is made and the referring agent feels disqualified and trapped. In the final stage, the referral is made when the referring agent has become exasperated.

The Milan group noted that when they accepted referrals like these without including the referring agent in the initial meetings, or at least without discussing the family's relationship with the referring agent, therapy was ineffective. The team slipped into fulfilling the same function as the referring agent. They dealt with this problem by prescribing continued contact with the referring agent and positively connoting all that he or she had done.

Selvini Palazzoli (1985) and her colleagues have also described the difficulties that arise in cases where a prestigious sibling of the problem person is the referring agent. Usually the sibling has a close relationship with one parent and holds a privileged and powerful position within the family. The demands of new relationships outside the family, however make the sibling feel tied down. He sees family therapy as a way of liberating himself from his exacting role. There is also the possibility that the prestigious referring sibling has begun to grow envious of the love and attention which the problem sibling commands. The key to the Milan group's approach has been to avoid slipping into the referring sibling's shoes by attempting to do therapy with the remainder of the family.

    Example 1. Selvini Palazzoli (1986) describes how she and the Milan Team first offered a family referred by a sibling an assessment, so as to check if they were suitable for family therapy. During the assessment, the pattern of interaction which surrounded the problem person and included the parents, the siblings and the referring sibling was established. At the conclusion of the assessment, the therapist then described this pattern, positively connoting the role of problem person in creating a prestigious position within the family for the referring sibling to occupy. She then said that family therapy was not indicated, since it would lead to improvement in the problem person which would destroy the privileged position of the referring person in the family and lead to him becoming depressed. The problem daughter spontaneously improved and referring sibling left home to live in his own apartment.

5. Failing to Identify System Members that Promote Stuckness. This error can occur when the therapist assumes that the nuclear family is the unit of treatment but where the boundaries of a nuclear family are fairly diffuse and family members rely on close ties with members of their community or the extended family for carrying out the tasks of day to day living.

    Example 1. A single parent of borderline intelligence and her 9 year- old son, who had mainly home-based conduct problems, were referred by the GP. An assessment showed that when the mother asked the boy to do something to which he objected, he would often throw a tantrum. The mother managed these tantrums inconsistently; it appeared that the tantrums continued because most of the time they got him what he wanted, it seemed that the mother's inconsistency persisted because she did not know what else to do. It was not related to emotional exhaustion since the mother was well supported emotionally, both by her sister who lived locally and by members of her church.

At the conclusion of first session the mother and son agreed to carry out two homework tasks. The first involved the mother spending half an hour a day with her son doing painting, his favourite activity. They understood that this regular period of positive interaction was to rebuild the positive side of their relationship which had become tainted with bitterness. The second task involved the boy going to *time out* under mother's supervision anytime he lost his temper, so that he could learn how to control it himself.

The mother and son consistently executed the temper control task incorrectly. Mother would let the boy out of his bedroom immediately he began swearing and cursing. Careful interviewing revealed that she abhorred swearing because of her religious beliefs. She would rather her boy got his own way than be eternally dammed for swearing—and she was certain that her vicar would take the same view. Thus the vicar (and possibly God) were up to this point *system members promoting stuckness* whom I had failed to identify. I made arrangements to meet the vicar and after some discussion about the rationale behind the tasks he convinced the mother to go along with the homework assignments. In the long run, he said, they would help her son avoid sin and keep to the path of righteousness.

The assumption that the boundaries of a problem system are rarely the boundaries of the family is helpful in identifying system members who promote stuckness. It helps inform clinical practice in various ways. For example, during assessment it becomes necessary to draw an ecomap as well as a genogram. It provides a context within which the therapist remains uncertain about the principal characters in the problem person's drama for longer. This helps the therapist to cling less tenaciously to an initial formulation or hypothesis.

System members who promote stuckness may reside not only out in the wider community but also in the memories of members of the nuclear family. When therapists focus on current patterns of interaction without reference to past relationships, and where introjects or ghosts are a significant part of the family drama, they may fail to identify these system members. These stuckness-promoting-system-members may be estranged or deceased and so physically absent from the problem system. However as introjects or ghosts, they continue to have a powerful constraining influence on the search for a workable solution to the presenting problem. Usually the member of the problem system influenced by the ghost will require a forum within which to complete unfinished business.

    Example 2. In an initial interview with the mother of a 13-year-old- girl referred because of her aggressive and defiant conduct, it emerged that the girl's problem behaviour only occurred in specific circumstances. When mother, stepfather and daughter were together and stepfather showed more interest in the girl than in his wife, or where mother believed that this scenario was imminent, mother and daughter would fight. So as to establish how the presenting problem would have been dealt with in the mother's family of origin, I asked the mother how her mother would have *shared her father*.

    The mother became distressed in response to this enquiry. It emerged that at 13 she had become involved in an incestuous relationship with her father and feared that her daughter and husband might be about to replicate this pattern. The deceased grandfather in the family was a ghost who promoted stuckness

    The parents of the 13-year-old were seen on a number of occasions without their daughter so that the mother could address the unfinished business with her incestuous deceased father. Concurrent family work focusing on straightforward parent-adolescent negotiation progressed without any major impasses.

6. Failing to identify system members who can promote change.
The belief that family therapy may be ineffective if one or more family members receive concurrent individual counselling, group therapy, psychotropic medication or are placed in a therapeutic or custodial institution led many family therapists to take a negative view of other treatment modalities. However, in doing so, therapists cut their clients off from many valuable resources. Numerous examples of effective multimodal treatment approaches where family therapy plays a central part in the programme or where concepts drawn from family systems theory are used to construct the overall treatment programme have been described. A statutory treatment package involving family therapy, peer group therapy for individual family members and the temporary placement of the father outside the family home has been used to

rehabilitate families where incest has occurred (Giaretto, 1982) . Family therapy, peer group therapy and neuroleptic medication is an effective treatment for schizophrenics who live in families where parents score high on the expressed emotion scale (Berkowitz, 1984). Concurrent individual play
therapy or behaviour therapy for the problem person may be effectively integrated with family-based treatment in child psychiatry or paediatric settings (Carr and Afnan, 1989; Carr, McDonnell and Afnan, 1989). These examples differ from the cases which led pioneering family therapists to outlaw concurrent involvement in other forms of treatment in two ways. First, the various therapeutic inputs are co-ordinated by co-operating professionals. Second, these interventions are guided by a systemic case formulation or hypothesis. If the activities of system members who can promote change are not co-ordinated in this way, the problem system may gradually lapse into patterns of behaviour that promote stuckness.

7. Replicating dysfunctional patterns which occur elsewhere in the problem system. When a referral is made to a therapist, the positions taken by various members of the problem system usually form a pattern which is dysfunctional in so far as it precludes the resolution of the presenting problem. Haley's (1967) perverse triad is one such pattern. The most commonly sighted instance of this, is the enmeshed mother child dyad and the peripheral father. The mother, within the context of an exclusive relationship protects the symptomatic child whom she sees as frightened, sick or sad. The father, who has little involvement in child care, views the problem child as naughty, manipulative or bad. A danger exists that when a therapist and team join this problem system, the therapist and the mother child dyad, for example, will become involved in an enmeshed and exclusive relationship to which the team (and the father) are peripheral (Westheafer, 1984).

   If a therapist and team accept that the tendency to replicate dysfunctional patterns is inevitable (particularly in highly dysfunctional problem-systems) and are prepared to consider them as an impediment to problem resolution when a case becomes stuck, then it is unlikely that they will lead to protracted impasses. First, the problem system will become stuck less often because the therapist and team will be anticipating pattern replication. Second, when the system becomes stuck, the therapist, the team and the family can map out the patterns of alliances that they experience and search for alternative solutions that do not involve these dysfunctional alliances.

   In larger problem systems that involve multiple agencies such as those which evolve in cases of child abuse, it is more difficult to anticipate alliances because the group members do not know each other

or each others' agencies' policies well (Carr,1989). Also, the process of
exploring patterns of alliances as a springboard for finding more
functional patterns of organization requires a basic level of interpersonal
trust and professional respect. In large groups of professionals this is
often difficult to achieve because the members do not know each other at
a personal level and professional rivalry rather than respect seems to be
quite common (e.g. Butler-Sloss, 1988).

This problem may be tackled by attempting to form positive
alliances with all those professionals within the district where the
therapist practices who are likely to become involved in large problem
systems. Thus a level of basic trust is established which permits
problem solving rather than polarization when agency groups begin to
replicate patterns present in highly dysfunctional families with which
they are involved

**8. Failing to distinguish the role of therapist from the role of
agent of social control.** An agency may have statutory functions but
also offer a therapeutic service. This is true of departments of social
services, probation, police, psychiatry and education. A social services
department, for example, is empowered by the state to protect children
by requesting that a court remove them from the custody of their
parents. The department may also offer a family therapy service, but if a
worker confuses these two functions, a good therapy will not be offered.
When workers exercise statutory powers, they act as social control
agents for the state. They define and control the limits of an individual's
or family's liberty. Inevitably, the client whose freedom has been
limited through the exercise of statutory power will feel antagonistic
towards the statutory worker. For these two individuals then to attempt
to develop a therapeutic alliance is difficult. It requires the client to
distinguish between the *worker as therapist* from the *worker as agent
of social control*. Maintaining this distinction requires a constant input
of energy from both parties over and above that necessary for therapy. If
the distinction is not maintained, the client may go through the
motions of therapy so as to appease their *statutory controller* or the
client may drop out of therapy.

There is also a danger of this process occurring even when the
statutory worker and the therapist are separate individuals. This is well
illustrated by the example given in paragraph number 3 of this section
where a mother and child referred to me by a social worker because of
attachment difficulties. Although I was in a different agency from the
referring social worker, and no threat of statutory action had been made,
the client still viewed both me and the referring agent as agents of social
control.

In cases where statutory action has been taken or is likely to occur and therapy is offered, the therapist must devise a set of strategies to convince the client that the therapy is distinct from the social control. One useful arrangement is for the statutory worker to set clearly defined and observable criteria which must be met before the statutory limits which have been placed on the client's freedom may be wholly or partially wit drawn. The worker may then refer the case to a therapist requesting that the client be offered a contract for therapy which involves searching for ways to meet the criteria posed by the statutory worker. The statutory worker may then periodically assess therapeutic progress according to the predefined criteria (Cottrell et al., 1990).

9. Failing to take account of the image projected by the agency to prospective clients. The image the agency projects will affect engagement and the therapy process. For example, clients may view probation offices and social work departments as being staffed by social control agents. Hospitals and private therapeutic institutes may be viewed as t e workplaces of helpful professionals. Family therapy was originally developed in the latter type of settings. However, a sizeable number of practitioners now practice within the former types of agencies.

In taking family therapy lock stock and barrel as practised in one agency context and attempting to replicate this in another without taking account of how the agency is perceived by the client group may lead to engagement problems. For example, Howe (1989) found that clients attending a social services staffed family therapy agency had difficulty participating in family therapy and experiencing benefit from the live supervision which was available to the therapist. In fact the live supervision provided by the team via close circuit television was one of the key factors leading to clients' sense of powerlessness. These difficulties occurred, in part, because the therapist and team assumed that their clients were well informed customers who wanted the form o intervention being offered. Howe's study suggests that many of the clients were frightened to voice their opinions and none asked to e referred to another practitioner. Howe's study points to the importance of redressing the perceived imbalance of power for clients who seek therapeutic services from statutory agencies through providing an brief educational induction programme prior to therapy. Such a programme should highlight the details of how the therapeutic process will proceed, the voluntary nature of the treatment contract and the other locally available treatment options (Pimpernell and Treacher, 1990) . If we are to be truly systemic in our outlook we must include therapist, team and agency in our initial formulations. We must make hypotheses about how we are perceived by our clients, test these out and take steps to correct misapprehensions. This is precisely the course of action taken by the team which Howe studied, although regrettably this information was omitted from his book (Reflection, 1989).

10. Failing to engage the agency's management and secure the support necessary for a high quality of clinical practice. While therapists and teams are providing a service for clients and their networks on the one hand, they should be in regular contact with management so as to secure and maintain the resources necessary for their practice on the other. They need their managers to provide them with the time, space, supervision ongoing training and facilities to do this type of work. If these needs are not met the therapist and team will develop burnout and the quality of the service offered will plummet. Therapists and teams must view securing resources and maintaining them as part of their function and use a variety of skills and tactics, including those drawn from an appreciation of systems theory.

Therapists should schedule time to assess and map out their organization in much the same way as one would map out any problem system. This map may include resources outside the agency such as training courses, other premises, trust funds etc. In the light of this assessment they should plan to secure appropriate resources.

If family therapy is being introduced into an agency from *the bottom up* a useful tactic is for therapist to describe some small aspect of clinical work in detail in an informal meeting with the person who holds the required resource. This gives the resource holder an opportunity to empathize with the therapist. The request for increased resources may then be made with reference to the clinical example. Negotiation is less likely to escalate into confrontation if it begins with empathy. Once the demand for family therapy has been established through such small pilot projects, other tactics may be used to consolidate and expand the service offered. Broadly speaking, the team and the referring agents who avail of the therapy service must present an argument to management indicating that the demand for family therapy outstrips the supply and that certain resourcing requirements must be met if the project is to continue (Lieberman, 1989).

DISCUSSION
Taken individually, each of the issues addressed in this paper has been a concern for many family therapists. However these difficulties have rarely been dealt with collectively as a constellation of problems requiring a cohesive set of interrelated solutions. The work of Carpenter and Treacher is a notable exception to this generalization (Carpenter et al., 1983; Carpenter and Treacher, 1989, Treacher and Carpenter, 1982). The relationship between the ideas set out in this paper and those of Carpenter and Treacher deserve some elaboration.

Carpenter and Treacher (1989, Chapter 1), in keeping with the position advocated in this paper, argue that it is unhelpful to assume that the boundary of the problem system is coterminous with the boundary of the problem person's family. The therapist must be prepared to consider other systems in her formulation. These include the clients extended family, work or school system, other agencies involved with the case, the therapist's own team and agency and the therapist s own family.

The second main area of overlap between Carpenter and Treacher's position and that taken here concerns the importance of the worker understanding their role when practising family therapy in their agency (Carpenter and Treacher, 1989, Chapter 2). In two important papers, Carpenter and Treacher identified four sets of difficulties which may inhibit therapeutic progress (Carpenter, Treacher et al., 1983; Treacher and Carpenter, 1982). First, factors related to the context of therapy and the therapeutic contract; of particular importance here is the accuracy with which the therapist identifies the customer and clarity with which the customer's presenting problem and related goals are defined. Second, therapy may become stuck because the style of therapy used or the way in which techniques are employed do not fit with the clients' needs. Third, the therapist may inadvertently (usually through the development of countertransference reactions) become sucked into the problem maintaining system or excluded from the problem resolving system. Fourth, the therapist and her supervisory team may develop a working relationship which inhibits the therapist from helping the clients resolve the presenting problem.

With the exception of the second set of factors (therapeutic style and technique), the difficulties associated with therapy becoming stuck identified by Carpenter and Treacher overlap substantially with those outlined in this paper. The central difference between Treacher and Carpenter's work and the position taken here, is the view that the catalogue of engagement difficulties described in the body of this paper can be viewed as arising from a failure to distinguish between the eleven elements of problem systems listed at the beginning of the article.

NOTES

1. Throughout this paper the term problem-system is used to refer to the social organization which comprises the problem person and those members of her social network who are trying to help her solve the presenting problem. Once a therapist accepts a referral, she and those colleagues from her agency involved in the case become part of this problem system.

REFERENCES

Barrera, M. (1988). Models of social support and life stress. Beyond the buffering hypothesis. In L. Cohen (ed.), *Life Events and Psychological Functioning.* Beverley Hills, CA: Sage.

Berkowitz, R. (1984). Therapeutic intervention with schizophrenic patients and their families a description of a clinical research programme. *Journal of Family Therapy,* 6, 211-233.

Butler-Sloss (1988). *The Cleveland Report.* London: HMSO

Carl, D., & Jurkovic, G. (1983). Agency triangles: problems in agency-family relationships. *Family Process,* 22, 441 451.

Carpenter, J. & Treacher, A. (1989). *Problems and Solutions in Marital and Family Therapy.* Oxford: Basil Blackwell.

Carpenter, J., Treacher, A., Jenkins, H. & O'Reilly, P. (1983). Oh no! Not the Smiths again' An exploration of how to identify and overcome 'stuckness' in family therapy, part II: Stuckness in the therapeutic and supervisory systems. *Journal of Family Therapy,* 5, 81-96.

Carr, A. (1986). Three techniques for the solo family therapist. *Journal of Family Therapy,* 8, 373-382.

Carr, A. (1989). Countertransference reactions to families where child abuse has occurred. *Journal of Family Therapy,* 11, 87-97.

Carr, A. & Afnan, S. (1989). Concurrent individual and family therapy in a case of elective mutism. *Journal of Family Therapy,* 11, 29-44

Carr, A., MacDonnell, D. & Afnan, S. (1989). Anorexia Nervosa: The treatment of a male case with combined individual behaviour therapy and family therapy. *Journal of Family Therapy,* 11, 335-351

Coleman, S. (1985). *Failures in Family Therapy.* New York. Guilford.

Cottrell, D., Jog, S., Jackson, E. (1990). Casework towards the family reintegration of a sexually abusive father - a single case study. *Journal of Family Therapy,* 12, 341-353.

Fisch, R., Weakland, J., & Segal, L. (1982). *The Tactics of Change. Doing Therapy Briefly.* San Francisco: Jossey Bass.

Foa, E. & Emmelkamp, P. (1983). *Failures in Behaviour Therapy.* New York: Wiley.

Giaretto, H. (1982). *Integrated Treatment of Child Sexual Abuse: A Treatment and training Manual.* Palo Alto, CA. Science and Behaviour.

Goolishian, H. & Winderman, L. (1988). Constructivism, autopoesis and problem determined systems. *Irish Journal of Psychology,* 9, 130-143.

Gurman, A., Kniskern, D. & Pinsof, W. (1986). Research on marital and family therapies. In S. Garfield and A Bergin (eds.), *Handbook of Psychotherapy and Behavior Change* (3rd. Edition.) New York: Wiley.

Haley, J. (1967). Toward a theory of pathological systems. In: G. Zuk and I. Boszormenyi-Nagy (eds.), *Family Therapy and Disturbed Families.* Palo Alto, CA: Science and Behaviour.

Howe, D. (1989). *The Consumer's Views of Family Therapy.* Aldershot, Hants. Gower.

Lieberman, S. (1989). The birth pains of establishing an NHS family therapy clinic. *Context,* 3, 8-10.

Mays, D. & Franks, C. (1985). *Negative Outcome in Psychotherapy and What to Do About it.* New York: Springer.

Pimpernell, P. & Treacher, A. (1990). Using a videotape to overcome clients reluctance to engage in family therapy. *Journal of Family Therapy,* 12, 59-71

Quinton, D. & Rutter, M. (1988). *Parenting Breakdown.* Aldershot, Hants: Avebury-Gower.

Reflection (1989). Howe's the FT consumer champion. *Context,* 2, 25-26.

Rutter, M.& Garmazy, N. (1985). Developmental psychopathology. In E. Hetherington (ed.), *Handbook of Child Psychology, Vol. 4. Socialization, Personality and Social Development.* New York: Wiley.

Selvini Palazzoli, M. Boscolo, L. Cecchin, G. & Prata, G. (1980). The problem of the referring person. *Journal of Marital and Family Therapy,* 6, 3-9.

Selvini Palazzoli, M. (1985). The problem of the sibling as the referring person. *Journal of Marital and Family Therapy,* 11, 21-34.

Skynner, A. R. C. (1968). The Minimum sufficient network. *Social Work Today,* 29.

Treacher, A. & Carpenter, J. (1982) . Oh no! Not the Smiths again! An exploration of how to identify and overcome 'stuckness' in family therapy, part I: Stuckness involving the contextual and technical aspects of therapy. *Journal of Family Therapy,* 4, 285-303.

Westheafer, C. (1984). An aspect of live supervision: the pathological triangle. *Australian Journal of Family Therapy,* 5, 169-175.

Wynne, L., McDaniel, S. & Weber, T. (1987). Professional politics and the concepts of family therapy, family consultation and systems consultation. *Family Process,* 26, 153-156.

CHAPTER 10

A FORMULATION MODEL FOR USE IN FAMILY THERAPY

ABSTRACT
A model for simplifying complex information about a given presenting problem and integrating it into a formulation is described in this paper. The model contains three columns. In the right hand column, the cycle of interaction containing the symptom or presenting problem in which the identified patient and members of the network are caught up, is set out. In the left hand column, factors which predispose participants in this cycle to persist in this repetitive sequence of interactions are noted. In the central column (where pertinent) cognitive factors which mediate the influence of predisposing factors upon the present cycle of activity are listed. A sample formulation is first given to demonstrate the way in which the model may be used to simplify and integrate information. The implications of the model, from a clinical perspective, for assessment, treatment planning and the management of resistance, are then illustrated with a detailed case example.

INTRODUCTION
A distinction is made by family therapists between circular and linear explanations (McGuirk, Friedlander & Blocher, 1987). Circular explanations highlight the way in which a family network's attempt to solve an index patient's problem can be viewed as a recursive pattern of social interaction which perpetuates the patient's difficulties. Linear explanations, in contrast, identify discrete historical events as causes of the patient's symptoms. Such factors may be physiological, intrapsychic, interpersonal or societal.

The formulation model set out in this paper represents a way of integrating circular and linear styles of explanation. It is based on the notion that people with behavioural problems and members of their social networks become embroiled in vicious cycles of problems and inappropriate solutions. Such cycles of interaction maintain presenting problems. Participants fail to break out of such cycles because certain personal or historical factors inhibit them from altering their roles in these stereotyped patterns of interaction.

The model was developed within a framework which reflects an integration of structural/strategic (Aponte & van Deusen, 1981; Stanton, 1981a, 1981b) and functional/behavioural (Barton & Alexander, 1981; Patterson & Chamberlain, 1988) approaches to family therapy. This framework takes account of the structure and development of the family over the course of the life cycle; the social network in which the family is embedded; extrafamilial stress; learning processes and symptom development; belief systems and styles of information processing in determining interpersonal behaviour within the family network; and risk factor research in developmental and adult psychopathology. Within this integrated framework, assessment and treatment are conceptualised as distinct stages. The goal of the assessment stage is to develop a clear formulation of each of the presenting problems. On the basis of these formulations a unique set of strategies is developed in each case for solving each of the presenting problems. These strategies are implemented during the treatment phase.

The problem formulation model described in this paper offers a way of simplifying complex information and integrating it in a clinically meaningful way. It allows the clinician to avoid information overload while maintaining a relatively comprehensive conceptualisation of a given presenting problem. The model dictates a clear set of information gathering tasks. The symptom must be clearly defined and the pattern of social interaction which surrounds it must be determined. Factors which predispose participants in this pattern to maintain their roles must be clarified and the cognitive factors which mediate these predisposing factors must be assessed.

The circular aspect of formulations based on this model will identify network members involved in problem maintenance. This information may be used to decide which network members must be contacted or invited to further assessment or therapy sessions. The circular aspect of this type of formulation will also contain information on ineffective solutions which members of the patient's network have tried, and those aspects of these solutions which maintain the presenting problem.

Table 10.1. Three Column Formulation Model

Predisposing Factors	Mediating cognitive factors	Cycle of interaction surrounding symptom
• Remote & recent stressful life events	• Maladaptive belief systems	• Symptom & related behaviour & feelings of identified patient
• Membership of stressful social systems	• Maladaptive styles of information processing	• Actions and feelings of others which precede and follow the symptom
• Debilitating somatic states		
• Genetically based vulnerabilities		

NOTE: Predisposing and mediating factors, when present, should be specified for each action of each member in the cycle of interaction surrounding the symptom.

This information will have implications for treatment tactics to avoid, and those worth pursuing so as to break the cycle of social interaction in which the symptom is embedded.

The linear aspects of formulations, based on the model described below, point to factors which impede interventions aimed at directly disrupting the cycle of interaction surrounding the symptom. That is, linear aspects of a formulation following this model define sources of resistance (Anderson & Stewart, 1983). They may also suggest ways of mastering this resistance.

FORMULATION MODEL

The Three Column Model for Case Formulation is presented in Table 10.1. In this section the model will be described and illustrated with a sample formulation which is presented in Table 10.2.

Table 10. 2.   Case formulation for Beth, a persistently tearful child whose family bad been involved in a relief care programme which has broken down

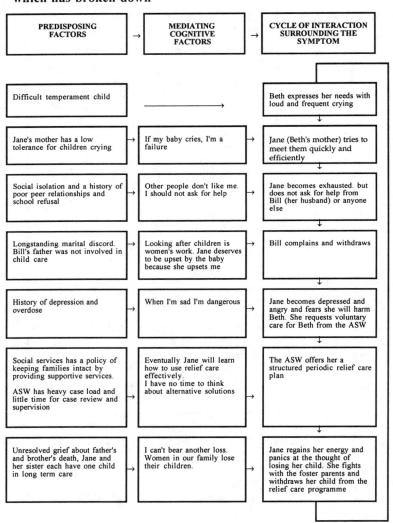

PREDISPOSING FACTORS	→	MEDIATING COGNITIVE FACTORS	→	CYCLE OF INTERACTION SURROUNDING THE SYMPTOM
Difficult temperament child				Beth expresses her needs with loud and frequent crying
Jane's mother has a low tolerance for children crying	→	If my baby cries, I'm a failure	→	Jane (Beth's mother) tries to meet them quickly and efficiently
Social isolation and a history of poor peer relationships and school refusal	→	Other people don't like me. I should not ask for help	→	Jane becomes exhausted. but does not ask for help from Bill (her husband) or anyone else
Longstanding marital discord. Bill's father was not involved in child care	→	Looking after children is women's work. Jane deserves to be upset by the baby because she upsets me	→	Bill complains and withdraws
History of depression and overdose	→	When I'm sad I'm dangerous	→	Jane becomes depressed and angry and fears she will harm Beth. She requests voluntary care for Beth from the ASW
Social services has a policy of keeping families intact by providing supportive services. ASW has heavy case load and little time for case review and supervision	→	Eventually Jane will learn how to use relief care effectively. I have no time to think about alternative solutions	→	The ASW offers her a structured periodic relief care plan
Unresolved grief about father's and brother's death, Jane and her sister each have one child in long term care	→	I can't bear another loss. Women in our family lose their children.	→	Jane regains her energy and panics at the thought of losing her child. She fights with the foster parents and withdraws her child from the relief care programme

Cycle of Interaction Surrounding the Symptom

The right hand column is reserved for a sequential description of how members of the index patient's social network behave and feel before and after an episode of problem behaviour. Such descriptions make specific reference to events which trigger problem behaviour, how the identified patient is treated while the problem behaviour or symptom is exhibited, how members of the network try to deal with the problem, the outcome of such attempted solutions for the identified patient, the network's response to the outcome and how time is spent by members of the network and the identified patient before the next triggering event occurs and the cycle repeats again.

In the example presented in Table 10.2, the referral letter stated that Beth's persistent crying and broken sleep were the main presenting problems. The cycle in which Jane (the mother), Beth (the child), Bill (the husband) and the Area Social Worker were caught up is described in the right hand column. An interview with the Area Social Worker (ASW) and Mary revealed the triggering factor (Beth's illness) and the ineffectual solution (a relief care programme, which had broken down in the way outlined in Table 10.2 on three occasions).

Predisposing Factors

In the left hand column of the model, factors which predispose participants to maintain their roles in the cycle of social interaction which surrounds the symptom are specified. Such factors fall into five subcategories. Remote or recent stressful life events constitute the first subcategory of predisposing factors. Poor maternal bonding, early multiplacement experiences or a personal history of neglect or abuse are examples of remote stressful life events (Wolkind & Rutter, 1985). Financial difficulties or changes in family composition are common recent stressful life events (McCubbin et al., 1982). Involvement in other social systems which make excessive demands on the individual, such as the school or workplace, are included in the second subcategory (Walker, 1985). Relevant temperamental characteristics or personality traits are included in the third subcategory (Rutter, 1987). Debilitating somatic states such as hemiplegia or obesity are contained in the fourth subcategory. The final subcategory includes functional vulnerabilities which have a genetic basis, such as those which have been documented for certain types of learning disabilities and certain psychoses (McGuffin & Gottesman, 1985).

In the left hand column of Table 10.2 factors which predisposed Jane, Beth, Bill and the Area Social Worker to become involved in the cycle outlined in the right hand column of the table are presented. For example, Jane's mother had a low tolerance for children crying. This predisposed Jane to respond quickly to Beth's crying.

Mediating Cognitive Factors
The impact of certain predisposing factors, for example prior stressful life events, on the behaviour of participants in the cycle of interaction surrounding the symptom, may be mediated by cognitive factors. Two categories of such cognitive factors are belief systems and styles of information processing. The defence mechanisms described by psychodynamic therapists (Ursano & Hales, 1986), distortions described by cognitive therapists (Beck, 1976) and the various attributional processes described by functional family therapists (Barton & Alexander, 1981) are examples of styles of information processing.

Belief systems comprising entrenched assumptions, attitudes and expectations which individuals hold about themselves and others which have implications for problem maintenance have been presented by therapists of many orientations, e.g. Beck, 1976; Laing, 1970; Byng-Hall, 1988.

The contents of the central column of Table 10.2 are cognitive factors which mediated the effects of predisposing factors in the left hand column on the behaviour described in the right hand column of the Table. For example, Jane's history of depression and overdosing led to her developing the belief, 'When I'm sad, I'm dangerous'. This belief led to her fear of harming Beth, and to her request for relief care for the child.

CASE EXAMPLE
In this section a more detailed case example will be presented to illustrate how the formulation model outlined above may be used to guide the collection, simplification and integration of information about a presenting problem. The implications of the formulation for treatment planning and the management of resistance will also be described.

Circumstances of Referral. The Doyle family which comprised Mr and Mrs Doyle, Sammy (10 years) and Sharleen (14 years) were referred by the G.P. Sharleen's longstanding conduct problems had recently reached a head when she threatened to stab her mother with a bread knife. Beyond this, little information was given in the referral letter other than the fact that Mr and Mrs Doyle were 'desperate for help'.

Initial Interview. All four members of the nuclear family attended the initial interview. Once a contract for family assessment had been established the main goal for the first session was to complete the right hand column of the formulation model. Most of the information gathering questions focused on the sequence of social interaction in which the problem behaviour, i.e. Sharleen's conduct problems, was embedded. Both direct and circular questions were used (Selvini-Palazzoli et al., 1980a) to obtain a specific description of Sharleen's problem behaviour and a blow by blow account of the interactions which preceded and followed this behaviour. The family were also asked about their explanations of the problem, their previous attempts to solve the problem which arose from these explanations and the effects of these attempts on the problem itself.

By the end of the first session the following sequence had been revealed:

1. Sharleen fights with her brother.
2. Her parents reprimand her and threaten to punish her.
3. She fights with them and these fights often involve an escalation from verbal abuse to physical struggles. These altercations lead to Sharleen feeling angry and rejected. Mr and Mrs D feel angry and guilty.
4. Sharleen absconds to the grandparents' house and the parents do not wholeheartedly try to stop her. She and her parents feel relief because this provides an escape from the escalating battle for all concerned. They are all likely to repeat this pattern again because they experience the relief as reinforcing.
5. Sharleen does not tell her grandparents about the fight and they pamper her. She experiences this as reinforcing and so is more likely to do it again.
6. She returns home the next day and is not confronted because her parents want to avoid another escalating battle.
7. The cycle repeats when Sharleen and her brother fight again. Sequences such as this may suggest whom to invite to the next session, insession activity and intersession interventions such as homework prescriptions.

In this example, given the critical position of the grandparents in the sequence, I asked Mr and Mrs D to invite them to the next session. The parents said it would be impossible for them to come. Since time had run out, the most immediate way of assessing this resistance was through a homework assignment. I asked Mr and Mrs Doyle to consider the implications of looking for help from grandmother in solving Sharleen's problems. A task was also given to Sharleen. She was asked to note her thoughts in those situations involving her brother which led to altercations between herself and her parents. Consent was obtained to contact Sharleen's school teacher, a social worker and a clinical psychologist with whom the family had previous contact.

Table 10.3. Case formulation for The D family and Sharleen, a girl who threatened to stab her mother

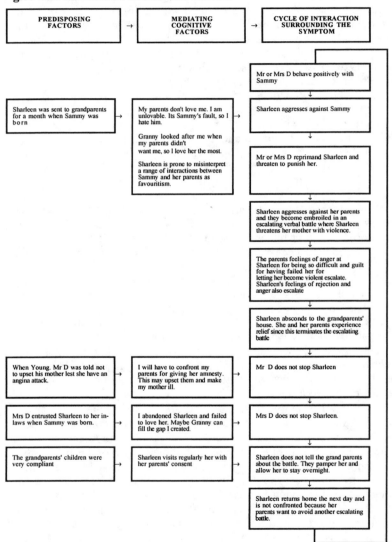

PREDISPOSING FACTORS	→	MEDIATING COGNITIVE FACTORS	→	CYCLE OF INTERACTION SURROUNDING THE SYMPTOM
				Mr or Mrs D behave positively with Sammy
Sharleen was sent to grandparents for a month when Sammy was born		My parents don't love me. I am unlovable. Its Sammy's fault, so I hate him.		Sharleen aggresses against Sammy
		Granny looked after me when my parents didn't want me, so I love her the most.		Mr or Mrs D reprimand Sharleen and threaten to punish her.
		Sharleen is prone to misinterpret a range of interactions between Sammy and her parents as favouritism.		Sharleen aggresses against her parents and they become embroiled in an escalating verbal battle where Sharleen threatens her mother with violence.
				The parents feelings of anger at Sharleen for being so difficult and guilt for having failed her for letting her become violent escalate. Sharleen's feelings of rejection and anger also escalate
				Sharleen absconds to the grandparents' house. She and her parents experience relief since this terminates the escalating battle
When Young, Mr D was told not to upset his mother lest she have an angina attack.		I will have to confront my parents for giving her amnesty. This may upset them and make my mother ill.		Mr D does not stop Sharleen
Mrs D entrusted Sharleen to her in-laws when Sammy was born.		I abandoned Sharleen and failed to love her. Maybe Granny can fill the gap I created.		Mrs D does not stop Sharleen.
The grandparents' children were very compliant		Sharleen visits regularly her with her parents' consent		Sharleen does not tell the grand parents about the battle. They pamper her and allow her to stay overnight.
				Sharleen returns home the next day and is not confronted because her parents want to avoid another escalating battle.

Contact with Involved Professionals. The primary reason for contacting involved professionals was to determine if they were currently involved in the cycle of interaction surrounding the symptom or if they had been in the past. If they were currently involved, then their role had to be determined. If they had been involved, the impact of their interventions on the cycle of interaction surrounding the symptom needed to be evaluated. Written reports were obtained from the Area Social Worker and the Clinical Psychologist. Sharleen's teacher was contacted by phone. The teacher and Area Social Worker confirmed that Sharleen's conduct problems were confined to the home. Her achievement, attendance and peer relations at school were broadly within normal limits and she had no record of police cautions or convictions. Previous referrals to the Area Social Worker and a psychologist had been made by the GP when Sharleen was aged 11 and 13 years respectively. Social Services had enrolled her in a summer activities programme and counselled the parents on the management of adolescents. The social worker saw Sharleen as a normal girl and the parents' inexperience in managing adolescents as the core problem. The psychologist had implemented a behavioural parent training programme. He saw Sharleen as a highly impulsive girl who would be difficult for any parent to manage and this was compounded by the parents' inconsistent management of her. Neither of these two previous interventions had led to more than a brief improvement in the girl's behaviour. In each instance the family dropped out of treatment after two to three sessions. From these reports I concluded that Sharleen's problems did not involve members of the community or the school, and were essentially family based. Sharleen had the capacity to behave within normal limits for extended periods of time outside the family context. I also deduced that the final formulation did not have to include other professionals in the cycle of interaction surrounding the symptom, although this is often not the case (Selvini Palazzoli et al., 1980b). Finally, I surmised that explanations of the Doyles' problems which excluded Sammy and the grandparents would probably lead to ineffective interventions.

Second Family Interview. A number of goals were set for the second phase of the assessment. These goals were dictated in part by the information already available on the Doyle family and in part by the formulation model. The first was to secure an interview with the grandparents so as to obtain their view of the symptom and the interactions surrounding it. The second was to identify those factors which predisposed the members of the Doyle family to become stuck in this cycle of interaction. The third was to uncover those cognitive factors which mediated the effects of the predisposing factors.

At the beginning of the next session, which was attended by

the nuclear family only, the homework tasks were reviewed. Mr and Mrs Doyle said that they could not involve the grandparents in solving the nuclear family's problems since the grandparents might feel blamed for wrongfully giving amnesty to Sharleen and they would find this stressful. The grandparents could not be exposed to stress because of their ill health. Sharleen said that she realised now that her infractions of house rules usually followed incidents where she saw her parents favouring Sammy over her. These answers which the homework assignments provided, uncovered the rudiments of the belief systems which were locking Mr and Mrs Doyle and Sharleen into their roles in the interaction pattern surrounding the symptom.

A developmental history was taken for each family member to determine the predisposing factors which underpinned these belief systems and to provide clues as to how the belief systems might be elaborated. The following significant information emerged. Mr Doyle was always told as a child not to upset his mother (Sharleen's grandmother) lest she have an angina attack. As a result he developed an unrealistic view of his parents' vulnerability and a primitive fear of killing them should he confront them about their behaviour towards Sharleen. Mrs Doyle said that she sent Sharleen to stay with the paternal grandparents for a month when Sammy was born. Since them she has felt guilty for abandoning her daughter. Mrs Doyle said sometimes she believes that Sharleen's jealousy of Sammy and her conduct problems are justified since she has failed to nurture her daughter adequately. This belief prevents her from stopping Sharleen absconding to grandmother's when she has misbehaved, since grandmother may provide the nurturance which she believes she has failed to give.

At the end of the session I said that the assessment could not continue without having a meeting with the grandparents. I assured Mr Doyle that such a session would be terminated if it became too stressful and that the children need not attend so that heated arguments could be avoided. Mr Doyle agreed to this arrangement. An individual session was also scheduled for Sharleen to obtain her view of the separation which occurred at Sammy's birth.

Interview with the Grandparents. Mr and Mrs Doyle and Mr Doyle's parents attended this meeting. I explained how the referral had occurred, the cycle of interaction surrounding the symptom and the predisposing factors and related belief systems which ensnared the Mr and Mrs Doyle in this pattern. I said that their comments on the partially completed formulation were essential if I were to develop an accurate understanding of the whole situation, as a basis for offering the Doyles sound professional advice on how to manage Sharleen's escalating violence.

The grandparents were shocked by the fact that they had never been told that Sharleen's visits to them were always to escape parental sanctions. As for their ill health, they confessed to Mr Doyle that grandmother's angina was a ruse they had used when he was a child to keep him in check so that they would not have to smack him. The fact that he and his siblings had been so compliant as children (in response to the threats about angina), made it difficult for the grandparents to appreciate the extent of their granddaughter's conduct problems.

This information suggested that the grandparents' role in the cycle of interaction surrounding the symptom was being maintained by their ignorance of Sharleen's conduct problems and by their son's reluctance to upset them. The grandparents agreed to participate in further sessions if necessary.

Individual Interview with the Identified Patient. Sharleen said that when Sammy was born she felt that he took her place as the centre of her mother's attention. Since then her feeling that she is unloved by her parents and unlovable by all but her grandmother has grown. She disclosed that she continually felt irritable and angry in Sammy's presence, especially when only her mother is present. It was these feelings, she said, which fuelled her aggression towards Sammy and her defiance of her parents. In this way, Sharleen clarified how her beliefs about herself in relationship to her parents, link a predisposing event to her current role in the cycle of interaction surrounding her conduct problems.

Formulation.

A diagrammatic formulation for this case is set out in Table 10.3. It conforms to the model set out in Table 10.1. What follows is a narrative statement of this formulation.

Cycle of Interaction Surrounding the Symptom. When Sharleen believed that her parents' behaviour meant that they favoured Sammy over her, she became jealous and was aggressive towards him. Her parents reprimanded her and threatened to sanction her aggressive behaviour, for example by stopping her pocket money. After a shouting match between the parents and the daughter, Sharleen would abscond to the grandparents' house. (These shouting matches periodically escalated to a level where physical violence was threatened, as in the incident with the bread knife which led to the referral). Both Sharleen and her parents were relieved by the immediate experience of separation and so they were likely as a group to repeat this action. The daughter was pampered by her grandmother during the visits and so was likely to seek amnesty there again. When Sharleen returned home after the visits, she was not confronted because Mr and Mrs Doyle wanted to avoid a recurrence of this aversive process. The cycle was repeated the next time the parents' behaviour confirmed Sharleen's belief that her parents favoured Sammy over her.

Predisposing and Mediating Factors. The family were locked into this cycle of interaction by certain beliefs which in turn had their roots in prior events. Sharleen, a first born child, was jealous of Sammy who usurped her position next to mother when she was four years old and he was born. At that time Sharleen was sent to spend a month with her grandparents. At the time of the assessment she doubted her own self-worth and her parents' love for her. She blamed her parents' apparent rejection of her on Sammy. Hence her readiness to aggress against him. She saw her grandparents as the only people who truly love her. Hence her choice of their house as a place of amnesty. Mr Doyle was reluctant for himself or his wife to confront his own parents because he believed, erroneously, that they were both in poor health did not want to upset them. His view of them as vulnerable derived from his childhood when he was warned, spuriously, never to upset his mother lest she have an angina attack. Mrs Doyle was reluctant for herself or her husband to physically restrain Sharleen when she tried to leave the house. She felt that she had failed her daughter and secretly believed that they may provide Sharleen with the love that she has failed to give.

The grandparents were unaware of their role as amnesty providers for Sharleen, hence their acceptance of the status quo.

Treatment Plan. The goals of treatment in this case were to alter the behaviour of each participant in the cycle of interaction described in the right hand column of Table 10.3 and thereby reduce the frequency of Sharleen's conduct problems. The formulation suggested both direct structural (Minuchin, 1981) and indirect or paradoxical (Stanton, 1981a) treatment programmes. It also contraindicated certain treatment strategies and offered an explanation of previous treatment failures.

Structural Treatment Programme. With this approach Sharleen and her brother could be helped to avoid jealous interchanges by substituting negotiation for accusation. This in turn would reduce the number of altercations between Sharleen and her parents and the concomitant need for limit setting. As a preliminary step to this, Sharleen's resistance to negotiating with her brother would have to be addressed by helping her to feel as valued by her mother as she believes him to be. Towards this end, Mrs Doyle and Sharleen could be instructed to schedule regular periods of exclusive time together (which would not be contingent upon Sharleen's good behaviour), during which they could carry out activities which promote positive feelings.

The second element of a structural programme would involve helping the parents and grandparents to work cooperatively in setting limits for Sharleen so that if she were to leave her parents' house, she would not receive amnesty at her grandparents. Mr Doyle's belief about the grandparents' vulnerability, one of the major sources of resistance to such a cooperative venture, had been neutralised during the assessment. However, Mrs Doyle would have to be convinced that she could meet her daughter's need for nurturance if she were to block Sharleen's escape to the grandparents' house. Appreciative feedback from Sharleen, about the exclusive time mother and daughter were to spend together, would be one way to help Mrs Doyle see herself as capable of meeting her daughter's need for nurturance and so reduce Mrs Doyle's resistance to a cooperative limit setting programme with the grandparents.

Paradoxical Treatment Programme. The structural programme described above would aim to solve the presenting problem by directly coaching the family to alter their behaviour so that it no longer maintained the presenting problem. An alternative indirect or paradoxical approach would involve describing the cycle of interaction surrounding the problem to the entire family, underlining the positive function of each participant's role in this cycle, and cautioning the family against change lest these positive functions be lost. The cognitive factors in the central column of Table 10.3 provide clues as to what themes might plausibly be used in connoting the behaviour of family members positively. In the D family the following themes were suggested by the cognitive factors set out in the central column of Table 10.3: (a) Sammy was favoured over Sharleen by the parents; (b) Mr Doyle feared for the grandparents' well-being; (c) Mrs Doyle felt grandmother could meet Sharleen's nurturance needs better than she could. These themes suggested the following positive connotations for the behaviour of the family members involved in the cycle of interaction surrounding the symptom.

Mr Doyle's reluctance to contact the grandparents in the past was an expression of his concern for their well-being. Mrs Doyle's reluctance to block Sharleen's escape was a self sacrificing recognition that Grandmother could meet her daughter's need for warmth better than she could. Sharleen's conduct problems and visits to grandmother were a way of allowing her parents to have exclusive time with Sammy whom they preferred to her, without having to take on the guilt associated with excluding her. Sammy's involvement in the fights with Sharleen and the grandparents' acceptance of her visits also resulted from a recognition that Mr and Mrs Doyle need to be able to spend exclusive time with Sammy without feeling guilt for rejecting Sharleen.

A paradoxical treatment approach would involve the

presentation of this positively connoted description of family functioning along with a caution against change. The aim of such an approach would be to alter the family's understanding of the intentions underpinning their roles in the cycle of interaction surrounding the symptom and the function of these roles. Such a new understanding could result in their finding new ways to fulfil the functions associated with these roles which maintain Sharleen's problem behaviour. In this way the cycle of interaction surrounding the symptom would be disrupted.

      Contraindicated Treatment Programmes. From the formulation it was predicted that a short or long term residential placement option (e.g. boarding school, relief care, placement of Sharleen with the grandparents, or hospitalisation) would exacerbate the problem by increasing Sharleen's belief that she was not valued by her parents. It would also increase Mrs Doyle's sense of guilt associated with her view that she had failed to nurture her daughter sufficiently. Individual therapy without concurrent family work was also contraindicated in this case (in my view), since it might foster within the family, an image of Sharleen as entirely responsible for the problem. Two previous, essentially educative interventions involving the parents only, were unsuccessful. In the light of the formulation set out in Table 10.3, this was not surprising since such interventions failed to account for the roles of the children and grandparents as active figures in the cycle of interaction in which the problem behaviour was embedded. Furthermore, as educative interventions they failed to take account of the parental resistances (suggested by the cognitive factors listed in the middle column of Table 10.3) to putting the acquired knowledge and skills into practice. Following the assessment sessions which have been described in this paper, the family were successfully treated with the structural treatment programme outlined, in a course of four therapeutic sessions.

DISCUSSION

The formulation model described above was developed as one of a series of clinician's tools (Carr, 1986) and as a device for use in therapist training (Carr, 1987). In formulations based upon this model, all elements which are not contained in the current cycle of interaction are compartmentalised into the linear categories of predisposing and cognitive factors. From a theoretical viewpoint this is a vast oversimplification of extant evidence (e.g. Breunlin & Schwartz, 1986; Cooklin, 1982; Dell, 1986). However, the clinical advantages of this simplification process have been enumerated in the introduction and illustrated with case material.

      At the recent NIMH/Family Process conference there was a

growing consensus among researchers working from behavioural/functional (e.g. Alexander, 1988) and structural/strategic (e.g. Stanton, 1981b) positions that distinct stages could be identified in effective family intervention (Wynne, 1988, page 260). It was recognised that the direct problem solving phase of therapy which focuses on breaking the cycle of interaction which surrounds the presenting problem, must often be preceded by a phase of therapy which targets the types of factors which fall into the linear categories of the formulation model described in this paper, e.g. work problems, negative attributions, etc. White (1986), arguing from a Batesonian perspective, has made a similar point. Families fail to break out of cybernetic cycles of problems and ineffective solutions because they are 'restrained' from discovering alternative solutions by certain beliefs or assumptions. White shows how the therapist may loosen these restraints through the use of certain therapeutic tactics grounded in Bateson's notion of 'double description'. These tactics help the family discover new and alternative ways of viewing their difficulties and consequently a way of breaking the cycle of interaction surrounding the presenting problem. The 'restraints' to which White refers are those cognitive factors which fall into the central column of the formulation model described in this paper.

The model also provides a bridge between individual and family based treatment modalities. Linear aspects of the hypothesis may sometimes suggest areas that might fruitfully be dealt with in individual therapy (e.g. Wachtel & Wachtel, 1986) or constitutional vulnerabilities that might usefully be treated pharmacologically (e.g. Falloon, 1985).

The model provides a way for incorporating (linear) research findings on individual risk factors into circular/systemic hypotheses. This is particularly useful in statutory work with child abuse cases (Gawlinski et al., 1988), or in cases where the identified patient is a suicidal adult (Hawton, 1987).

As the first example illustrated, this model of problem formulation allows the role of professionals (including the formulator) in the cycle of interaction surrounding the problem to be specified.

Finally, as research (Patterson & Chamberlain, 1988; Barton & Alexander, 1981) work has shown, a formulation model such as the one described here provides a useful template for asking clinically meaningful research questions, e.g. What types of cycles of interaction evolve around particular types of presenting problems? What types of factors prevent the index patient and members of the network from breaking out of these recursive patterns of social interaction which maintain the symptom?

164 Family Therapy and Systemic Practice

Family Therapy and Systemic Practice

REFERENCES

164 *Family Therapy and Systemic Practice*

164 Family Therapy and Systemic Practice

164   Family Therapy and Systemic Practice

164   Family Therapy and Systemic Practice

164   Family Therapy and Systemic Practice

REFERENCES

Alexander, J. (1988). Phases of family therapy process: A framework for clinicians and researchers. In L. Wynne (ed.), *The State of the Art n Family Therapy Research.* New York: Family Process.

Anderson, C. & Stewart, S. (1988). *Mastering Resistance.* New York: Guilford.

Aponte, H. & VanDeusen, J. (1981). Structural family therapy. In A. Gurman & D. Kniskern, (eds.), *Handbook of Family Therapy.* New York: Brunner/Mazel.

Barton, C. & Alexander, J. (1981). Functional Family Therapy. In A. Gurman & D. Kniskern, (eds.), *Handbook of Family Therapy.* New York: Brunner/Mazel.

Beck, A. (1976). *Cognitive Therapy and Emotional Disorders.* New York: Meridian.

Breunlin, D. & Schwartz, R. (1986). Sequences: Toward a common denominator of family therapy. Family *Process,* 25, 67-87.

Byng-Hall, J. (1988). Scripts and legends in family therapy, *Family Process,* 27, 167-179.

Carr, A. (1986). Three techniques for the solo family therapist. *Journal of Family Therapy,* 8, 373-382.

Carr, A. (1987). *Constructing Hypotheses to Guide Systems interventions.* National Conference of the Association for Family Therapy, York, UK

Cooklin, A., 1982. Change in here and now systems vs systems over time. In A. Bentovim, G. Barnes & A. Cooklin (eds.), *Family Therapy: Complementary Frameworks of Theory and Practice (Volume 1).* London: Academic Press.

Dell, P. (1986). In defence of lineal causality. *Family Process,* 25, 513-528

Falloon, I. (1985). *Family Management of Schizophrenia.* Baltimore: Johns Hopkins University Press.

Gawlinski, G., Carr, A., Irving, N. & McDonnell, D. (1988). Thurlow House Assessment Programme for Families with Physically Abused Children. *Practice,* 2, 208-220.

Hawton, K. (1987). Assessment of suicide risk. *British Journal of Psychiatry,* 150, 145-153.

Laing, R.D. (1970). *Knots.* Middlesex: Penguin.

McCubbin, H., Patterson, J. & Wilson, L.(1982). Family Inventory of Life Events and Changes. In D. Olson et al. (eds.), *Family Inventories.* University of Minnesota, MN: Family Social Science Departmental Press.

McGuffin, P. & Gottesman, I. (1985). Genetic influences on normal and abnormal development. In M. Rutter & L. Hersov (eds.), *Child and Adolescent Psychiatry* (2nd. ed.). Oxford: Blackwell.

McGurk, J., Friedlander, M. & Blocher, D.H., (1987). Systemic and nonsystemic diagnostic processes: An empirical comparison. *Journal of Marital and Family Therapy,* 13, 69-76.

Minuchin, S. & Fishman, C. (1981). *Family Therapy Techniques.* Cambridge MA: Harvard University Press.

Patterson, G. & Chamberlain, P. (1988). Treatment Process: A problem at three levels. In L.C.Wynn (ed.), *The State of the Art in Family Therapy Research.* New York: Family Process.

Rutter, M. (1987). Temperament, personality and personality disorder. *British Journal of Psychiatry*, 150, 443-458.

Selvini-Palazzoli, M., Boscolo, L., Cecchin, G. & Prata, G., (1980a). Hypothesizing - circularity - neutrality: Three guidelines for the conductor of the session. *Family Process*, 19, 3-12.

Selvini-Palazzoli, M., Boscolo, L., Cecchin, G., & Prata, G. (1980b). The problem of the referring person. *Journal of Marital and Family Therapy*, 6, 3-9.

Stanton, D. (1981a). Strategic approaches to family therapy. In A. Gurman & D. Kniskern (eds.), *Handbook of Family Therapy.* New York: Brunner/Mazel.

Stanton, D. (1981). An integrated structural/strategic approach to family therapy. *Journal of Marital and Family Therapy*, 7, 427439.

Ursano, R. & Hales, R. (1986). A review of brief individual psychotherapies. *American Journal of Psychiatry*, 143, 1507-1517.

Wachtel, E. & Wachtel, P. (1986).*Family Dynamics in Individual Psychotherapy.* New York: Guilford.

Walker, A. (1985). Reconceptualizing family stress. *Journal of Marriage and the Family*, November, 827-837.

White, M., (1986). Negative explanation, restraint and double description: A template for family therapy, *Family Process*, 2, 169-174.

Wolkind, S. & Rutter, M. (1985). Separation, loss and family relationships. In M. Rutter & L. Hersov (eds.), *Child and Adolescent Psychiatry* (2nd ed.). Oxford: Blackwell.

Wynne, L. (1988). *The State of the Art in Family Therapy Research: Controversies and Recommendations.* New York: Family Process Press.

CHAPTER 11

SYSTEMIC CONSULTATION AND GOAL SETTING

ABSTRACT
Over two decades of empirical research conducted within a positivist framework has shown that goal setting is a particularly useful method for influencing task performance in occupational and industrial contexts. The conditions under which goal setting is maximally effective are now clearly established. These include situations where there is a high level of acceptance and commitment, where goals are specific and challenging, where the task is relatively simple rather than complex, and where progress is regularly monitored. Participation in goal setting has also been found to be vital for enhancing performance. Setting both individual and group goals improves performance providing both sets of goals are compatible. In this paper these findings, constructed though the lens of goal theory, are considered from a social-constructionist perspective and their implications for systemic practice are outlined.

INTRODUCTION
The concept of change is at the heart of systemic consultation and therapy. During consultation and therapy changes occur in the way the team, therapist and client co-construct their relationships to one and other, the problem situation and the possibilities for resolving it.

During consultation both the therapist's skilled inquiries and invitations to action, and the clients responses to these lead to the co-construction of a new reality: a reality which empowers clients to entertain new possibilities for thinking, feeling and action; a reality which entails new possibilities for being-in-the-world.

A core tenet of systemic practice is that it is not a useful distinction to view the therapist as responsible for causing beneficial changes in clients since both therapist and client are part of the same system which co-creates a shared reality during the consultation process.   Rather, the therapist empowers the client to explore possibilities or perturbs the system and co-creates a reality that affords transformation (Pearce, Concha & McAdam, 1992; Burnham, 1992). It is therefore not surprising that the process of goal setting and reviewing goal attainment does not occupy a central position in current systemic practice, since both are usually associate with the positivist practice of viewing the therapist as an agent who *does things to* the client to *make the client change.*

However, the process of goal setting and goal attainment monitoring fit with systemic practice within the domains of both explanation and production (Lang, Little and Cronen, 1990). Firstly, within the Explanations Domain, inquiries about desired futures facilitate the co-construction of new realities that may offer clients useful possibilities for change and transformation. Indeed, key figures in the systemic tradition such as Peggy Penn (1985) pioneered feed-forward questions as a routine type of circular inquiry nearly 10 years ago with precisely this argument in mind. Feed forward questions hold much in common with goal setting. They invite clients to detail future scenarios and the implications of these for system members. Secondly, within the Explanations Domain inquiries about goal attainment and beliefs related to different levels of attainment also help create realities which both open possibilities while at the same time taking account of clients constraints and affordances. Third, within the Productions Domain, goal setting and goal attainment review are a useful technology for managing tasks and executing duties which fall outside of therapy and the Explanations Domain but which, nevertheless, many practitioners and clients must complete.

An interesting question is the conditions under which goal setting and review empower people to achieve desired outcomes. Over two decades of empirical research, conducted within a positivist framework, has shown that goal setting is a particularly useful method for facilitating task performance in occupational and industrial contexts (Guzzo et al, 1985, Locke et al, 1981, Locke et al, 1990). Indeed of all the management practices researched, goal setting and review was by far the most effective. This literature contains findings which suggest ways in which therapists, working within a social-constructionist framework, may enrich their approach to goal setting in clinical practice. What follows is an outline of the positivist framework within which this research was conducted, a summary of the key findings and the implications of these for consultation and therapy.

GOALS AND PERFORMANCE

Goal setting is a process where members of a social system define a desired outcome, agree to work towards that outcome and agree to review progress towards that desired outcome. Goal setting may be conducted in an autocratic way, with one member of the system dictating the goals others must strive for, or it may be conducted in a participative way where all members of the team contribute to goal definition. Goals may vary in their clarity and the detail with which the desired outcome is described. System members may vary in their acceptance of, and commitment to goals.

In any system, both group and individual goals may be described.

Goals lead to improved task performance if certain conditions are met. First, a person has to accept the goal and be committed to attaining it (Hollenbeck, 1987). Commitment entails a high level of acceptance and also having a personal stake in the outcome of goal directed action plans. Commitment will be given to an accepted goal if it is consistent with a person's values and world view and if the benefits of goal attainment are, in the individuals estimation, worthwhile.

Second, specific goals lead to better performance than vague goals (Tubbs, 1986). *To improve performance and do your best* is a vague goal. *To complete all current client reports by 5.30 on Fridays* is a specific goal. When people set specific goals, it is possible to specify precisely what an observer would see if they attained the goals. Furthermore, specific goals allow degree of goal attainment to be quantified.

Third, challenging goals lead to maximal performance. If a goal is too easy and does not challenge a person then he or she will not find pursuing the goal rewarding. Goal attainment may be experienced as boring. If the goal is too challenging an individual may find the process of trying to reach the goal frustrating. If a goal is optimally challenging, maximal performance will occur (Shalley et al, 1987).

Fourth, participation in goal setting (in contrast to being assigned goals) is important insofar as it ensures that the defined goal will be specific, moderately difficult and accepted (Shalley et al, 1987). It may also be the case that participation in goal setting gives people a sense of control over the potentially stressful process of goal attainment, and this sense of control is stress reducing (Carr and Wilde, 1988)

Fifth, where more than one person is involved, in the case of work teams or families, group goal setting is as important as individual goal setting. The ideal is to set both individual goals and group goals which are congruent with each other (Matsui et al, 1987; Gowen, 1985).

Sixth, when goal attainment is explicitly assessed, goals are pursued more diligently. People like to be evaluated positively, so they do their best when they know their performance and goal attainment are being monitored (Locke & Latham, 1990).

Goal setting leads to better performance for relatively simple rather than for complex tasks. For example, goal setting had a stronger effect on performance where goal attainment involved simple brainstorming exercises compared to when it involved conducting complex scientific research (Wood et al, 1987).

Specific psychological processes underpin the relationship between goal setting and performance (Earley & Lituchy, 1991).

Goals improve performance because they highlight the discrepancy between a person's current position and the position they aspire to. This creates dissatisfaction which serves as an incentive. The incentive leads a person to act in a way that reduces the discrepancy (Wood & Bandura, 1989). This process involves obtaining feedback on performance and comparing this with the desired goal.

When individuals achieve goals and obtain feedback about this success, their view of themselves changes. They view themselves as being more competent and effective. In Bandura's terms, they view themselves as having higher self-efficacy (Bandura, 1981).

These increased self-efficacy beliefs then influence the types of goals a person is prepared to aspire to in the future. People with high self-efficacy beliefs set or accept further goals that present them with a high degree of challenge. In this way, a positive feedback loop is set up.

A person's ability level sets a limit on the amplification of this positive feedback loop. At some point a person may set a goal that is too challenging and fail to achieve it because it is beyond their ability level. This will in turn decrease their self-efficacy beliefs in relation to such goals (Earley & Lituchy, 1991).

GOAL SETTING IN CONSULTATION AND THERAPY
Within the positivist framework, goal setting and review is not accepted as merely another lens through which to construct the world. Rather, goals and related constructs are accorded the status of objects to be discovered and the findings described as evidence for the existence of these entities. From a social-constructionist viewpoint, goal theory and its findings are a story: a frame within which certain types of events may usefully be given meaning and significance. Fortunately the goal theory story and the conclusions drawn from it have clear clinical implications for practitioners who wish to use goal theory as one lens through which to view aspects of the consultation process. Here are some of the more useful implications for systemic practice.

Help clients to set specific, moderately challenging goals which take account of their ability levels and current self-efficacy beliefs.
Here are two examples of goal setting that met these criteria.

> **Example 1.** An intelligent middle class couple who had a five year history of marital discord had lost faith in their ability to resolve any conflicts, no matter how simple. They set the following goal as their first in a series of progressively more difficult therapeutic goals: To complete a supermarket shopping trip without becoming involved in an angry stand-off.

> **Example 2.** A 30 year old recovered alcoholic had been dry for three years. He lived alone in Dublin, rarely visited his family of origin and had no network of friends outside of AA. He worked as a clerk in an engineering firm and was bright and socially skilled. However, he felt that he was not doing enough with his life and so sought counselling. He stated explicitly in the first fifteen minutes of the intake interview that he knew he could improve his lifestyle if he only put his mind to it. His therapy goals included: Visiting his mother and brother in the west of Ireland at least once a month; attending a course of night classes in photography and developing a career plan.

Do not help clients consider ways of reaching goals until it is clear that they accept and are committed to them.
A variety of future scenarios, possibilities and goals should be explored. When clients express a preference for one goal or set of goals, three key questions may be asked to check for acceptance and commitment:

- *Do you want to work towards these goals?*
- *What's in it for you if you achieve these goals and what will you lose if you don't?*
- *What's in it for you, if you stay as you are and what will you lose if you pursue these goals?*

If the clients say they want to work towards the goals and can clearly articulate the costs of not doing so and the benefits of achieving the stated goals, then they probably accept the goals and are committed to them. If clients cannot address the acceptance and commitment questions positively, then goal attainment is unlikely. The following example illustrates this point.

> **Example 3.** A single mother with a non-compliant six year old was referred by a concerned social worker for therapy. During

the intake interview the mother said that she and her son had about six big fights a day. The mother agreed to an initial goal of reducing the fights to no more than 4 a day. But when she was asked to explore what she would gain for herself by achieving this goal, she couldn't give a clear congruent answer even after much exploration. She also had no clear view of what the future would look like if she failed to achieve this goal. She feared having her child taken into care, but did not believe that she would ever physically harm the child.

In family work, set both personal goals and overall family goals that are compatible.
One of the major challenges in family therapy is to evolve a construction of the presenting problems that opens up possibilities where each family member's wishes and needs may be respected when these different needs and wishes are apparently conflicting. Helping family members articulate the differences and similarities between their positions in considerable detail and inviting them to explore goals to which they can both agree, first, is a useful method of practice here.

> **Example 4.** Polly, a 15 year old girl referred because of school difficulties said that she wanted to be independent. Her parents wanted her to be obedient. Both wanted to be able to live together without continuous hassle. Detailed questioning about what would be happening if Polly were independent and obedient revealed that both Polly and her parents wanted her to be able, among other things, to speak French fluently. This would help Polly achieve her personal goal of working in France as an *au pair* and would satisfy the parents goal of her obediently doing school work.   Getting a passing grade in French in the term exam was set as a therapy goal. It reflected the family goal reducing hassle and the individual goals of Polly and her parents.

Regularly assess progress towards these goals.
Ideally progress towards goals should be assessed in an observable way or in a quantitative manner. Frequency counts of the number of events that occurred are useful. For example: the number of fights, the number of wet beds, the number of compliments, the number of successes. Ratings of internal states are useful ways to quantify progress towards less observable goals. For example: ratings of anger, sadness, fear, confidence etc... on a ten point scale.
If this feedback is positive, discuss it in sufficient detail for

clients' to assimilate it into their world views. This will lead to enhanced beliefs in the family's ability to solve its own problems and increased solution focused behaviour in the future. This practice holds much in common with the problem solving school (Watzlawick et al, 1974), the solution focused approach (deShazer, 1988) the strategic school (Haley, 1976), the AGS commission model (Salamon et al, 1993) and behaviourally based practices (e.g., Martin, 1990) although the rationale for the use of feedback in strategic and behavioural approaches would be framed within a traditional positivist framework.

Distinguish between goal attainment failures due to lack of commitment and those due to lack of ability.
If clients fail to achieve a goal, the therapist must determine whether failure was due to a lack of acceptance and commitment or due to the goal being too difficult for the clients skill and ability level. Commitment may be assessed by asking the three related questions outlined previously concerning the costs and benefits of goal attainment versus the maintaining the status quo. Whether clients have the requisite abilities and skills to achieve a goal may be investigated in three ways. First, ask if similar goals have been achieved in the past. If they have, then the client probably has the required skills. Second, ask the clients to pursue the goal in the session and then observe their skills in action. Finally, ask for a blow-by-blow account of what went wrong when clients tried to achieve the goal that they set. This will throw light on skills deficits or commitment problems.

If failure was due to a lack of acceptance or commitment, then a new goal must be sought to which clients are strongly committed or the pro's and con's of goal acceptance need to be re-explored.
In multiproblem cases a common therapeutic mistake, illustrated by Example 5, is to select a goal to which the therapist is committed but to which the client is not.

> **Example 5.** A therapist selected improving family communication as a primary goal whereas the parents were adamant that getting better housing was their number one goal.

The related error is to set a goal without fully exploring the pro's and con's of goal attainment or relinquishing the status quo. In the following example exploration of the consequences of goal attainment had been too brief.

> **Example 6.** A nine year old boy and his mother experienced extreme reciprocal separation anxiety when the boy tried to

leave his mother at the school gate and attend class. The episode had begun when the boy changed school and after his aunt, to whom the mother was particularly close, had been hospitalised for surgery. The first goal that was set involved the boy travelling to the school gate with his father while the mother remained at home. The goal was not attained. Careful interviewing showed that the boy and his parents were not fully committed to him returning to school because of the anxiety this caused the mother and because of the impracticality of the father being involved in taking the son to school and missing work. Further interviewing focused on the pro's and con's of the mother and son staying close together and the mother and son gradually separating. Eventually, the same goal was set once more, but this time with a higher degree of commitment.

Failure to progress towards a goal due to lack of commitment may also occur because the client is not a customer for any therapeutic change whatsoever . If this is the case, then it is critical to assess the network and identify the customer. A catalogue of such situations and methods for dealing with them is described elsewhere (Carr, 1990). Example 3, above, typifies one such scenario. The customer for change was the worried social worker, not the mother of the non-compliant child. The minimum sufficient network for therapy, in this instance, therefore included the social worker in addition to the mother and the child.

If failure to make progress towards a goal is due to a lack of ability or skill, then a new goal consistent with the clients' ability levels must be set.
A common error, illustrated by Example 6, is to assume that clients have the micro-skills necessary to complete macro-assignments. In these cases smaller goals, ideally goals that will lead to skill development, need to be set.

> **Example 7.** Members of a chaotic distressed family with a handicapped child set the goal of having a weekly family outing. They consistently failed to achieve this goal because they lacked the communication skills or conflict management skills necessary to plan the outing without serious conflict occurring. This goal was put on the back burner and an intermediate goal introduced which was more consistent with their ability level: to complete a family active listening assignment on a weekly basis for a month.

Sometimes failure to achieve a goal that was apparently consistent with a client's ability level when it was set can occur because of an unforeseen change in a client's circumstances as is the case in Example 8. Here the therapist must help clients assimilate the event into their belief systems in a way that allows the failure to be attributed to external factors. If the failure is misattributed to personal shortcomings, this will undermine self-efficacy beliefs. The literature on attributional style and family adjustment has underscored the tendency of members of distressed families to attribute failure to internal, stable and global factors (Munton & Stratton, 1990).

> **Example 8.** Over a series of six sessions, two fosterparents failed to achieve the goal of helping a teenage fosterchild on short term placement complete an evening meal without engaging in verbally-abusive conflict. The failure was in large part associated with the erratic and stormy series of unscheduled and unforeseen visits that occurred between the fosterchild and his natural parents during the period in which the therapy was occurring. The relationship between the lack of goal attainment and the visits were an important therapeutic focus in the sixth session. The way in which the visits activated the teenager's sense of insecurity and ambivalent feelings about both the fosterparents and his natural parents was explored. A contract for further therapy was established. The first goal set was to develop a strategy with the social worker and the teenager's natural parents for arranging a more predictable schedule of visits. The original goal of eating a peaceful evening meal was deferred until this first goal was achieved.

DISCUSSION

The empirical findings from over two decades work on goal theory and task performance and related implications for clinical practice shed light on a number of debates within the fields of systemic consultation and family therapy.

The Unplanned Conversation Debate. Hoffman's recent paper has created a danger within the field of novice therapists advocating and pursuing goalless conversations (Hoffman, 1990). A further problem with the direction taken in Hoffman's paper is that it may discourage therapists from explicitly reviewing progress regularly, a process which enhances goal attainment. While an unplanned approach to the therapeutic process may be useful in promoting a sense of participation and collaboration between therapist and client, the overall therapy process may usefully be aimed at a specific goal. Perhaps Pearce and Cronen's (1980) Co-ordinated Management of Meaning model offers a useful explanatory framework here. Where *a series of consultations* is the context marker, goal directedness may be important for transformation and movement towards new possibilities. However, where *a particular therapeutic conversation* is the context marker, a less directive way of being may be more appropriate for the therapist.

Goals and Neutrality. One argument against goal setting is that the therapist becomes overly committed to certain therapeutic outcomes and so abandons a position of therapeutic neutrality. This type of argument is a bit like saying that therapists should not evolve hypotheses because they might 'fall in love with them'. Using goal setting and review within systemic practice need not lead the therapist to become overly committed to one set of goals and thereby compromise a position of neutrality. Rather, the reality within which goals are articulated must be carefully and skilfully co-constructed and goals should be treated with the same irreverence as a good working hypothesis.

The Ordeal Debate. Milton Erickson and subsequently Jay Haley argued that in some instances therapy should present the client with an ordeal or challenge (Haley, 1984). Others, notably the MRI school, have emphasised the importance of small therapeutic goals which nevertheless are noticeably different from the status quo and signal movement towards a larger goal (Watzlawick et al, 1974). The findings reviewed above suggest that optimally, goals should be set at the limits of a persons competence. This is in keeping with the Ordeal concept. However, the tasks that lead to goal attainment should be simple, not complex. This fits with the MRI position.

The Power and Deception Debate. Whether therapists should conceal or reveal their expert knowledge has been a central debate within the field. Allied to this has been the debate about whether therapy is a strategic competitive battle or a collaborative and co-operative problem-solving process (Carr, 1991). The work reviewed in this paper underlines the importance of participation in goal setting. This entails a view of therapy as co-operative and open venture rather than a competitive and deceptive enterprise.

The individual's needs and the common good. The subordination of individual needs to the needs of the family has been a central problem within the family therapy field. The goal setting literature points to way out of this dilemma by demonstrating that setting both individual and group goals improves performance provided both sets of goals are compatible. One clinical challenge is to pursue therapeutic inquiries that bring forth compatibility.

REFERENCES

Bandura, A. (1981). Self-efficacy mechanisms in human agency. *American Psychologist*, 37, 122-147.

Burnham, J. (1992). Approach - Method -Technique. Making distinctions and creating connections. *Human systems: Journal of Systemic Consultation and Management*, 3, 3-26.

Carr, A. (1990). Failure in family therapy: A catalogue of engagement mistakes. *Journal of Family Therapy*, 12, 371-386.

Carr, A. (1991). Power and influence in systemic consultation. *Human Systems: Journal of Systemic Consultation and Management*, 2, 15-30.

Carr, A., Gawlinski, G., MacDonnell, D., Irving, N. & Docking, S. (1989). Thurlow House Adolescent Assessment Programme. *Practice*, 2, 60-190.

Carr, A. & Wilde, G. (1988). The effects of actual and potential stressor control on physiological and self-reported stress responses. *Journal of Social and Clinical Psychology*, 6, 371-387.

de Shazer, S. (1988). *Clues: Investigating Solutions in Brief Therapy*. New York: Norton.

Earley, P. & Lituchy, T. (1991). Delineating goal and efficacy effects: A test of three models. *Journal of Applied Psychology*, 76, 81-98.

Gowen, C. (1986). Managing work group performance by individual goals and group goals for an independent group task. *Journal of Organisational Behaviour Management*, winter, 5-27.

Guzzo, R., Jette, R. & Katzell, R. (1985). The effects of psychologically based intervention programmes on worker productivity: A Meta-analysis. *Personnel Psychology*, Summer, 275-291

Haley, J. (1976). *Problem solving therapy*. New York: Harper & Row.

Haley, J. (1984). *Ordeal Therapy*. San Francisco: Norton.

Hoffman, L. (1980). From System to discourse. *Human Systems: The Journal of Systemic Consultation and Management*, 1, 5-8.

Hollenbeck, J. & Klein, H. (1987). Goal commitment and the goal setting process: Problems, prospects and proposals for future research. *Journal of Applied Psychology*, 72, 212-220.

Lang, P., Little, M. & Cronen, V. (1990). The systemic professional: Domains of action and the question of neutrality. *Human Systems: The Journal of Systemic Consultation and Management*, 1, 39-55.

Locke, E., Shaw, K., Saari, L. & Latham, G. (1981). Goal setting and task performance:1969-1980. *Psychological Bulletin*, 90, 125-152.

Locke, E. & Latham, G. (1990). *A theory of goal setting and task performance*. New York: Prentice-Hall.

Martin, P. (1990). *Handbook of Behaviour Therapy and Psychological Science*. New York: Pergamon.

Matsui, T., Kakuyama, T. & Onglato, M. (1987). Effects of goals and feedback on performance in groups. *Journal of Applied Psychology*, 72, 414.

Munton, A. & Stratton, P. (1990). Concepts of causality applied in the clinic: Interactional models and attributional style. *Journal of Cognitive Psychotherapy*, 4, 197-209.

Pearce, W.B., Concha, E. & McAdam, E. (1992). Not sufficiently systemic: An exercise in curiosity. *Human Systems: The Journal of Systemic*

Consultation and Management, 3, 75-87.

Pearce, W. B. & Cronen, V. (1980). *Communication, Action and Meaning: The creation of Social Realities.* New York: Praeger.

Penn, P. (1985). Feed-forward: future questions, future maps. *Family Process,* 24, 299-310.

Salamon, E. , Grevelius, K. & Andersson, M. (1993). Beware the Siren's Song: The AGS Commission Model. In S. Gilligan & R. Price (Eds.). *Therapeutic Conversations.* New York. Norton.

Shalley, C., Oldham, G., Proac, J. (1987). Effects of goal difficulty, goal setting method and expected external evaluation on intrinsic motivation. *Academy of Management Review,* 12, 559-572.

Tubbs, M. (1986). Goal-setting: a meta-analytic examination of empirical evidence. *Journal of Applied Psychology,* 71, 474-483.

Watzlawick, P., Weakland, J., & Fisch, R. (1974). *Change: Principles of Problem Formation and Problem Resolution.* New York, Norton.

Wood, R. & Bandura, A. (1989). Social cognitive theory of organisational management. *Academy of Management Review,* 14, 361-384.

Wood, R., Mento, A., Locke, E. (1987) Task Complexity as a moderator of goal effects: A Meta-analysis. *Journal of Applied Psychology,* 72, 416-425.

CHAPTER 12

GIVING DIRECTIVES EFFECTIVELY: THE IMPLICATIONS OF RESEARCH ON COMPLIANCE WITH DOCTOR'S ORDERS FOR FAMILY THERAPY

ABSTRACT
Research on factors that facilitate the co-operation of patients with medical treatment regimes points to guidelines that may enhance family therapy practice. A number of such guidelines, which concern giving therapeutic directives, are described and their implications for systemic work with families are considered.

INTRODUCTION
Practice and theory in family therapy may be enhanced by drawing on relevant material from neighbouring disciplines (Carpenter, 1988). In this paper an attempt is made to apply findings from the social psychology of the doctor-patient relationship to the field of family therapy practice.

On average, medical patients forget about 50% of the information about their illnesses and related treatment regimes given to them by their physicians. About 40% of medical patients do not co-operate with medical treatment regimes. This situation has inspired scientific enquiry into the circumstances under which patients are most likely to co-operate with doctor's orders. This impressive body of research has previously been reviewed by Haynes (Haynes et al, 1979) in the USA and more recently by Ley (1988) in the UK. The findings of these reviews have implications for giving directives within any psychotherapeutic context. This paper considers twelve well-established conclusions from the research on doctor-patient communication and in each case explores the usefulness of the conclusion w applied to family therapy. It is shown that principles derived from the intensive controlled study of a highly defined situation (the doctor-patient consultation) are remarkably productive when applied to the very different context of a system family consultation.

GUIDELINES FOR GIVING DIRECTIVES
1. Help the family appreciate the seriousness of the presenting problem.
Clients who view their problems as serious are more likely to follow therapeutic directives (Janz & Becker, 1984). If clients' assessments of the seriousness of their problems is inaccurate, the therapist can enhance the likelihood of co-operation with therapeutic directives by giving information about prognosis, mortality or vulnerability. For example an angina patient, referred for family therapy with a view to smoking cessation and weight reduction, could be given information on his vulnerability to having a heart attack by listing the risk factors present in his case. Minuchin often gave information about the consequences of untreated anorexia nervosa in a dramatic way to mobilise families into adopting a more adaptive family structure (Minuchin et al, 1978).

2. Show the family that you care about the resolution of the presenting. Showing flexibility about appointment scheduling and seeing patients punctually for appointments is an important way of demonstrating care and concern for the seriousness of the problem. For example, only 30% of patients who were left waiting longer than an hour in an arthritis clinic complied with doctor's orders compared with 67% who waited less than half an hour (Geersten et al, 1973). Flexibility may also be demonstrated through offering emergency telephone contact or appointments on short notice at critical periods in therapy (e.g. Gawlinsky, Carr et al, 1988).

3. Use a directive and structuring interviewing style initially to help the   family understand their role within the context of the therapy sessions. Studies in both medical and psychotherapeutic contexts show that clients are better able to co-operate with treatment and benefit from it if the therapist initially uses an active structuring interviewing style (e.g. Heller, 1968; Stiles et al, 1979; Bennun, 1989). This style probably facilitates therapy by allowing the therapist to convey to the client what is expected of her within the therapeutic relationship. A directive and structuring style may also help the client to view the therapist as competent. The perception of the therapist as competent and as having the resources to help the client find a solution to the presenting problem, has been identified within the social-psychology literature as an important aspect of the effective therapeutic relationship (e.g., Strong & Claiborn, 1982).

4. Help each family member describe the problem their explanation for its occurrence and their expectations about its resolution. Patients who feel misunderstood do not comply with medical advice (Haynes et al, 1979). Some patients expect to be asked to take responsibility for their health. Others expect the physician to do this. Where patient have such expectations and these are not assessed and dealt with, usually patients fail to co-operate with treatment regimes (Watts, 1982).

In family therapy each family member has a personal view on each of these issues. Each view is usually partial and linear. Often, collectively the views entail conflicting expectations about the role of the therapist and family members in problem resolution. For example, a school-refuser's mother may see her as depressed and requiring bedrest and medication. Here, the expectation is that the family should take little responsibility in problem resolution. The father in the same family may view the child's problem as misconduct requiring a firm hand. The expectation here may be that the therapist will point out the error of the mother's position and so give the father a free hand to implement a solution involving strict discipline. The therapist must allow each family member to have the experience of being understood where the issues of problem evolution and responsibilities for problem resolution are concerned.

5. Obtain enough information about the problem and the context within which it occurs to develop a hypothesis or rationale from which your directives will follow logically. In medicine most physicians approach this task in roughly the same way. The relatively advanced state of medical science and the relatively uniform approaches to medical training have some bearing on this issue. In family therapy there is a wide variability in approaches to family assessment because of the youthfulness of our science and art. The variability is also due to the lack of uniformity in our training (Gurman and Kniskern, 1981)

6. Offer your explanation of the problem to the family and point out how it is consistent with the information that you have obtained. Show how your explanation entails a rationale for the directive which you invite the family to follow. Most family therapists develop hypotheses about presenting problems, although there is some debate about the usefulness and ethics of sharing these hypotheses with clients (Walrond-Skinner and Watson, 1987). The evidence from the patient-compliance literature is unequivocal about the importance of offering a rationale within which the treatment regime may be comprehended (Ley, 1988, p. 75). By implication, directives offered within a family therapy context are more likely to be followed if the hypothesis guiding them is also described by the therapist and understood by the client (e.g. Carr and Afnan, 1989). The following example illustrates this guideline.

It was suggested to the parents of a teenager whose diabetes was poorly controlled that the boy knew full well how to control his illness, but that he avoided doing so for their sake. We guessed that he wanted them to continue to feel the satisfaction of knowing that they were vital to his survival. We said that we were almost certain that the boy had assessed their reasons for helping him monitor his diabetes incorrectly. We took the view that they really wanted him to grow up and be healthy and independent. We therefore advised that they stop inquiring about the boy's symptoms and reminding him to do his blood tests. Instead, we suggested that they provide him with an opportunity to develop independent control of his diabetes by avoiding discussion of the illness altogether.

We believe that the parents' compliance with this directive was in part due to the rationale which we gave for it. Incidentally, other members of the extended family and network had offered this directive previously, but without our rationale, and the family had been unable to accept it.

7. Help the family appreciate the costs and benefits of accepting or rejecting the directive. In the medical sphere it has been found that two-sided messages lead to greater compliance with doctor's orders than one-sided messages which point only to the dangers of violating medical advice (Ley, 1988, p.154). One explanation for this is that the two-sided message offers the patient a cognitive framework which can accommodate conflicting information about compliance with doctor's orders, while allowing the patient to continue to regard the physician as competent. Where only a one-sided message is given, information which contravenes doctor's orders cannot be accommodated without viewing the physician as incompetent. (The importance of the patient or client viewing the professional as competent has already been mentioned under guideline 3 above).

In keeping with this guideline a behavioural family therapist might help a family explore the positive and negative events which would happen in the home if the parents set about teaching their eight year old son to control his temper through using *time out* . A strategic family therapist might offer the same family feedback following a midsession break indicating that the team were divided on whether the use of *time out* was a good idea or not. In both situations the family would have an opportunity to familiarise themselves with the costs and benefits of following the directive. A variety of ways in which the solo-therapist may routinely offer such split-messages are described elsewhere (Carr, 1986).

8. Use language which the family can understand when offering directives and check that the family have understood the rationale and directives that have been given. Jargon should be avoided. Short words and short sentences should be included. Feedback and clarification should be encouraged (Ley, 1988, p. 25). Family therapists often use terms like *ambivalence*. They also present complex hypotheses in lengthy sentences. Where possible these practices should be avoided. After directives have been given, some schools of family therapy, such as the structural school (Minuchin, 1974), encourage feedback and clarification. Others, for example the original Milan team (Selvini Palazzoli et al, 1978), discourage this process. The literature on patient compliance suggests that this is an erroneous position to adopt.

9. Present the rationale and the directives in a way that allows the family members to remember what you have said. The directive should be brief. Information should be simplified and categorised. Directives should be specific and not vague. The directive should be repeated. The important aspect of the directive should be given first and its importance should be stressed (Ley, 1988, p. 174-176).

An example is presented here to illustrate some of the points entailed by this guideline. This directive (which draws heavily on Minuchin's (1974) work) was offered to a family where the son presented with social withdrawal and school failure.

> *There are three things that we are suggesting you do between now and the next session. First, John and Dad should spend one hour together each evening. This is vital if he is to regain his confidence. Not three hours, not two hours. One hour and one hour only. OK? Second, Mr and Mrs Longfellow, we advise that you visit the school together as a team on Wednesday evening. You have to go together! Third we suggest that you clarify with the school how you can best help John with his homework. Have you any questions about these three suggestions? John and Dad's daily hour, the school visit and the questions for the school.*

In this example the directive is fairly brief and simple. The directive contains very specific suggestions. Particular family members are invited to do particular things at specific times for specific durations for specific purposes. The three separate elements of the directive are clearly categorised. The important point concerning father-son contact is presented first and emphasised. The core elements are repeated twice. These features of effective directives culled from the patient compliance research literature are strikingly similar to those advocated by Milton Erickson and his followers (Haley, 1973).

10. Back up orally presented information concerning rationales and directives with easily comprehensible written information. The written information should be simply presented, using short words and short sentences (Ley, 1988, p. 139). Family therapists working within behavioural or psycho-educational frameworks often present clients with extensive information packages to back up work done in therapeutic sessions. While this is a laudable practice, reviews of such materials from the fields of medicine and behaviour therapy unfortunately reveal that the text contained in such packages is often too difficult for clients to understand (e.g. O'Farrell & Keuther, 1983).

The original Milan Team were strong advocates of backing up the orally presented end-of-session intervention with a written letter (Selvini-Palazzoli, 1978). Many systemic and strategic therapists incorporated this use of written material in this way into their practice (e.g. Weeks & L'Abate, 1982). Ensuring that these letters are kept simple so that clients can readily understand them will increase the chances of the client responding appropriately to the directive.

11. Include all significant members of the family and the network in the process of giving directives. In Haynes' review (Haynes et al, 1979) of the literature on patients' compliance with doctor's orders, he examined the relationships between compliance and 100 patient characteristics, 49 physician-patient interaction characteristics, 13 disease related factors and 13 regime related factors. Second to beliefs about illness and health (mentioned above under guidelines 1 and 4), the involvement of family, friends and members of the patient network was identified as the second most important correlate of compliance with doctor's orders. This finding provides substantial justification for the family therapy practice of routinely including members of the identified patient's network in treatment sessions. It also underlines the importance of offering each family member a clearly defined part to play when a family task is given as homework (e.g. Carr and Afnan, 1989).

12. Explicitly monitor the family's response to the directive. Patients have been found to co-operate well with doctor's orders when three conditions, related to monitoring, have been met (Meichenbaum and Turk, 1987). First, clients must be asked to monitor their own symptoms and their compliance with treatment between sessions. This monitoring often takes the form of keeping some form of diary. Second, clients must be asked to employ specific signals to remind them to monitor their symptoms and their compliance with the treatment regime. For example, a patient might be asked to note routinely their symptoms and whether they had remembered to take their pills last thing before retiring each night. To remind them to do this they could place a note on their bedside alarm clock. Third, the physician must inquire about compliance at each follow-up consultation and reinforce clients for co-operation with the treatment regime.

It follows from this that family therapists might fruitfully build into the directives offered, an invitation for one or more family members to monitor the occurrence of the problem and also the family's co-operation with various aspects of the homework tasks. What follows is an illustrative example.

We asked the sister of a boy suffering from hysterical pain and paralysis to note between sessions the conditions under which her brother showed the greatest amount of muscular movement and apparently normal behaviour. We also asked that the parents keep a diary of the number of mealtimes where they successfully avoided talking about the boy's condition. The diaries were to be filled in every day after supper.

Where family therapists have given directives to their clients in one session, a portion of the next session should be devoted to exploring whether or not the directive was followed. If the directive has been followed and the expected alteration in the presenting problem has occurred, then the family should be reinforced for their efforts.

Where directives have not been followed, therapists should explore the beliefs and expectations of the family members which underpinned their negative response to the directive. That is, they should go back to guideline 4 and work from there onwards. This exploration may lead the therapist to maintain or alter the working hypothesis. If the original hypothesis is maintained, then efforts may be made to help the family to share the therapist's understanding and the same directive may be given again. If the hypothesis is altered, a new directive and rationale may be given. The following example illustrates how non-co-operation with a directive can lead to a revision of the hypothesis and a consequent change in the types of directives given.

A single parent and her seven year old daughter, who was described by the referring GP as extremely disobedient, were referred for therapy. After a preliminary assessment, the guiding hypothesis was that the parent-child boundary was blurred largely because it was a single-parent family. The mother therefore needed help in re-establishing parental authority and clarifying this boundary. The mother chose mealtime interaction as a focus for change. Mother and daughter frequently became involved in mealtime battles. The daughter would frequently leave the table during the evening meal and rarely finished her meal. The mother was concerned that the daughter was failing to learn good table manners and also that she was being undernourished. The mother and daughter were invited to participate in this task.

First, the mother was to serve from the main serving dishes in the dining room at the table, rather than in the kitchen as was the usual practice. Second, the mother was only to serve one spoonful of dinner for her daughter. Third, the daughter had to eat this serving before a further helping could be requested. Her mother was then to serve only one more spoonful. If the daughter left the table during the meal, then no more food could be served.

I informed the mother that this would teach the girl how to finish a portion dinner, since at each sitting she would have an opportunity to finish a number of potions. Also, the task would almost guarantee that the girl would never leave the table until she had finished what was on her plate. The mother and daughter co-operated with this task for a week. In the second session I suggested that the size of the portions be increased to two spoonfuls. In the third session the mother said that she had not done the task, except on one occasion.

Further exploration revealed that the mother had always known that her daughter could be well behaved at table and that the girl was not undernourished. The mother had given these as reasons for wanting to alter the way she and her daughter behaved at mealtimes because she thought I would be critical of her if she revealed the real reason. She explained how she believed that her friends and acquaintances were critical of her capacity to meet her child's needs alone, because she had no husband. Her daughter was thin and she constantly feared that she would be accused of not feeding the daughter properly and that this would be held up as an example of how she was failing as a single parent. I saw the woman without her daughter for a series of further sessions which focused on the way she evaluated herself as a parent. She was given tasks in which she was invited to check out how her friends and her family of origin evaluated her adequacy as a parent. She co- operated well with these tasks. Concurrently, the friction between herself and her daughter diminished and the mother-daughter boundary became more clearly defined.

DISCUSSION
In this paper conclusions drawn predominantly from research on patients' compliance with medical advice have been used as a basis for

guidelines that family therapists might use when giving therapeutic directives. This raises the question of the validity of generalising from one context to another. The validity of the guidelines rests on the similarity and differences between the twos contexts, i.e. the doctor-patient relationship and the therapist-family relationship. Both are helper/helpee relationships. In both contexts the helper has expert training, knowledge and qualifications. In both contexts the helper is governed by a code of ethics which prizes the client' s welfare . There are two main differences between the contexts. Physicians are probably perceived by clients as more powerful and as having greater status that family therapists. They are also more likely to take autocratic responsibility for the patient's difficulties. It could be argued that these differences would mask rather than expose specific factors related to co-operating with directives. In the light of these considerations, my view is that the guidelines set out above are reasonably valid.

Of course, the ideal test of the validity of these guidelines would be to assess empirically their impact within a family therapy context. This is a worthwhile area for further research.

Within the structural, strategic and behavioural schools of family therapy, family tasks are usually given to alter directly the behaviour which comprises the pattern of social interaction surrounding the symptom (Lange and van der Hart, 1983). The metaphors of power or instruction are used to conceptualise the relationship between the therapist and the family. The guidelines set out in this essay may easily be incorporated into the practice of therapists working within these frameworks.

Within the systemic-constructivist schools of family therapy, tasks, e.g. family rituals, are offered as opportunities for the family to experiment with new ways of behaving (Hoffman, 1988). These experiments are usually offered to provide families with opportunities to alter their belief systems. Alterations in the pattern of interaction surrounding the symptom are expected to follow from changes in the family's belief system. The metaphors of co-operation and curiosity are often use to describe the therapist-client relationship. The therapist is interested in the meaning of the family's acceptance or rejection of an invitation to carry out prescribed task, not compliance with directives for their own sake. The guideline set out in this essay are useful to therapists working within this framework insofar as they provide a set of conditions under which most clients would accept invitations to behave differently. If clients fail to accept an invitation to carry out a task, and the guidelines set out here have been followed, then it is plausible to assume that an exploration of the family's refusal may throw light on aspects of their belief system pertinent to resolving the presenting problem.   This paper has focused largely on the

188   *Family Therapy and Systemic Practice*

technicalities of giving directives. There is a danger that it may convey an image of the therapist as naive and bossy if well-intentioned. To guard against such dangers the reader is referred to the following accounts of the pitfalls that need to be avoided in forming sound hypotheses and in recognising the role of the therapist in the overall network within which specific therapeutic directives are given (Carr, 1989a; 1989b; Carr, 1990; Gawlinski, Carr et al, 1988).

REFERENCES

Bennun, I. (1989). Perceptions of the therapist in family therapy. *Journal of Family Therapy* , 11, 243-255

Carpenter, J. (1989). Editorial: Contributions to family therapy. Journal *of Family Therapy*, 10, 203-206

Carr, A. (1986). Three techniques for the solo family therapist. *Journal of Family Therapy* , 8: 373-382

Carr, A. (1989). Countertransference reactions to families where child abuse has occurred. *Journal of Family Therapy*, 11, 87-97

Carr, A. and Afnan, S. (1989). Concurrent individual and family therapy in a case of elective mutism. *Journal of Family Therapy*, 11, 29-44

Carr, A. (1990). A model for formulating problems in family therapy. *Australian and New Zealand Journal of Family Therapy*, 11, 85-92.

Carr, A., McDonnell, D. and Afnan, S. (1989). Anorexia Nervosa: The treatment of a male case with combined individual behavioural therapy and family therapy. *Journal of Family Therapy*, 11, 335-351

Gawlinski, G., Carr, A., McDonnell, D. Irving, N. and Docking, S. (1989). Thurlow House assessment programme for families with physically abused children, *Practice*, 2, 208-220

Geersten, H., Gray, R. & Ward, J . (1973). Patient non-compliance within the context of seeking medical care for arthritis. *Journal of Chronic Diseases*, 26, 689-698

Gurman, A. and Kniskern, D. (1981). *Handbook of Family Therapy*. New York: Brunner Mazel.

Haley, J. (1973). *Uncommon Therapy*. New York: Norton.

Haynes, R., Taylor, D., Sackett, D. (1979). *Compliance in Health Care*. Baltimore: John Hopkins University Press.

Heller, K. (1968) Ambiguity in the interview interaction. In J. Schlein (ed.), *Research in Psychotherapy, III*. Washington DC: APA.

Hoffman, L. (1988). A constructivist position for family therapy. *Irish Journal of Psychology*, 9, 110-119

Janz, N. & Becker, M. (1984) The health belief model: a decade later. *Health Education Quarterly*, 11, 1-47

Lange, A. and van der Hart, O. (1983). *Directive Family Therapy*. New York: Brunner Mazel.

Ley, P. (1988). *Communicating with Patients: Improving Communication Satisfaction and Compliance*. London: Croom Helm.

Meichenbaum, D. and Turk, D.C. (1987). *Facilitating Treatment Adherence: A Practitioner's Guidebook*. New York: Plenum.

Minuchin, S. (1974). *Families and Family Therapy*. Cambridge MA: Harvard

University Press.
Minuchin, S., Rosman, B., and Baker, L. (1978). *Psychosomatic Families.* Cambridge MA: Harvard University Press.
O'Farrell, T. and Keuther, N. (1983). Readability of behaviour therapy self-help manuals. *Behaviour Therapy,* 14, 449-454
Selvini-Palazzoli, M., Boscolo, L., Cecchin, G. & Prata G. (1978). *Paradox and Counterparadox.* New York: Jason Aronson.
Stiles, W., Putnam, S., Wolf, M. & Sherman, A. (1979). Interaction exchange structure and patient satisfaction with medical interviews. *Medical Care*, 17, 667-681.
Strong, S. and Claiborn, C. (1982). *Change Through Interaction: Social Psychological Processes or Counselling and Psychotherapy.* New York: Wiley.
Watts, F. (1982) Attributional Aspects of Medicine. In C. Antaki & C. Brewin (eds.), *Attributions and Psychological Change.* London: Routledge and Kegan Paul.

CHAPTER 13

INVOLVING CHILDREN IN FAMILY THERAPY AND SYSTEMIC CONSULTATION

ABSTRACT
After reviewing the rationale for including children in therapy and reasons for the widespread practice of excluding them a variety of strategies for engaging children in various aspects of family therapy are described and illustrated with case examples. These include: making the therapeutic context attractive, explaining the therapeutic process and systemic ideas in concrete terms, tracking patterns of interaction using dolls and drawings, using genograms and lifelines to assess perception of family structure and development, using face drawings to assess perception of emotional atmosphere, tracking perceived changes using visual analogue scales, teaching turn taking, using personification and externalisation of problems and strengths to solve problems, reframing problems using stories and metaphors, coaching children in new skills and providing children with advocacy.

INTRODUCTION
Family therapy has evolved into a modality largely suited to the articulate adult client with a facility for abstract reasoning. With some notable exceptions, family therapy takes scant account of the cognitive and linguistic developmental limitations of children (Ackerman, 1979; Bloch, 1976; Carpenter & Treacher, 1982, Dare & Lindsey, 1979; Satir, 1967; Keith & Whittaker, 1981; Wachtel, 1987; O'Brien & Loudon, 1985; Zilbach, 1986)).

This virtual exclusion of children from family therapy is

common practice. In a major US survey Korner & Brown (1990) found that 40% of therapists excluded children from therapy sessions and 31% only included them in a token way. This is a serious problem.

WHY INCLUDE CHILDREN?

Children need to be included in family therapy for seven main reasons. First, with child focused problems a useful evaluation of the nature and severity of the problem or the meaning of the problem for the child cannot be assessed without asking children for their view of the situation. This may occur either in the family session or in an adjunctive individual session. Obtaining the child's point of view is crucial during the assessment of high risk cases where depression, self-harm, or abuse may be present (Carr et al, 1989). Second, children participate in patterns of interaction that surround presenting problems. If children are not present the therapist can neither observe these patterns nor ask children about their experience of these cycles of interaction and the beliefs that trap children within these patterns (Carr, 1990a).

Third, children often give more spontaneous and less guarded accounts of family problems. These both help the therapist's assessment and loosen constraints on adults within the family by drawing attention to unspoken issues. Metaphorically speaking, children can declare innocently that the emperor is not wearing any clothes. Fourth, children are often aware of emotional themes in family life which adults have repressed into the unconscious. When they speak about these in family therapy they open up new options and possibilities for solving family problems (Bloch, 1976). Fifth, children's ability to play: to deal with problems through the medium of drawings, toys, stories and games offer many avenues for bypassing adult defences and exploring new ways of resolving the presenting problem (Keith & Whittaker, 1981).

Sixth, direct (rather than indirect) coaching of parents in child-management skills or adolescent-negotiation skills is possible when children are included in therapy (Minuchin, 1974). Seventh, family sessions offer a forum where the therapist can facilitate the development of supportive relationships between parents and children.

WHY ARE CHILDREN EXCLUDED?

Therapists exclude children from sessions for a variety of reasons. Many therapists feel poorly prepared by their training to work directly with children (Korner & Brown, 1990). Pre-adolescent children are difficult to engage in therapy because of their cognitive and linguistic immaturity. Before about the age of 12, children cannot easily be engaged in problem solving conversations involving abstract concepts. This is the type of conversation with which most therapists feel comfortable. Pre-adolescent children use enactments and images rather abstractions and concepts to solve problems. Engaging them in activities and conversations about sensitive or complex matters using concrete images is very challenging.

Children can be difficult to involve in therapy because of their emotional state or behavioural characteristics .In the extreme children may be either obstinately silent and withdrawn or disruptive and aggressive. Therapists may fear loosing professional credibility with parents if they try to include children in therapy and fail (Carpenter & Treacher, 1982).

Therapists may believe that the presenting difficulty is basically a marital problem expressed through the children and therefore argue that the exclusion of the children is warranted on theoretical grounds. These beliefs may often be a rationalisation to defend against difficult emotions elicited by involving challenging children in therapy (Dare & Lindsey, 1979). Marital difficulties may co-occur with child problems (Frude, 1990). Good practice requires that separate therapeutic contracts be offered for each of these problems. The child problems cannot be ignored. Two ways are recommended for dealing with families that present with both marital and child problems. Whole family therapy may be followed by couples therapy after a resolution of the child's problem (Kniskern, 1981) or concurrent child and couples therapy may be offered (Kaslow and Racusin, 1990). Unfortunately no empirical research has been conducted to assess the relative efficacy of these practices.

TECHNIQUES FOR INVOLVING CHILDREN IN FAMILY THERAPY

A compendium of techniques drawn together from various sources over the past 15 years is presented below. Like most therapeutic techniques, none of those described here are completely new. However, the collection of the practices into a compendium and its presentation a solution to the problem of involving children in therapy is novel. The methods described here have been used with children between the ages of 3 and 12 in a number of contexts including an outpatient child and family centre in Ontario Canada; an NHS outpatient child and family centre, an NHS Paediatric ward in the UK; and private practices in the UK and Ireland. They have evolved within the context of an integrative approach to family therapy and systemic consultation (Carr, In Preparation). However, all of the techniques described below may be incorporated into the practice of most forms of family therapy.

MAKE THE PROCESS OF ATTENDING THERAPY SESSIONS ATTRACTIVE FOR CHILDREN

Children find attending family therapy initially threatening (Carr et al, In Press). Their anxiety may be initially reduced by arranging a child oriented play area in the waiting room and by offering refreshments such as orange juice and biscuits. After each session children may be issued with stick on badges with smiling faces on them or other positive images. After a course of therapy children may be issued with a certificate to show that they have completed treatment.

EXPLAIN WHAT HAPPENS IN THERAPY IN CONCRETE TERMS

Children's anxiety about therapy may be reduced by explaining in concrete terms the role they will be expected to play in therapy and what therapy will involve in concrete terms. This also helps them to contribute to the process more productively. In the following example the therapist explains the consultation process to a six year old with abdominal pain for which no physical basis could be found.

> **Example 1.**
> *Therapist:* You and I and your mum and dad are going to talk together in this room for about an hour or so. That's the same length of time as Sesame street is on. Do you watch Sesame street?
> *Child:* Yes. Sometimes at granny's.
> *Therapist:* Your mum and dad told me that they are worried about the pain yoke getting in your tummy. You know the one.
> *Child:* (Nods.) mmmm
> *Therapist:* Well I may be able to help you with that. OK.
> *Child:* (Nods.) mmm (looks tearful)
> *Therapist:* But the thing is this...I want you to know...You're at the doctor's. But there I don't give injections or use pills to make tummy aches better. So you needn't worry that I'm going to open up this drawer here (opens desk drawer)and take out a syringe and .....eh..give you an injection. You were worried about that maybe..?
> *Child:* Yes. I don't like needles.
> *Therapist:* But sometimes I ask people to do special exercises and things to help them get rid of aches and pains.
> *Child:* What sort of exercises?
> *Therapist:* The boy I saw this morning had to do some deep breathing exercises with his mum. That sort of thing. I'll see him again next week to check how he got on with the exercises. Do you do breathing exercises in PE.

Child: Sometimes.

Therapist: OK. So you know what I mean. Right ? But first I want you to draw a picture of yourself and show me where the pain is on the picture and what eh..colour it feels like..Ok....

EXPLAIN COMPLEX SYSTEMIC CONCEPTS USING CONCRETE MODELS

Systemic concepts and the language used to express systemic ideas are complex. Nevertheless if children are to fully participate in therapy it may be important for them to understand some of these complex ideas such as the interdependence of family members, the cumulative effects of stress, and the effects of criticism and emotional overinvolvement (two of the main elements contributing to expressed emotion (Stubbe, 1993). These are best addressed through the use of concrete models (O'Brien & Loudon 1985).

The Mobile. A fish mobile is a useful way to explain interdependence. Siblings of referred children, often ask why they have to attend therapy since they are not sick, sad or bad. I ask them to move one fish on the fish family mobile hanging in my office. Then I ask if the other fish were effected by this. This leads on to an exploration of how they are effected by their brother or sister having problems and how they can help with solving them.

Balloons. Where youngsters are under pressure, they may be given a balloon to blow into the balloon once each time a stress factor that effects them is mentioned. The therapist then engages the rest of the family in an exploration of stresses that the youngster faces. Eventually the balloon bursts, dramatising the cumulative effects of the various stresses on the child. Where parents have difficulty empathising with the stresses a child faces this is a particularly valuable intervention.

The Scales. Where parents criticise one child exclusively and ignore the shortcomings of the other children, a plastic balancing scales designed for teaching maths concepts is a useful way of dramatising the effects of this on the children. Each child can have a turn of using the scales while the therapist asks the parents about that child's daily behaviour. The child holding the scales must put one counter on the right side each time the parents say a positive remark and one counter on the left side for each critical comment. The unbalanced amount of criticism that the scapegoated child has to bear becomes evident and the need for balance in praise and criticism can then be explored.

The Rope. Where a parent continually talks for a child, the child may be asked to hold one end of the rope and the parent to hold the other. Each time the child notices the parent talking for him, he has to pull the rope. This is a useful method for reducing enmeshment and emotional overinvolvement.

ASK ABOUT PATTERNS OF INTERACTION USING DOLLS, PUPPETS AND DRAWINGS

Tracking sequences of interaction with children is a useful way of including them in therapy. Often children notice things in behavioural sequences to which adults will not admit or of which they are unaware. Important sequences are those in which the presenting problem is embedded and those exceptional patterns of interaction which are slightly different but where the problem does not occur. Comparing these sequences may then throw light on ways in which the problem may be resolved (Carr 1990a; 1990e). With young children these sequences may be dramatised using dolls or puppets or drawn on a whiteboard or flipchart. This helps children to keep whole sequences of interaction in memory when two or more sequences are being compared. This technique, adapted from play therapy, also allows children to express things that they may not be able to express in words (O'Connor, 1991).

DRAW A GENOGRAM AND FAMILY LIFELINE ON A WHITE BOARD

The genogram and family lifeline, longstanding family evaluation methods, offer many opportunities for children to be involved in therapy particularly if these assessment methods are described as games. Drawing a genogram is a game the object of which is to draw a map of everyone in the family. The rules are that squares are for boys and circles for girls. Every circle or square must have a name and an age in it. And so on. The therapist can then ask questions of individual children or divide the family into teams with adults and children on each team and conduct a game show quiz. During the process of drawing a genogram gaps in family members knowledge and differences of opinion about family life may become apparent and require further inquiry. When the basic genogram is finished, more detailed information about key family members may be included and patterns identified (McGoldrick & Gerson, 1985; Carr et al, 1989)

A developmental family history can be represented pictorially on the whiteboard as a family lifeline. A game show quiz format may be used to involve the children in contributing to its construction. Gaps in knowledge and discrepancies between accounts may be explored when the lifeline is complete.

ASK CHILDREN ABOUT EMOTIONS USING HAPPY, SAD, SCARED AND ANGRY FACE DRAWINGS

Draw faces representing these four emotions on a white board and ask the children in the family what emotions they represent. Then ask each child one at a time to give their opinion about who is most sad, happy, scared and angry now. Follow this with questions about who is least sad, happy, scared and angry. Then inquire whether there has been a noticeable change in the way anyone has been feeling recently or since the onset of the problem. This will give a clear picture of how children experience the emotional climate of the family.

The children's understanding of the belief systems that family members hold can now be explored by asking questions about why each of the children think different people feel differently. For example a therapist may ask: Why do you think Mum is sad but Dad is angry?

TRACK CHANGES FROM SESSION TO SESSION USING VISUAL ANALOGUE SCALES OR BAR CHARTS DRAWN ON THE WHITE BOARD

Tracking client's perception of change is a crucial aspect of therapy. Discussion of perceived change provides feedback necessary for developing more adaptive ways of coping. Visual techniques are particularly useful in helping young children describe and discuss their perception of changes in both the symptom and the family system.

Visual analogue scales are useful for helping children express perceived changes in the *intensity* of a problem or an emotion. They are particularly useful for detecting changes in pain, fear, anger, sadness and happiness. They can also be used to help children express changes in interpersonal factors such as how close children feel to their mother or how warm they feel about a family member. To use visual analogue scales meaningfully, anchor points must be agreed upon and held constant from session to session. Here is an example to illustrate the process.

Example 2.
Therapist: You see this line? It goes from 1 to 10. Now I want to know..eh..how ..eh sad or happy you've been feeling since last week. OK?
Child: Just ..a bit sad.
Therapist: OK. You said that last week so I'm going to ask you to use this line to help me see if you still feel the same or different. Worse or better. Now One stands for the sadness you felt when you had to go into hospital. Do you remember that feeling.
Child: Yes. I was really sad then.
Therapist: 10 is how you felt in Spain last year. Really happy. OK. 1 is sad in hospital and 10 is happy in Spain hospital. Got that.
Child; Yes.

Therapist: Put a mark on the line for how sad you are now.
Child: ...mmmm...here.
Therapist: Now put in a mark for how you felt last week. Better or worse than now.

Bar charts are useful to track changes in symptoms or events that can be expressed as *frequencies* such as the number of nightmares, the number of times a youngster vomited, the number of tantrums or the number of fires set. These are of most value if the parents keep an ongoing record of the events as they occur and then in each session the child can draw a bar chart for each week on the board and see the change in frequency herself.

The explicit tracking of symptoms and aspects of systemic functioning in a graphic way is common practice in many forms of cognitive and behavioural therapy (Gordon & Davidson, 1981)

TEACH TURN TAKING
Silent children and disruptive children have difficulty participating in therapy. In both cases there is a need to introduce a concrete method for showing that it is the child's turn to speak. In Golding's *Lord of the Flies* in meetings of the council children were only allowed to speak if they held a large sea shell which symbolised authority: the conch. This practice is also useful in family therapy. The rules of turn taking need to be clearly spelled out. Everybody gets a turn. When it's their turn they hold the conch and speak. No-one can interrupt except the therapist if they speak for more than 4 minutes. When a person has finished talking they hand the conch back to the therapist who then passes it to the person whose turn it is next.

PERSONIFY AND EXTERNALISE PROBLEMS AND STRENGTHS
Many psychological difficulties involve internal conflict. The person feels torn between two sets of feelings, beliefs or courses of action. An important part of therapy is to articulate the conflicting inner states and then explore alternatives for handling the dilemma. Children (and indeed many adults) find the process of externalising these competing inner states and naming them as people useful in managing this process.

> **Example 3.** Theresa, a nine year old, was referred because she consistently failed to complete her homework despite staying up studying till after 10 pm. most evenings. She looked pale and tired during the intake interview. She said she wanted to finish her homework but the harder she tried to finish it, the less she got done. She was a very bright girl with an excellent academic record. Her difficulty was confusing for herself, her

parents and her teachers. I asked her to write a brief essay about her family in the session and tell me what she was thinking when she became stuck. With careful prompting she eventually identified how her need to improve each sentence she composed in her mind was preventing her from writing fluently. She externalized this urge by translating it into one half of a dialogue with the part of herself that wanted to write the essay. Here is part of the dialogue.

> There are four people in my family.
> No that's not quite right.
> In my family there are my parents, my brother Paul and myself.
> No that's the wrong way to start. What about the house.
> My family lives in a bungalow in Malahide.....

I then invited her to personify this urge to re-edit everything she composed. She named the urge *Miss Right*. The goal of therapy became developing a relationship with *Miss Right* so that Theresa could ask her to go away and let her do her homework in peace and then come in afterwards and check that it was correct, rather than hovering over every sentence.

The externalisation and personification of urges to engage in problem behaviour is useful in obsessive-compulsive disorders, such as Theresa's, in phobias, with tics and with enuresis and encopresis. The key to working with urges to engage in negative behaviour is not to destroy this aspect of the self but to 'make friends with it' and integrate it into the child's sense of self.

Strengths and competencies can also be externalised and personified. Aggressive children who need to learn temper control or shy children who need to learn assertiveness may begin by externalising and personifying a character that has these new skills. The child can then be invited to let this character have a place in their life.

Example 4. Trevor, aged 10, was extremely shy and had difficulty making friends. However, he was a good cyclist. During therapy we developed a character called The Spin. The Spin was a brilliant cyclist and trickster who loved cycling with other people. However, he would only talk to people about bikes. No matter what you said to The Spin, he would always answer in terms of cycling. So if you said 'Hello', The Spin would say 'Hi, great day for wheelies.' If you said 'Goodbye', The Spin would say ' Bye, and hope you never get a puncture'. For home work I asked Trevor to cycle to the playground each day for gradually increasing periods of time and pretend to be The Spin. He found that when he did this he was able to overcome his shyness. Eventually, he made two close friends. They talked a lot about bikes at first but later Trevor found that he talked about other things too. He no longer needed to pretend to be The Spin with his friends. However, he would bring The Spin back into his life whenever he felt threatened or shy.

Finally therapists can externalise and personify aspects of themselves that help engage children in therapy. Andrew Wood's (1988) co-therapist King Tiger is a   delightful example of this approach. Andrew tells children that he will talk to King Tiger about their problems or strengths. King Tiger then writes the child a letter which Andrew   delivers. The letters are all written from a child centred viewpoint and may be used to help the child reframe their situation, identify personal strengths, acknowledge accomplishments and so forth. The child is encouraged to write back to King Tiger and build a penfriend relationship.

The processes of externalisation and personification are widely used in the psychotherapy field. The Gestalt Therapy empty chair technique is a common case in point (Yontef & Simkin, 1989).

USE STORIES AND METAPHORS FOR REFRAMING

The use of parables, myths and fairy tales to help people find solutions to problems of living is a custom that has its roots the oral storytelling tradition.   Within the family therapy field, Milton Erickson, is recognised as the key figure to integrate this ancient tradition into modern clinical practice (Haley, 1985). He and his many followers use therapeutic storytelling with both adults and children.

The key to good practice in this area is to take the salient elements of the clients situation and build them into a story which arrives at a conclusion that offers the client an avenue for productive change rather than a painful cul-de-sac. The story is a metaphor for the client's dilemma, a metaphor that offers a solution. This age old technique is particularly useful for involving children in therapy.

> **Example 5.** Sabina, a 7 year old girl was referred because of recurrent nightmares in which she dreamt her house was being burgled and her parents assaulted. The nightmares followed an actual burglary of the families shop, over which they lived. The girl dealt with the nightmares by climbing onto the end of her parents bed so as not to wake them trying to think of something else. During the day she refused to talk about the nightmares or the burglary. To some degree, her parents went along with this process of denial. Sabina was in the brownies

and was learning about first aid when she was referred. Towards the end of the first session I offered the following story.

Two brownies were on an adventure in the woods. They decided to have a race. They were both the same height and looked alike except that one had blond hair like yours and one had dark hair. While they were racing, and they were neck in neck all the way, they both tripped over the same branch and each of them cut their knee. The cuts hurt a lot and both girls felt like crying. The dark haired girl tried to stop herself from crying and her leg hurt more. The blond girl allowed herself to cry and felt relieved. The crying made her knee hurt less. Both girls went to the stream and bathed their cuts. Both girls had small first aid kits in their pockets. The dark haired girl put a bandage from her kit on her cut straight away. The blond girl could have done this also but she did not. She let her cut air. Both girls went home for tea. After tea they went to bed. The dark haired girl couldn't sleep because the cut hurt so much. She turned on the light. She took off the bandage and noticed that the cut had become infected. It was all yellow with puss. The dark haired girl washed the cut quickly and put on another bandage over the puss. The blond girl, woke in the middle of the night because her knee was hurting her. She woke her mum and her mum helped her bathe the cut in hot water to draw the puss out. This was painful, but she knew it would make her better. Three days later her cut was better. But her friend was still wearing a bandage. Her knee still had puss in it. She still woke up in the middle of the night night with the pain.

In the conversation that followed, Sabina and her parents began to talk openly about the robbery and the nightmares and the parents spontaneously invited Sabina to wake them when she had nightmares. I asked Sabina to draw pictures of the nightmares and explain them to myself and her parents. After three sessions, over a period of a month, the nightmares had almost disappeared.

This story took account of Sabina's interest in first aid and racing. A physical trauma (cutting her knee) was used as a metaphor for the psychological trauma she had suffered (being burgled). The story included one course of action taken by the dark haired girl which resembled the pattern of coping she had adopted. It also contained an alternative. This other more adaptive route was taken by the blond girl. The girl whose hair was the same colours as Sabina's. This detail was included to make it easy for Sabina to identify with her. The story reframed Sabina's dilemma from 'How can I distract myself from memories of the robbery and get rid of these nightmares so I can feel good.' to 'How can I squeeze all of this psychological puss out of my mind so the wound will heal?' This reframing offered a new avenue for coping.

ASK THE CHILD TO REHEARSE SKILLS NECESSARY FOR HOMEWORK IN THE SESSION

Children delight in mastering new skills. This may be capitalised upon in family therapy by using sessions as a forum for teaching new skills that are to be practised as homework. Commonly these new skills will involve interacting with parents in particular ways.

Within the structural family therapy tradition Minuchin (1974) used to advise a peripheral father to spend special time with the problem child as homework but insist that the father and son begin planning the use of the special time in the session. If the father and son had poor communication skills, Minuchin would coach them in how to communicate more effectively.

With young children this coaching process can be applied to teaching children to play a variety of games or engage in a variety of activities with their parents, while avoiding unnecessary conflict. The skills include checking if the parent is available to play, planning an alternative time if the parent is unavailable, selecting a game, asking the parent to select a game, rule following, accepting interruptions without tantruming, accepting that the special time period is limited, showing appreciation and arranging to play again.

With young children behavioural parenting skills such as using time out or token systems can be taught with a high degree of child involvement if they are reframed as helping the child to learn self-control or self directed behaviour.

> **Example 6.** Sean, a six year old, was referred because of tantrums and defiance. A time out and token system was developed with him and his parents in the following way. His temper was personified and externalized as Mister Fire. We spent some time talking about how hard it was for Sean to control Mr Fire and how useful it would be to be able to do so. It would help him to avoid rows with his parents. It would prevent him from feeling shame and in sports he could ask Mr Fire to help him to run fast and kick the football harder. At the close of this conversation Sean said he wished he could learn to control Mr Fire. I explained that any time Mr fire started coming out and making Sean be rude or naughty, he should run up to his room, let Mr fire have a good shout and then tell

him to calm down. Sean agreed to do this. I said that he would need his mother's help some times. She could remind him to bring Mr Fire upstairs or help him get Mr Fire back into the room if he escaped before he had calmed down. She agreed to this.

To tackle the problem of defiance, we first worked on Sean's refusal to tidy his toys up each evening. He loved to go to the adventure playground at weekends with his father, but this rarely happened. We discussed the playground at length and what incentives Dad might need to bring him there. After some prompting, Sean suggested that dad would love a Saturday Newspaper which cost 50p. The question then was, what chores could he do to earn this. A number were explored, and we settled on tidying the playroom each night at 6.00pm. Mum would pay him 10p if he completed the job successfully.

The parents kept routine behavioural records. The frequency of tantrums decreased rapidly after an initial increase and Sean regularly tidied the toys up for 6 weeks running. He also began to take responsibility in other areas.

In this example, the parents implemented routine behavioural time-out and token programmes (Gordon & Davidson, 1981). However, Sean participated in their development and implementation. He also construed them as an opportunity to learn how to control his temper and how to arrange to go the adventure playground with his father.

In paediatric settings children can be trained in the skills necessary to manage their own health and well-being. This is particularly important for children with chronic conditions like diabetes and asthma. Children need to understand their condition in terms that are age appropriate, be given a rationale for treatment that they can make sense of and be given very clear instructions and coaching in medical self care skills. In addition they need to be regularly monitored and their parents need to support and understand the child's self-care responsibilities. These guidelines are extrapolated from the extensive literature on compliance with medical advice (Carr, 1990d, 1990f).

Example 7. Pearse developed asthma as a young child and was admitted to the Paediatric ward on a number of occasions with severe attacks. To control his condition he was required to use a volumatic inhaler on a twice daily basis to take three actuations of Salbutamol (Ventolin) and Beclomethasone (Becotide). At the age of five he was trained in how to do this himself under parental supervision. It was first explained to him that the tight feeling in his chest and the difficulty drawing breath was because the little sponges in his lungs that soak up air were not working in the same way as a bike will cease up if you don't oil the chain. The inhalers were then presented as special gases that uncease the little sponges in the lungs so that little bits of oxygen could get into the blood and make his muscles work so he could run and play.   This led to a discussion about how the little bits of oxygen hitched a ride on the blood boats that travelled around the rivers of blood that flowed in the arteries and veins. We drew a diagram on the board and looked at a diagram in an anatomy atlas. We also discussed the consequences of not having enough oxygen. It would make him feel exhausted and unable to play. Once Pearse understood the rationale, he was eager to learn the very best way to use the inhaler. He was instructed in how to say "ready, steady , go" and use these mental self-instructions to co-ordinate the actuation with a deep intake of breath.

PROVIDE CHILDREN WITH AN ADVOCATE

In complex multiproblem cases, especially if there is multiagency involvement , there is a danger that the child's voice will become lost in the complexities of the problem determined system (Carr, 1990b, 1990c; Carr et al, 1989). This is often true of cases involving child abuse, foster care, parental criminality or psychiatric difficulties, bereavement, hospitalisation or special education. Providing the child with a key worker or advocate in such situations is an important way of ensuring that the child may participate in family therapy or broader systemic consultation meetings in a meaningful way. The advocate may involve the child in a series of individual sessions to help clarify the child's point of view. The advocate may then help the child present this view in family or network consultations.

> **Example 8.** Cindy was originally referred for neuropsychological assessment and counselling by the Paediatrics Department in a District Hospital in the UK following a road traffic accident in which she sustained a closed head injury and in which her father was killed. Subsequently, her mother, Christine, a poorly controlled diabetic, had great difficulty caring for Cindy (aged 9) and her younger brother , Kevin, (aged 6). After a year, and a series of crises where Christine was unable to cope with the children, respite care was arranged with Social Services. Cindy and Kevin spent between 2 and 4 days a week with foster parents in a nearby village. This respite care evolved into full time care when Christine was hospitalised for surgery following the

diagnosis of breast cancer. When Christine was discharged from hospital, an agreement was reached that the children should stay in full time care, but that they would have regular visits with Christine, who felt unable to cope with them on a full time basis. In addition to the stress of bereavement, single parenthood, poorly controlled diabetes and cancer, Christine was also engaged in litigation for compensation in relation to the accident in which her husband was killed and her daughter injured. Throughout the five years I worked with this case, more than thirty professionals were involved. These included paediatricians, family doctors, school doctors, psychiatrists, nurses, occupational therapists, physiotherapists, social workers, remedial teachers, solicitors, barristers, foster parents, home aid workers and managers from the departments of Social Services and Education. Many of the systemic consultation meetings that were convened involved up to a dozen of these professionals along with Cindy, Kevin and Christine. A key element in involving both Cindy and Kevin in these consultations and allowing their opinions and views to be heard was providing them with advocacy throughout the process.

DISCUSSION

The approach to involving children in family therapy described here is based on three principles. First, at an ethical level children have a right to participate in the process of solving problems of living which they and their families face. Second, at a pragmatic level therapy has a better chance of success if those involved in the problem, including children, participate in the solution. Third, at a theoretical level, methods of engaging children in therapy must be based on an integration of both the therapeutic literature and the child development literature.

This approach to including children in therapy can be adopted by therapists from any professional background that includes a grounding in the basic therapeutic skills needed to engage children in a helping relationship. The skills outlined here can be refined in brief intensive training workshops. Of course, being a parent helps too, but its not essential.

REFERENCES

Ackerman, N. (1970). Child participation in family therapy. *Family Process*, 9, 403-410.
Bloch, D. (1976). Including the children in family therapy. In P. Guerin (Ed.) *Family Therapy: Theory and Practice* . New York: Gardiner.
Carpenter, J. & Treacher, A. (1982). Structural family therapy in context: Working with child focused problems. *Journal of Family therapy*, 4, 15-34.

Carr, A. (1990a). A formulation model for use in family therapy. *The Australian and New Zealand Journal of Family Therapy*, 11, 85-92.

Carr, A. (1990b). Failure in family therapy: A catalogue of engagement mistakes. *Journal of Family Therapy*, 12, 371-386.

Carr, A. (1990c). Power and influence in systems consultation. *Human Systems*, 2, 15-29.

Carr, A. (1990d). Giving directives effectively. The implications of research on compliance with doctors orders for family therapy. *Human Systems*, 1, 115-127.

Carr, A. (1990e). From problems to solutions: Report on a workshop by Steve de Shazer and Insoo Kim Berg from the Milwalkee Brief Therapy Centre, USA. *Context, Newsletter of the Association for Family Therapy*, Summer, No.6, 12-15.

Carr, A. (1990f). Compliance with medical advice. *British Journal of Medical Practice*, 40, (No. 338), 358-360.

Carr, A., Gawlinski, G., MacDonnell, D., Irving, N. & Docking, S. (1989). Thurlow House Adolescent Assessment Programme. *Practice*, 2, 60-190.

Carr, A. (1995). *Positive Practice with families and other systems: An Integrative Approach to Systemic Consultation.* Reading: Harwood.

Carr, A., Mc Donnell, D. & Owen, P. (1994). Audit and family systems consultation: Evaluation of practice at a child and family centre. *Journal of Family Therapy, 16*, 143-157,

Dare, C. & Lindsey, C. (1979). Children in family therapy. *Journal of Family Therapy*, 253-269.

Frude, N. (1990). *Understanding Family Problems.* New York: Wiley

Gordon, S. & Davidson, N. (1981). Behavioural parent training . In A. Gurman & D. Kniskern (Eds.), *Handbook of Family Therapy.* New York: Brunner Mazel.

Haley, J. (1985). *Conversations with Milton H. Erickson, MD. (3 Vols).* New York. Triangle.

Kaslow, N. & Racusin, G. (1990). Family therapy or child therapy: An open or shut case. *Journal of Family Psychology*, 3, 273-289.

Keith, D. & Whitaker, C. (1981). Play therapy: A paradigm for work with families. *Journal of Marital and Family therapy*, 7, 243-254.

Korner, S. & Brown, G. (1990). Exclusion of children from family psychotherapy: Family therapists beliefs and practices. *Journal of Family Psychology*, 3, 420-430.

Kniskern, D. (1981). Including children in marital and family therapy. In A. Gurman (Ed.) *Questions and answers in the Practice of Family Therapy* . New York. Brunner/Mazel.

McGoldrick, M. & Gerson, R (1985). *Genograms in Family Assessment.* New York: Norton.

Minuchin, S. (1974). *Families and Family Therapy.* Cambridge, MA. Harvard.

Mussen, P., Conger, J., Kagan, J. & Huston, A. (1990). *Child Development and Personality* (7th. ed). New York: Harper Collins.

O'Brien, A. & Loudon, P. (1985). Redressing the balance. Involving children in family therapy. *Journal of Family Therapy*, 7, 81-98.

O'Connor, K. (1991). *The Play Therapy Primer.* New York: Wiley/

Satir, V. (1967). *Conjoint Family Therapy.* London: Souvenir Press.

Stubbe, D., Zahner, G., Goldstein, M., & Leckman, J. (1993). Diagnostic specificity of a brief measure of expressed emotion. *Journal of Child Psychology and Psychiatry,* 34 (2), 139-154.

Watchel, E. (1987). Family systems and the individual child. *Journal of Marital and Family Therapy,* 13, 15-25.

Wood, A. (1988). King Tiger and the roaring tummies: A novel way of helping young children and their families change. *Journal of Family Therapy,* 10, 49-63.

Yontef, G & Simkin, J. (1989). Gestalt Therapy . In R. Corsini & D. Wedding (Eds.) *Current Psychotherapies* (Fourth edition). Itasca, Ill: Peacock.

Zilbach, J. (1986). *Young children in Family Therapy.* New York: Brunner Mazel.

CHAPTER 14

RESISTANCE, DILEMMAS AND CRISES IN FAMILY THERAPY: A FRAMEWORK FOR POSITIVE PRACTICE

ABSTRACT

When clients believe that they have not got the personal resources to cope with the demands of either living with their problems or taking steps towards the resolution of these, stating their therapeutic dilemma may precipitate a therapeutic crisis. A therapeutic dilemma is a concise statement of the disadvantages and difficulties associated with leaving the presenting problem unresolved and the disadvantages and risks entailed by solving the problem. Invariably, therapeutic crises involve some family members doubting an interactional formulation of the family's problems and redefining these as individual difficulties of a specific family member. That is, someone in the family becomes defined as *bad, sad, sick* or *mad*. The pressure to collude with the family and other network members in abandoning an interactional construction of the problem and accepting an individual description is usually very intense. When therapists follow this route they become part of the problem maintaining system. In this paper a framework for conceptualizing therapeutic crises and guidelines for their management are described. These guideline allow the therapist to avoid becoming involved in problem maintenance and to retain a position from which to promote problem resolution. The framework and guidelines evolved within the context of a brief integrative approach to consultation with families who require help with child-focused psychosocial difficulties.

INTRODUCTION
Positive Practice is a brief integrative approach to consultation with families who require help with child-focused psychosocial difficulties (Carr, 1995). The approach looks to the tradition of Milan systemic family therapy for its central clinical framework (Campbell et al, 1991). Aspects of psychodynamic therapy (e.g. Malan, 1979) and social learning theory (e.g. Falloon, 1991) are integrated into this core approach to practice along with elements drawn from the wider fields of family therapy (Gurman & Kniskern, 1991) and brief therapy (Gilligan & Price, 1993). Within this approach a clear distinction is made between the stages of assessment and treatment. Clients formally contract for both phases of consultation (Carr, 1990a). In each phase, treatment plans are based on an integrative formulation. Formulations are constructed in a way that allows therapists and clients to map information about the pattern of interaction around the presenting problem, beliefs that constrain family members from altering their roles in these problem maintaining patterns and factors that have predisposed family members to hold these beliefs (Carr, 1990, b). Positive Practice offers methods for evolving new behavioural patterns and belief systems within sessions and for arranging homework tasks for clients between sessions. It also incorporates methods for dealing with resistance; for managing therapeutic crises; for convening individual sessions (Carr, 1994) and broader network meetings; for disengaging from the consultation process and for recontracting for further episodes of therapy. In this paper, the focus is on the midphase of therapy and the issues of resistance and crises that may occur when the dilemmas entailed by resistance are explored.

RESISTANCE
Between contracting for consultation and disengagement many hitches occur in most family therapy cases. For example, family members may miss appointments, not complete homework assignments, participate in therapy sessions in ways that prevent progress or revert to an individualistic formulation of the problem (Anderson and Stewart, 1983). Let us here become acquainted with a case example which will be followed throughout the paper to illustrate points made. The Barrow family comprised two teenage children, Caroline (14) and Mat (18) and their parents Dick and Sheila. Caroline was referred to a child and family clinic in the UK concurrently by a paediatrician and an educational psychologist.

Their respective concerns were Caroline's abdominal pains for which no medical explanation could be offered and her school non-attendance. With the Barrows, resistance was first apparent in the third session when Sheila reported that she failed to complete the task of allowing Caroline to autonomously manage her abdominal pains. Resistance intensified in session four. Dick failed to attend the session. He also failed to follow through on his agreement to phone Sheila each morning at 8.30 to help her deal with the difficulty she experienced in allowing Caroline space to manage her pain independently. In addition, Sheila and Caroline did not visit the family doctor on three mornings when the intensity of the abdominal pains led to school non-attendance. The agreement was that in such situations, the judgement about Caroline's medical fitness for school attendance would be left with the GP.

In Positive Practice resistance is dealt with in a systematic manner. The discrepancy between what clients agreed to do and what they actually did is described. Second, inquiries are made about the difference between situations where they managed to follow through on an agreed course of action and those where they did not. Third, their beliefs about factors that blocked them from making progress are explored. Fourth, their beliefs about whether and how these blocks may be overcome are examined. Fifth, strategies for getting around the blocks are brainstormed. Sixth, the pros and cons of these courses of action are delineated. Seventh, a therapeutic dilemma is framed in which the costs of maintaining the status quo and the costs of circumventing the blocks are juxtapositioned.

DILEMMAS AND CRISES

If clients see that they have not got the personal resources to cope with the demands of either living with the problem or taking steps towards its resolution, stating the therapeutic dilemma may precipitate a therapeutic crisis. A therapeutic dilemma is a concise statement of the disadvantages and difficulties associated with leaving the presenting problem unresolved and the disadvantages and risks entailed by solving the problem. It is rarely enough to say that the symptoms are bad but the prospect of change is worse. Rather, when articulating the therapeutic dilemma it is important to relate the way in which family members are trapped in the cycle of interaction around the presenting problem to their belief systems that underpin their roles in this cycle and also to note that these belief systems have roots in their personal histories, their families of origin or their membership of other systems such as work or school. It is also important to specify or give examples of the types of action that might lead to resolving the presenting problem in the future and the emotional costs of these.

Stating the therapeutic dilemma may precipitate a therapeutic crisis. If clients see that both the problem and its resolution entail emotional pain and that the responsibility for resolving the problem is largely theirs, they will experience a crisis if they believe that they have not got the personal resources to cope with the demands of this responsibility.

Invariably, therapeutic crises which follow the articulation of a therapeutic dilemma, involve some family members doubting the interactional formulation of the problem (Carr, 1990b) and redefining the problem as an individual difficulty rather than as an interactional phenomenon. This happened with the Barrows following the fourth session. Dick attempted to force Caroline to attend school and she responded with aggression, fearfulness and threats of self-harm. In a phone call to the therapist, Dick insisted that Caroline's difficulties reflected an underlying individual psychopathological condition rather than an interactional difficulty and requested hospitalization and sedation for her. Details of the management of this crisis phonecall will be outlined in the next section.

In later sessions when we discussed the episode that preceded the crisis phonecall, it became apparent that Dick chose to disregard a complex interactional systemic understanding of the problem and construe Caroline as a *bad* girl who needed firm handling, and   forcibly return her to school. When Caroline bit Dick, crooned and rocked back on forth like a baby on the car seat in response to his treatment of her as a disobedient child, he was extremely distressed and began to doubt his framing of her as *bad* and the wisdom of the firm and ineffective approach he took in returning her to school.

In response to the doubt, he chose another simplistic individualistic framing of Caroline's behaviour. He chose to see his daughter not as *bad* but as *mad.* This is not surprising. Under stress all of us choose cognitively simple rather than complex framings of challenging or threatening situations (Kelly, 1955). Also, we all choose to avoid emotionally distressing situations. When Dick reframed Caroline's difficulties as *madness* and the solution as *hospitalization and sedation* he selected a framing that would help him to avoid considerable emotional distress. By selecting an individualistic framing rather than the interactional formulation, he chose a way of conceptualizing the problem that would allow him to continue to avoid the painful process of negotiating a shared understanding of the problem with Sheila. If

Caroline were *mad* then she needed expert help, *hospitalization, and sedation.* His role in the management of the problem would be peripheral. He could therefore avoid emotional pain and possibly protect Sheila from emotional pain also. He could also preserve a view of himself as a good father who was doing the best he could for his *mad* daughter.

Invariably, therapeutic crises involve some family members doubting the interactional three column formulation of the problem and redefining the problem as an individual difficulty rather than as an interactional phenomenon.

That is, someone in the family becomes defined as *bad, sad, sick* or *mad.* There is usually some attempt by a member of the problem-system to convince the therapist that an individual definition of the problem is true and an interactional definition of the problem is false. Often, another professional is coopted into the system to help the family convince the therapist of the truth of the individual formulation, or to disqualify the therapists interactional formulation. This pressure to collude with the family and other network members in abandoning an interactional construction of the problem and in accepting an individual description is usually very intense. Without a framework for understanding these crises and guidelines for managing them, therapists are easily *sucked into* colluding with those members of the problem-system who wish to label one person as the problem (Selvini-Palazzoli and Prata, 1982).

PROBLEM MAINTAINING AND PROBLEM RESOLVING THERAPEUTIC SYSTEMS

Figure 14.1 is a map of a therapeutic system which faces a crisis and evolves in such a way that ultimately the therapeutic process maintains the presenting problem. In systems such as these, the therapist abandons a systemic or interactional framing of the problem and accepts the family's individualstic framing of their difficulties. Subsequent consultations premised on this individualistic framing, maintain rather than resolve the family's problems (Anderson, Goolishan & Windermand, 1986).

In Figure 14. 2, the evolution of a therapeutic system which remains premised on an interactional problem formulation is presented. The therapist and family avoid an individualistic framing of the problem because the therapist has followed a series of guidelines which maximize the chances of creating a context within which a systemic interactional formulation of the problems can be privileged. It is to these guidelines that we now turn.

GUIDELINES FOR MANAGING THERAPEUTIC CRISES

The overriding goal in managing a therapeutic crisis is to help clients retain an interactional construction of the problem which opens up possibilities for achieving their long term therapeutic goals. By implication this involves avoiding collusion with an individualistic construction of the problem which would lead to short term relief but hinder long term goal attainment. What follows are guidelines for dealing with crises. They are framed *as if* the crisis takes the form of a phonecall from a parent. Of course this is not always the case. Some crises occur during a consultation. Others are mentioned through letters from involved professionals. However, the majority of crises in my practice have taken the form of phonecalls from parents, and so it is in this context that the guidelines are framed.

1. Assess and manage danger. Family violence, abuse, self-injurious gestures, running away, staying out late, theft, and the discovery of substance abuse are some of the incidents that occur when a therapeutic crisis is reached. In Positive Practice the clinician's first duty is to establish if anyone in the family is a danger to themselves or to other people. If there is a high risk of danger, an immediate family consultation should be scheduled. The goal of this is to help the family manage the immediate danger.

Figure 14.1. Map of a problem maintaining therapeutic system

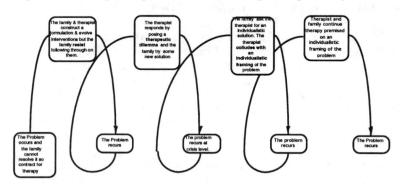

Figure 14. 2. Map of a problem resolving therapeutic system

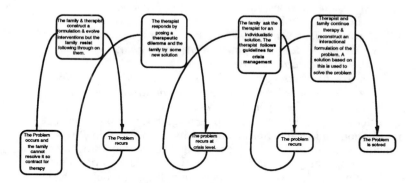

2. Empathize with the caller's emotional pain without colluding with their simplistic solutions. Parents typically make crisis calls if they perceive the demands of the situation to outweigh their capacity to cope. If their child has run away or slashed their wrists, or if their spouse has screamed at them and hit a child, they may believe that these are situations with which they cannot deal. Often, in such circumstances, patents are overwhelmed by fear, sadness or anger, and these intense emotions have compromised their capacity for clear thinking and systematic problem solving. They find themselves locked into black and white thinking, unable to tolerate the complexities or ambiguities of their problem situation. So, for example, with the Barrows, Dick saw Caroline as mentally ill and was unable to entertain a complex three column formulation or even a simple reframing of her difficulties as part of a broader pattern of interaction that included the family and involved professionals. In Positive Practice it is recognized that parents need a chance to ventilate overwhelming emotions, often by discussing simplistic black and white descriptions of the problem and simplified solutions like hospitalization or reception into care. The expression of empathy for the overwhelming feelings with which parents are faced is therefore important. However, this empathy and support must be given without accepting the simplistic problem definitions and solutions that accompany the intense emotions. Here are some typical examples of constructive empathy and contrasting examples of collusion in black and white thinking and individualistic problem formulations and solutions. This is constructive empathy.

• *It sounds like you're really worried about her. You're driven*

    to distraction wondering what she will do next.
- *You have both been in a battle and now she has walked out.*
  This has left you with a deep feeling of loss and failure.

This is destructive collusion

- *It sounds like you see her as really agitated and needing
  something to calm her down. Well, I will phone the GP and
  ask that he consider medication.*
- *You see her running away as a sign of delinquency and you
  see boarding school as a way of containing that. I can
  suggest two places you could call.*

It is not intended in these examples to give the impression that
medication and residential placement have no place in Positive
Practice. Far from it. Many excellent examples of how these
interventions may be integrated into systemic approaches to
formulating and resolving a variety of very difficult problems have
been described (e.g. Falloon et al, 1993; Manor, 1991). Rather, the
central point is that it is not Positive Practice to use these
interventions within the context of a formulation that labels one
system member as *bad, sad, sick* or *mad* and the other members of
the system as being uninvolved in the maintenance or resolution of
the problem.

**3. Acknowledge that labelling one person as the problem
would provide short term relief but may lead to long term
difficulties.** Defining complex interactional problems in simple
individual terms usually provides short term relief for parents.
Individual problem definitions (like *sad, bad, sick* or *mad*)
usually entail clear unambiguous solutions. These allow parents a
way of avoiding the emotional pain which goes with exploring an
interactional problem formulation and carrying out the solutions
that follow from it. However, in the long term simplistic solutions
to individual framings of interactional problems may lead to major
difficulties.

    For example, when children are defined as *sad* o r
depressed, the simplistic solution is to cheer them up by arranging
for them to join the scouts, go to a sports club or take up a hobby
to make them happy. In the long term, the child may find that
scouts, sports and hobbies leave them as sad as ever. Both the
parents and the child may be left with a sense of despair that the
depression is unresolvable, and anger that the solution did not
work.

    Punishment is the simplistic solution for *bad* o r
delinquent children. In the long run, sustained punishment
untempered by understanding and warmth leads children to become

alienated from their parents. This alienation may lead to further conduct problems. Punishment may take many forms from physical or verbal abuse to threats of abandonment or actual placement of the child in care or a boarding school situation. That is not to say that residential and foster care or boarding schools are necessarily alienating or destructive. Rather, the point is, that if the child sees the placement as an act of punishment, then it may lead to alienation and this may further compound the problem.

Hospitalization, individual assessment or therapy and medication are the more common simple solutions suggested when youngsters are defined as *mad, sick,* or mentally ill. All three of these interventions, when used outside of an interactional systemic framing of the problem, run the risk of confirming the youngster's identity as a problem person, victim, or invalid. Once youngsters accept this type of problem- saturated identity, their problem behaviour may increase and the quality of their relationships with their parents may deteriorate.

In my clinical experience no parents want to reap the potentially disastrous consequences that may arise from individualistic framings of their children's problems. They do not want to run the risk of casting their children into despair, destruction, alienation or invalidity. However, they are often unaware that individualistic framings have these long term consequences. An important part of crisis management in Positive Practice is to acknowledge parent's understandable wish to avoid the emotional pain that pushes parents to adopt individualistic framings of the problem, and to point out to them the destructive long-term consequences that may inadvertently arise from their individualistic construction of their children's problem behaviour.

4. Offer an urgent appointment and a plan. When a crisis occurs, parents may feel helpless and threatened yet aware that they must take action. Once they have ventilated their feelings and seen that individualistic problem definitions and simplistic solutions are inappropriate, they will feel supported. However, they may still be at a loss to know how to proceed. In Positive Practice, it is crucial to help parents form an immediate action plan. It has already been mentioned that this plan should offer precedence to managing risks of danger. A second priority is that it will maximize the chances of them accepting the interactional problem formulation and related solutions.

A useful place to start constructing such a plan is to decide on a date for the next appointment. This should be as soon as possible. During crises, people are open to accepting new framings of old problems. Usually, the further from a crises a family moves, the less open it will be to change. A second consideration is who should attend the post-crisis consultation. In Positive Practice, significant members of the wider network, including involved professionals and important members of the extended family, may be included in the consultation. With the Barrows, Caroline's year-head, the GP and the school nurse were invited to the post-crisis consultation. Where important members of the network are unavailable for this consultation, the therapist may phone them beforehand, inform them of the situation, request comments and relay this information to those who attend the consultation. These absent network members should be briefed after the consultation as to the outcome and about the plan.

Once a decision has been reached on the time, place and composition of the post-crisis consultation, the parents or children may be offered a plan to carry out between the phonecall and the consultation. Often the most appropriate plan is to monitor a specific aspect of the situation or to avoid engaging in escalating patterns of behaviour. With Caroline, she talked explicitly to me about the importance of being left alone in her room and asked that her parents respect her right to do this during the forty-eight hour period before the post-crisis consultation. Here are some examples of tasks given to family members during crisis phonecalls.

- *Between now and the meeting tomorrow, there are a couple of things that you can do that may provide useful information for yourself and your family. First, notice those situations where the sense of tension in the house subsides and keep a note of the time and circumstances surrounding these episodes. Second, if you feel yourself being drawn into a typical bickering session, tell Marie that you have been asked by me to avoid this until after tomorrow's meeting and then make a cup of tea instead of continuing.*

- *We will meet in three days. Tonight, tomorrow night and Thursday night may be stressful for you. You may want to know what is the best thing to do. May I suggest this? Follow your usual routine of putting the kids to bed, doing the story and then watching the news. But after that, phone Colin and tell him in detail about how you managed the strong feelings of anger that you felt during the routine. Rate these on a ten point scale. We can discuss the fluctuations in your feelings at the meeting on Friday.*

- *You may find that the urge to run away becomes very strong. If you don't know what to do, here is something that another boy in your sort of situation found useful. He would lock himself in his room and then write a letter to me telling me why he had to run away and why he found it difficult to do so. You may find this sort of thing useful. If you do decide to write me some letters, we can set aside time on Monday for you and I to read them privately. Or you may wish to keep them a secret. Its up to you. But the thing is, the writing itself may help you contain the urge to run away.*

DISCUSSION

The approach to managing crises presented in this paper draws on ideas from a variety of sources. Some of these deserve elaboration. The idea that resistance in therapy is an expression of a perceived imbalance between therapeutic demands and client resources is taken from the field of health psychology (e.g. Sarafino, 1994). The notion that under stress most people automatically revert to cognitively simple rather than complex constructions of problems is drawn from a body of research conducted within the constructivist tradition which grew from the work of George Kelly (Jankowicz, 1987; Kelly, 1955). The idea that well intentioned therapeutic interventions may exacerbate problems is drawn from the work of the MRI associates (Watzlawick et al, 1994; Segal, 1991) and this idea was expanded by Anderson, Goolishan & Windermand (1986) when they distinguished between problem maintaining and problem resolving therapeutic systems.

Figure 14.3. Guidelines for managing crisis phonecalls

1. Assess and manage danger
2. Empathize with the caller's emotional pain without colluding with their simplistic solutions
3. Acknowledge that labelling one person as the problem would provide short term relief but may lead to long term difficulties
4. Offer an urgent appointment and a plan
5. Significant network members should be included in the post-crisis consultation
6. The plan for managing the situation until the post-crisis consultation should include symptom monitoring tasks and tasks that prevent the escalation of destructive interactional spirals

Finally, within both the structural family therapy tradition (Colapinto, 1991) and the therapeutic approach adopted by the original Milan associates (Campbell et al., 1991) there was an emphasis on promoting therapeutic change actively working precipitate crises (Jenkins, 1989). Salvador Minuchin, founder of Structural Family Therapy, invited families to enact their routine solutions to presenting problems in the consulting room, but encouraged family members to progress further with these solutions than they would typically go. For example, in families with anorexic teenagers, he invited the parent who saw the child as bad or disobedient and who favoured force feeding, to show him how this solution worked in practice by making the anorexic girl eat food during the consultation. When this enacted solution ended in a crisis of failure, he would invite family members to consider other ways of reframing the problem and other solutions (Minuchin, Rosman and Baker, 1978). The original Milan associates precipitated family crises by articulating the necessity of the family members' roles in maintaining the presenting problem and pointing out the costs of changing the family game (Campbell et al, 1991). Therapeutic approaches which aim to precipitate a crisis, challenge clients to act-out or think-through their current framing of the problem and its solution. When the limitations of this are seen and the intense sadness, fear or anger associated with this realization are foreseen or experienced, clients begin to doubt their original framing of the problem.

While this paper has focused on an approach to crisis management, it should be stressed that within the Positive Practice approach to family therapy, it is accepted that a therapeutic crisis does not have to occur in every case. If the responsibilities that the therapist invites clients to take on are well within their capacity to cope, then no resistance will occur, no therapeutic dilemma will be framed and no crisis will occur. Certain types of client are less likely to experience a therapeutic crisis. Where clients have single rather than multiple problems and mild rather than severe difficulties then they are less likely to experience a therapeutic crisis. A crisis is also less likely where clients have good coping skills and where their social support network is well established. There are certain things that a therapist can do to minimize the chance of a therapeutic crisis occurring. Therapists can help clients co-construct a formulation that entails solutions which can be broken down into a number of manageable tasks. For example with behavioural training in problem solving skills, clients begin by being trained in how to solve emotionally neutral problems and only when they have mastered these skills are they invited to move on to tackle emotionally loaded issues relevant to the presenting problem (Falloon et al, 1993).

REFERENCES

Anderson, C. and Stewart, S. (1983). *Mastering Resistance.* New York: Guilford.

Anderson, H., Goolishan, H. and Windermand, L. (1986). Problem determined systems: Toward transformation in family therapy. *Journal of Strategic and Systemic Therapies,* 5 (4), 1-14.

Campbell, D., Draper, R. and Crutchley, E. (1991). The Milan Systemic Approach to Family Therapy. In A. Gurman, and D. Kniskern (eds.) *Handbook of Family Therapy . Volume 2.* New York: Brunner/Mazel.

Carr, A. (1990a). Failure in family therapy: A catalogue of engagement mistakes. *Journal of Family Therapy,* 12, 371-386.

Carr, A. (1990b). A formulation model for use in family therapy. *The Australian and New Zealand Journal of Family Therapy,* 11, 85-92.

Carr, A. (1990c). Giving directives effectively: The implications of research on compliance with doctor's orders for family therapy. *Human Systems: Journal of Systemic Consultation and Management,* 1, 115-127.

Carr, A. (1994). Involving children in family therapy and systemic consultation. *Journal of Family Psychotherapy,* 5, 41-59.

Carr, A. (1995). *Positive Practice. A Step-by-step Guide to Family Therapy.* Reading: Harwood.

Colapinto, J. (1991). Structural Family Therapy. In A. Gurman, and D. Kniskern (eds,), *Handbook of Family Therapy . Volume 2.* New York: Brunner/Mazel.

Falloon, I. (1991). Behavioural Family Therapy. In A. Gurman, and D. Kniskern (eds) *Handbook of Family Therapy . Volume 2.* New York: Brunner/Mazel.

Falloon, I. Laporta, M., Fadden, G. and Graham-Hole, V. (1993).*Managing Stress in Families.* London: Routledge.

Gilligan, S. and Price, R. (1993) *Therapeutic Conversations.* New York: Norton.

Gurman, A. & Kniskern, D. (1991). *Handbook of Family Therapy. Volume 2.* New York: Brunner/Mazel.

Jankowicz, A. (1987). Whatever became of George Kelly. *American Psychologist, 42,* 481-487. A review of recent research.

Jenkins, H. (1989). Precipitating crises in families: Patterns which connect. *Journal of Family Therapy,* 11,99-109.

Kelly, G. (1955). *The Psychology of Personal Constructs. Volumes 1 and 2.* New York: Norton

Malan, D. (1979). *Individual Psychotherapy and the Science of Psychodynamics.* London: Butterworths.

Manor, O. (1991). Assessing the work of a family centre. Services offered and referrers' perceptions: A pilot study. *Journal of Family Therapy,* 13, 285-294.

Minuchin, S. Rosman, B. and Baker, L. (1978). *Psychosomatic Families: Anorexia Nervosa in Context.* Cambridge, MA: Harvard

University Press.

Sarafino, E. (1994). *Health Psychology: Biopsychosocial Interactions* (2nd. ed.). Chichester. Wiley.

Segal, L. (1991). Brief Therapy: The MRI approach. In A. Gurman, and D. Kniskern (eds.), *Handbook of Family Therapy . Volume 2*. New York: Brunner/Mazel.

Selvini-Palazzoli, M. and Prata, G. (1982). Snares in family therapy. *Journal of Marital and Family Therapy*, 8, 443-453.

Watzlawick, P. Weakland, J. and Fisch, R. (1974). *Change*. New York: Norton.

CHAPTER 15

THREE TECHNIQUES FOR THE SOLO FAMILY THERAPIST

ABSTRACT

Three techniques are described which may be used by family therapists working without the aid of a co-therapist or team. These are: (I) the use of a *ghost co-therapist;* (2) the use of the Gestalt therapy *empty chair* technique in developing a systemic hypothesis; and (3) the use of self, the opinions of significant others and research findings to allow conflicting views of the family's dilemma to be presented.

INTRODUCTION

Like many family therapists, I conduct part of my clinical work as a team member, and part as a solo therapist. The three techniques outlined below are ones that I have found particularly useful when working alone. From a pragmatic viewpoint, they represent ways in which a therapist can draw on personal resources to fulfil functions which would otherwise be executed by a co-therapist or team (e.g. Ferrier, 1983; Hoffman and Gafni, 1984). In this respect, they fall into the same category as Simon's (1985) mythical consultant technique.

GHOST CO-THERAPY

Often when I am working with particularly difficult, or what to me seem to be powerful families, I set out an extra chair in the comer of the room for my ghost co-therapist. I usually do this unobtrusively and do not refer to my partner when working with the family. The technique involves vividly imagining, in the period preceding the therapy session, a real and trusted co-worker being present in the room in the empty chair. Later during the first or second part of the interview, if I find myself being pulled into the family dance (Minuchin and Fishman, 1981), I mentally turn to my ghost co-therapist and ask for support or guidance.

The following example illustrates the use of, this technique. A particularly wealthy family was referred to me by a paediatrician. The son, a bright ten-year-old, presented with a range of somatic symptoms including headaches, abdominal pains and dizziness for which no physical basis could be found. He was being withheld from school and peer group activities by his parents, both of whom where inappropriately overinvested in their son. According to them, he was their special child: his mother's final offspring and his father's protégé. The boy's intractable symptoms had only amplified the parents' concern. They clearly had high academic and athletic expectations of their son which they denied, but which, nevertheless, were communicated in subtle indirect ways. Part of my hypothesis was that the son's symptoms allowed him a way out of fitting the mould his parents had built for him without overtly rebelling and thereby losing their approval. He also derived a variety of creature-comfort secondary gains from his sick role. From the parents' viewpoint, the son's symptoms provided a social}y acceptable focus for their inappropriate overconcern. The goals of therapy included removal of the symptoms, enabling the family to move towards a less enmeshed position and fostering the direct expression of negative feelings and disagreement within the family.

In the second session, I asked the parents to outline what they believed their son would lose if he gave up his sick behaviour. The son, halfway into his parents' list of secondary gains, began to moan dramatically and complain of abdominal cramps. At my request, both parents initially tried to ignore the disturbance, but when their son rolled on the floor and began to bang his head and limbs against the wall, they turned to me for further advice. It was clear that they were asking me to support their wish to give him comfort in what they viewed to be his hour of need. Usually it would have been fairly easy for me to withhold such support and insist on the parents continuing to ignore their son's persistent moaning. However, in this instance the father, because of his appearance, manner, wealth and power, evoked in me the desire to please which I usually feel towards my own father. My resolve weakened. Fortunately, before the session I had taken the precaution of setting out my ghost co-therapist's chair. I turned to her and listened to what she had to say: *You have been in situations similar to this hundreds of times before. Today it's not any different. Stick to your guns. Mr X. bears a strong resemblance to your dad and this is clouding your vision. Remember, this family functions just like all those others you've worked with.* In response to this I felt my body relax, my vision clear, and my resolve strengthen. With renewed vigour, I set about encouraging the parents to withhold recognition from their son in response to his dramatic display of illness and pain.

The family complied with the directive, and eventually the child's moans of agony became screams of rage. He threw a temper tantrum. While the parents felt unsure and behaved in an overconcerned way when faced with their child's *pain behaviour*, they felt competent and set limits effectively in handling this tantrum. The session ended before the boy finished his display of anger. At their next appointment, the symptom chart which the family were keeping revealed that the frequency and intensity of the boy's somatic complaints had dropped dramatically. Concomitantly, the previously overprotective parents encouraged their son to spend more time playing away from the house with his friends. Further abnormal tantrums did not occur, although the son became more assertive in expressing his mixed feelings with regard to his parents' high expectations of him.

USING THE EMPTY CHAIR TO FORMULATE A SYSTEMIC HYPOTHESIS

The empty chair technique is a procedure much used by Gestalt therapists to facilitate the integration of conflicting aspects of the personality (Simkin, 1979). A chair is allocated to each aspect (or persona) involved in the intrapsychic conflict. The client then rôle plays, in an affectively charged manner, the position of each persona. In effective *chair work*, an integrative *aha* experience marks the closure of a session.

I often use a variant of this procedure as an aid to developing a systemic hypothesis during the intra-session break (Selvini Palazzoli et al., 1980) . I set out a number of empty seats in the intra-session room and then move from chair to chair, persuasively presenting a different linear hypothesis from each position. I have found this process of acting out the various linear views to be more effective than simply thinking them through. The empty chair technique allows for a greater degree of affective involvement and so facilitates the brainstorming procedure which is the precursor of good systemic hypothesis. As in team work, the discovery of an accurate systemic hypothesis is often something of an *aha* experience when this technique is used. A case of school refusal will be presented to illustrate this approach to the development of a systemic hypothesis.

The L. family was referred to the clinic by their GP. The thirteen-year-old son, J., had refused to go to school for the preceding sixteen weeks. He is a pupil at private grammar school. J has two sisters. His twenty two year old sister has left home, and his eighteen year old sister was about to graduate from high school. In the first part of the initial interview, I obtained information about the problem and the courses of action the family had taken to solve it. Some pertinent historical information was also obtained.

Following the interview, I returned to the intra-session room and set out three empty chairs (labelled A. B and C below). From each of these, I argued in turn a particular linear view of the case:

A. This kid is not going to school because he is acting like a baby. He is too old to be disobedient like this. He might be looking for what babies get when they are disobedient. He is not just frightened of going outdoors because he goes out to visit his friends at weekends.

B. This kid is not going to school because his mother is not strict enough. She should lay down the house rules and enforce them.

C. This kid is not going to school because his dad will not support his mum in laying down the house rules and getting him back to school.

B. The mother knows she should lay down the rules, but she is not doing it because she has always thought J. was a sickly child and has always felt that she is not giving him enough love and care, so how can she be strict with him? She comes from a family that values emotional closeness, so it is hard for her to push J. away from her out to school.

C. Mr L. does not help his wife push J. out to school because that is not the way they divide the labour. In this family, the mother does the child-rearing and the father brings home the bacon. Also, Mr L. comes from a family where the emotional distances were much greater than in Mrs L.'s family of origin. If he were to help his wife get J. back to school, he would have to get fairly close to her and work co-operatively with her and he is not used to this.

A. This kid is *staying young,* as shown by his not going to school to keep things the way they were. He thinks his parents will not be able to live with each other without children. One of his sisters is grown up and gone, his second sister is on her way. He is the only one left so he had better stay at home.

On the basis of these linear propositions, I formed the following systemic hypothesis. From a developmental perspective, the family was viewed as having difficulty in moving from the *household with adolescents* stage to the *empty nest* stage. From a structural perspective, it appeared that L. had to refuse to go to school so that his mother would have a focus for her energy (now that she only had one child and was used to looking after three). The mother repeatedly failed to solve the problem because she was frightened of losing her child and being left alone with her husband. Dad (who had devoted most of his married life to providing for the family and had become somewhat peripheral) was forced to come a little closer to mother (but not too close) and console her in the face of these failures. The threat of marital intimacy inhibited the parents from taking a concerted approach to their child's misbehaviour. The fear of parental separation fuelled the child's continual school refusal. Fear of ridicule when he returned to school and a wish to continue to enjoy the special comforts available to him while at home maintained the symptomatic behaviour. This systemic hypothesis served as a basis for further work with the family.

Briefly, the therapy followed the structural-strategic model for intervention with school-refusing families. It involved strengthening the parental subsystem by facilitating the development of a simple, behaviourally based return to school plan (Blagg and Yule, 1984) and strengthening the spouse subsystem through the use of a brief intervention derived from Selvini Palazzoli's *invariant prescription* (DiNicola, 1984). Although initially successful, this approach to treatment was ineffective in the longer term. The family relapsed after four months. At this point, I shifted from direct structural to (apparently) indirect strategic therapeutic tactics. The whole family was invited to a meeting where I presented the systemic hypothesis, positively connoted the behaviour of each family member and prescribed the behaviour described in it. Follow-up contacts at three and six months with the EWO (school attendance officer) revealed that the child returned to school that day and has attended consistently since.

THE SPLIT VIEW
Bateson (1969) has argued that the introduction of information (news of difference) into a system may lead to systemic change. From a family's viewpoint (within a therapeutic context), such information may be obtained through being presented with two descriptions of the same event or sequence of events which are coded differently. This theoretical position has given rise to the practice of presenting the family with a number of alternative views concerning their problem (e.g. Papp, 1980). These different descriptions of the same problem are often generated by a team who have been observing one of its members interviewing a family. These opinions are the building blocks from which a systemic hypothesis (discussed in the last section) is constructed. A variety of ways have been developed for presenting alternative views of the presenting problem and the network of relationships in which it is embedded to the family. For example, after the intra-session break the therapist may inform the family that *the team think X for the following reasons, but I think Y because . ...* When this format is used. usually one opinion argues for homeostasis and the other against it. Occasionally, the therapist may attribute opinions to subsystems of the team which are isomorphic with subsystems within the family. For example, *the older women on the team agreed with the*

mother's position that .... the men on the team are in agreement with father for the following reasons ....The trainee on the team has sympathy with the daughter's position ... This use of the split view technique is a way of *prescribing the system.*

A number of models of family therapy based on systems theory highlight the importance of training families in problem solving skills (e.g. Haley, 1980; Barton and Alexander, 1981; Epstein and Bishop, 1981). An assumption underlying such approaches is the view that dysfunctional families lack the requisite skills for problem clarification, the exploration of options and the negotiation of solutions. In the course of problem-solving training, split view techniques may be used by a team to facilitate the learning process. For example, the therapist may say: *One of the team members was impressed by the long and detailed list of possible solutions to the problem you drew up, Mr X. Although your list was shorter than your husband's, Mrs X., another team member was particularly intrigued by your thoughtfulness in developing such clever potential solutions to this difficult predicament in which your family finds itself.*

In the previous section, a way in which a solo therapist may generate alternative descriptions of the same events was described. Here, the problem of whom the solo therapist may attribute these views to will be dealt with.

A stance of personal conflict may be adopted. For example, the therapist, having presented the outline of his hypothesis, may say: *One part of me agrees with this arrangement that you, as a family, have come to; but the other part of me wonders if the symptom is too big a price to pay.*

Research findings may also be introduced as a hook on which to hang the alternative world view. (My preference is to rely on genuine results, but I know of one report which advocates the use of fictitious research findings to achieve therapeutic goals (Farrelly & Brandsma, 1974).) In he following example real research findings were used. The couple, who were *chronic fighters* had shown marked improvement after four sessions and reached what they defined in the first session as the minimum acceptable level of change. They enthusiastically proposed a new treatment goal . In response I said *You tell me you are only fighting once a day now, but that you would like to get that down to once or twice a week. You know there are a lot of people who would agree with you on that score. Some very carefully controlled research done in Oregon showed that, on average, couples who fight less are happier and that their kids do better in school. But there is something I have to tell you and it's this: I think you're not an average family. No, I think you're very special and that you use your fights as a way of showing your passion for each other. The way I look at it is this: no fights, no passion. Can you afford to give up fighting?* The couple took me to task and set about proving, over the next three sessions, that fights were unnecessary, and that passion could be expressed in ways other than argument.

A third vehicle for presenting alternative world views are opinions and observations made of one's own family, other families seen in treatment and colleagues or friends. For example, in developing a limit-setting programme with a family where the identified patient was a conduct disordered child, the parents had great difficulty in agreeing on a set of house rules. They continually turned to me to pass judgement on which of them was right. Rather than be sucked into the system, I took the following position: *Deciding on a set of house rules for P. is a pretty difficult job, and it's flattering that you ask me to decide which rules are right and which rules are wrong. But the thing is this: I can't tell you because there is no right or wrong here. Take meals for example. G, who works in the office next to me, likes to give his kids a choice of things to eat at each meal, and he and his wife will sometimes cook special stuff for each of their kids if they ask. In other families, like the one I grew up in, it's a lot different. Kids eat what they get, and asking for something different is seen as complaining and is disapproved of. Neither way of handling meals is right or wrong. The important thing is that the kids get something to eat, and the way this is arranged is decided by mum and dad.* In this case, where I was using problem-solving training and primarily structural (rather than strategic) tactics, I made interventions similar to this one in many of the early sessions. When the family finally accepted the view that house rules are fairly arbitrary, parental negotiation styles became the bone of contention. Split view techniques were used to illustrate a variety of negotiation styles, arguments for and against their general usefulness, and how appropriate they were for the family in treatment.

DISCUSSION

A number of theoretical constructs unite these apparently disparate therapeutic techniques. Firstly they each involve concrete svmbolization, a process which lies at the heart of active experiential therapies such as psychodrama and Gestalt therapy (Simkin, 1979; Fine, 1979). This is the process which occurs when the therapist actively generates an *imaginary team'* to whom he can look for support, with whom he can debate, and to whom he can attribute alliterative points of view. Novelists who report that their characters take on a life of their own and contribute to the development of the plot are describing this process (e.g. Fowles, 1969; O'Brien. 1939). Concrete symbolization makes previously unconscious response patterns available to the therapist. I have often been surprised by the extent to which I have held my ground when using the *ghost co-therapist technique*; the unexpected connections I have made using the *empty chair hypothesis construction technique*; and the variety of perspectives I have been able to present using the *split view technique*.

A second unifying theoretical theme underpinning these techniques is that of reframing (Watzlawick et al., 1974). *The empty chair hypothesis construction technique* allows the therapist to generate multiple reframings of subsets of a group of observations. In turn, these are synthesised into a comprehensive and therapeutically useful reframing of the families' situations. i.e. a systemic hypothesis. Regulating proximity, a function fulfilled by the *ghost co-therapist technique*, primarily involves moving between two distinctly different framings of the same set of events. These are: the family's view of reality on the one hand, and an alternative therapeutic reframing of observations of the family on the other. The *split view technique* allows the therapist to offer the family multiple reframings of family events. In short, the techniques described in this paper help the solo therapist to construct and present reframings of the family's situation and to move between this frame and that endorsed by the family.

Taken together, the use of the three techniques allows the therapist to construct the third corner of the family/therapist/team triangle. The procedures allow the therapist to develop an affiliation with the *imaginal team* and maintain an appropriately clear boundary between himself and the family. In this way, the dangers of inappropriate therapist/family coalitions may be somewhat lessened. Systems theorists argue that such inappropriate coalitions, if present in the family system, are likely to reproduce themselves in the family/therapist/team system, and so must be guarded against (e.g. Westheafer, 1984).

A similar point has been made by theorists whose models are predominantly intrapsychic in design. From the development of the concept of countertransference onwards (Freud, 1958), it has frequently been noted that therapists responses to certain classes of clients or client behaviours may be influenced by factors outside their awareness and which have their roots in the therapists family of origin experiences (e.g. Lieberman, 1982; Stewart. 1980) The techniques described here provide the therapist with ways of combating these influences and seeing around his or her *therapeutic blind spots*.

REFERENCES

Barton. C. & Alexander. J. (1981). Functional family therapy. In A. Gurman & D. Kniskern (eds.), *Handbook of Family Therapy*. New York: Brunner/Mazel.
Bateson, G. (1969.) Pathologies of Epistemology. Paper presented at the

Second Conference on Mental Heath in Asia and the Pacific at the East-West Centre Hawaii. Reprinted in G. Bateson (1972). *Steps to an Ecology of Mind.* New York: Ballantine.

Blagg. N. R. & Yule. W. (1984). The behavioural treatment of school refusal- a comparative study. *Behaviour Research and Therapy*, 22,119-127.

DiNicola. V. (1984). Road map to schizoland. Mara Selvini Palazzoli and the Milan model of systemic family therapy. *Journal of Strategic and Systemic Therapies*, 3, 50-61.

Epstein N, & Bishop. D. (1981). Problem centred systems therapy of the family. In A. Gurman & D. Kniskern (eds.), *Handbook of Family Therapy.* New York: Brunner/Mazel.

Farrelly. F. & Brandsma. J. (1974). *Provocative Therapy.* Cupertino, CA: Meta Publications.

Ferrier. M. (1983). *Teamwork: Process, Problems and Perspectives.* Participants Conference in Family Therapy. University of Calgary. April 29-30.

Fine. L. (1979). Psychodrama. In R. Corsini (ed.), *Current Psychotherapies* (2nd edition). Itasca, Illinois: Peacock.

Fowles, J. (1969). *The French Lieutenant s Woman.* London: Cape.

Freud. S. (1958). The dynamics of transference. In *Standard Edition of the Complete Psychological Works of Sigmund Freud* (Vol. 12). London: Hogarth Press.

Haley, J. (1980). *Leaving Home.* New York: McGraw Hill.

Hoffman. S. & Gafni. S. (1984). Active interactional co-therapy. *International Journal of Family Therapy*, 6, 53-58.

Lieberman, S. (1982). Going back to your own family. In A. Bentovim et al. (eds.), *Family Therapy: Complementary Frameworks of Theory and Practice.* (Vol. 1). London: Academic Press.

Minuchin, S. & Fishman. H. (1981). *Family Therapy Techniques.* Cambridge MA: Harvard University Press.

O'Brien, F. (1939). *At Swim Two Birds.* London: Longmans.

Papp, P. (1980). The Greek chorus and other techniques of family therapy. *Family Process*, 19, 45-58.

Selvini-Palazzoli, M., Boscolo, L., Cecchin, G. and Prata, G. (1980). Hypothesizing - circularity - neutrality: Three guidelines for the conductor of the session. *Family Process*, 19, 3-12.

Simkin, J. (1979). Gestalt therapy. In R. Corsini (ed.), *Current Psychotherapies* (2nd edition). Itasca, Illinois: Peacock.

Simon. D. (1985). Dr Boxford: a mythical consultant. (A note on the use of non-real resources). *Journal of Family Therapy*, 7, 387-390.

Stewart. R. (1980). Psychoanalysis and psychoanalytic psychotherapy. In: H. Kaplan et al. (eds.), *Comprehensive Textbook of Psychiatry* (Vol 2. 3rd edition). Baltimore: Williams and Wilkins.

Watzlawick, P., Weakland, J. & Fisch, R. (1974). *Change.* New York: Norton.

Westheafer, C. (1984). An aspect of live supervision: the pathological triangle. *Australian Journal of Family Therapy*, 5, 169-175.

CHAPTER 16

CARRYING PARCELS AND MAKING PUDDINGS: TWO CO-OPERATION STYLES

ABSTRACT
Parcel carrying and pudding making are two styles of co-operation. In work and family contexts mis-matches may occur between people who hold differing co-operative styles. This may accentuate parcel carrying and pudding making behaviour. Consultation to such systems involves helping participants articulate the belief systems that underpin both co-operative styles and negotiate a novel plan for co-operation that allows both styles find expression.

INTRODUCTION
Everybody has their own way of co-operating. Parcel carrying and pudding making are two extreme co-operation styles.

PARCEL CARRIERS
Parcel carriers like to co-operate by taking a parcel and delivering it. They like to be given the parcel, the delivery address and nothing more. They take pride in finding their way and delivering the parcel alone. They like reading the map and planning the journey in privacy. They love the clarity of the delivery process. They revel in the adventure of the solitary journey. They like to meet with their companions afterwards and bask in the appreciation which follows a delivery well done.

PUDDING MAKERS

Pudding makers like to co-operate by helping with the nitty gritty of measuring and mixing all the ingredients for the pudding. They like to pass the raisins to you. They like to weigh the flour while you pour the milk. They love to take their turn at stirring the mixture. They like to discuss whether some more of this or a little of that should be added. They like to consider and reconsider how best to finish the job. They are warmed by the chat that goes with sharing a kitchen. They thrive on the complex ways people making a pudding can vary the recipe form minute to minute. They love to sit back and have a cup of tea afterwards and enjoy the companionship that follows from making a pudding with someone else.

MIS-MATCH

Problems occur when parcel carriers assume that pudding makers hold the same world view as they do and visa versa. Here are two typical examples of this type of mismatch.

> **Example 1.** Robert and David, while on a communications training programme mentioned the following difficulty. Both men worked together in a management consultancy. Robert liked to work at close-quarters with David, conducting joint interviews with clients, writing reports jointly and operating in a shared office environment. He was continually frustrated by David's reluctance to work in this way, since joint work often yielded their most creative results. David conducted as many interviews as possible alone and always retired to an isolated office to write reports or took his work home with him. He was annoyed that Robert wanted to work jointly all the time and sometimes suspected that Robert was trying to freeload. This made him more adamant about working on discrete aspects of joint projects in isolation.

> **Example 2.** Tony and Susan during marital therapy revealed that most of their arguments occurred on weekends, when Susan would suggest joint shopping expeditions or joint completion of the housework. Tony would go along with these suggestions but gradually feel angrier and angrier over the course of the joint work. This would lead to bickering and periodically to explosive rows, where he insisted on a clear division of labour at week ends and no further joint completion of chores. Susan would interpret this as rejection and go to great lengths to cajole Tony into joint shopping and

housekeeping. Tony would eventually accommodate to joint approaches to homemaking tasks and the cycle would repeat.

Figure 16.1. Carrying parcels & making puddings: Two co-operation styles

In the first example, David, a parcel carrier, demanded that Robert conform to his style of co-operation. In the second example, Tony, a parcel carrier by nature, was trying to conform to Susan's requirement that he be a pudding maker. Both mismatches led to the participants feeling misunderstood and also to them drawing erroneous conclusions. For example, David concluded that Robert wanted to freeload and Susan believed that Tony wanted to reject her. These erroneous beliefs sparked more extreme parcel carrying or pudding making behaviour.

CONCLUSIONS
Mismatches between parcel carriers and pudding makers at work or in family life can rarely be avoided. However, the negative consequences of such mismatches can be minimised. Consultants and therapists can first help parcel carriers and pudding makers articulate their differing belief systems about co-operation. A clear articulation of both world views will help dispel erroneous beliefs that come from a partial understanding of each position. Co-operative planning about which style of co-operation to use in which situation follows on from this first step.

SECTION 3

EMPIRICAL FOUNDATIONS

In this section a collection of four papers which deal with empirical work of particular relevance to the practice of family therapy is presented. An audit of practice at Thurlow House Child and Family Clinic is presented in Chapter 13. (Audit and family systems consultation: Evaluation of practice at a child and family centre). The auditing system reported in this paper, and on which Penny Owen collaborated, was the forerunner of the system presented in the *Positive Practice* book in 1995.

In Chapter 18 (Milan Systemic Family Therapy: A review of 10 empirical investigations) a review of all major empirical studies of Milan systemic family therapy that I could locate in 1990 is presented. These studies are important since the work of the original Milan group was a central influence on the development of *Positive Practice*. As far as I can determine, the paper was the first review of empirical work on Milan systemic family therapy.

In Chapter 19 (Psychotherapy research) some of the main lessons that may be learned from process and outcome studies of individual and family approaches to psychotherapy are presented. The findings reported in this paper, such as the stages of the change process and the contribution of specific and non-specific factors to psychotherapy outcome all influenced the development of the model of practice presented in the 1995 *Positive Practice* textbook.

In Chapter 20 (Family Psychology. The emergence of a new field) some of the main areas of psychology of particular relevance to the practice of family therapy are briefly reviewed.

REFERENCES
Carr, A. (1995). *Positive Practice: A Step-By-Step Guide to Family Therapy.* Reading: Harwood.

CHAPTER 17

AUDIT AND FAMILY SYSTEMS CONSULTATION: EVALUATION OF PRACTICE AT A CHILD AND FAMILY CENTRE

ABSTRACT

This audit of practice at a child and family centre included a 16 month case note review covering 319 cases, a postal survey of 45 families and an interview survey of 10 GPs who typically referred cases to the centre. The audit furnished information from three different perspectives on the referral process, the consultation process, and outcome for clients attending the centre. The referral rate was about one new case per day and peak referral times were the beginning of the autumn and winter school terms. Almost half the referrals came from GPs and the remainder were largely from Paediatrics, Education and Social Services. Most clients were seen within two months. Half of the families referred had serious psychosocial difficulties including multiple problem members, multiproblem children, multi-agency involvement, psycho educational difficulties, child protection problems or child placement difficulties. The majority of cases received six hours of consultation. Families where child abuse had occurred or families containing a multiproblem adolescent received a more intensive service. Between a half and three quarters of cases had positive outcomes as rated by staff and parents.

This paper was jointly written with Penny Owen and Dermot MacDonnell Revised copies of the audit sheets are contained in Carr, A. (1995). *Positive Practice: A Step-By-Step Guide to Family Therapy*. Reading: Harwood.

The service was viewed by GPs to be highly satisfactory. On the negative side, many parents felt ill-prepared for the consultation process and most children did not enjoy the experience.

INTRODUCTION

Few audits of family therapy or systems consultation have been reported (Allman et al, 1989; Chase & Holmes, 1990; Dangan & Fish, 1991; Frude & Dowling, 1980; Thomas & Hardwick, 1989; Mashal et al, 1989, Manor, 1991). This is unfortunate because audit studies throw light on overall patterns of practice that occur in regular clinical settings. Published audit reports provide benchmarks against which other clinical teams can assess their work. The information provided by these studies complement the results of controlled treatment outcome studies. While the latter have high internal validity, audit studies have high ecological validity.

From a clinical team's view point, the results of a service audit are particularly valuable. They provide answers to questions like. How many cases are we seeing? Who refers them? What proportion of our cases are really complex and difficult? How many sessions do we see them for? Who drops out? What do our clients think of us? What do our referring agents think of us? How could we improve our service?

It was precisely a curiosity about these types of questions that spawned the audit described here. This curiosity was potentiated by a climate which was increasingly requiring clinicians in our field to provide evidence of therapeutic efficacy and quality service provision. At a National level we were being advised to develop audit systems to help us document and improve the quality of our services (Parry-Jones, 1992). At a local level a similar demand was made all the more poignant because our parent Hospital was preparing for Trust status (which it has since achieved). To place the audit in context, a description of the clinic follows.

THE CLINIC

Our Child and Family Centre provides a mental health service for a predominantly rural catchment area in the east of England. The population under 16 is 40,000. The Centre is based in a free standing building and is administratively attached to a large District General Hospital. Services are provided on site and at a satellite clinic in a small hospital 15 miles away. The satellite clinic is based in a small market town.

During the period when the audit described here was conducted, there was one senior staff member in each of the following disciplines: Psychiatry, Psychology, Occupational Therapy and Social Work. In addition there were part time junior or senior staff members in all four disciplines along with a number of trainees on placement. The total staff compliment was never more than 9 Whole Time Equivalent clinicians. While each member of the clinical team had loyalty to a different therapeutic tradition, a family-systems orientation was the overarching framework which unified practice (e.g. Carr et al, 1989a; 1989b; 1989c; Gawlinski et al, 1988).

The questions to which we wanted answers have already been mentioned. What follows is an outline of the methods we chose to secure the data to answer them.

METHOD
Data were collected from three sources: the case notes, patients and referring agents.

Case Notes: The Thurlow Evaluation Survey Schedule (TESS) was used to abstract information from the files of all new cases referred to the clinic between September 1986 and December 1987. The TESS data are an information set which describes a cohort of new patients attending the Thurlow House Child and Family Centre over a 16 month period.

TESS was developed by clinic staff in the early months of 1986 and used routinely as a face sheet in new patients' files during these 16 months. TESS was based on an instrument used in a survey one of previously conducted (McDonnell, 1973). All TESS sheets used in this period were checked for completeness before data analysis.

Postal Survey of Clients: A Postal Survey Questionnaire was sent to a cohort of 46 families who attended the clinic between September 1986 and November 1986. Of theses, 20 were returned. In addition, this questionnaire was sent to a cohort of 41 families who attended the clinic between September 1988 and November 1988. Of these 25 were returned completed. Because the two surveyed groups did not differ significantly on Postal Survey or TESS variables, data from both groups were analysed as a single data set. The non-response rate of about 50% was typical of surveys of this type (Stallard & Chadwick, 1991).

GP Interviews: Ten GPs who routinely referred cases to the clinic were interviewed using a semistructured interview schedule in the first half of 1990. The interviews were conducted by one of us (PO), a research assistant to the audit project who was not a member of the clinical team. The group of GP's interviewed provided 'consumer panel information' of the type that can best be provided by frequent users of the service. Their views were not intended to be representative of other referring agents such as social workers or GPs who referred infrequently.

DATA ANALYSIS AND RESULTS

Data from the Thurlow Evaluation Survey Schedule, the Postal Survey and the GP interview schedule were verified and analysed on an Amstrad PC 1640 using Systat software. The Chi Square test was used to test for all significant differences referred to in the results section and Spearman's rho was used for all correlation's.

THE REFERRAL PROCESS

Referral Rate. In the 16 month period between September 86 and December 87, 362 families were referred to the clinic. Of these, 319 attended their first appointment. This represents an attrition rate of only 12% and an annual first attendance rate of 239 cases per year. One third of these, that is 80 cases per year, were multiproblem families. In summary, a new family is referred to the clinic each working day of the year and a failure to attend a first appointment only occurs about once a fortnight. About seven multiproblem families are referred each month.

If it is conservatively assumed that each of the 80 multiproblem cases referred per year contained only two problem members, then the annual intake of people attending with problems is about 319.

Source of Referrals. Almost half of the cases (47%) were referred by GPs. The remainder were referred by the Paediatric Department of the District General Hospital (20%), the Local Authority's Education (12%) and Social Service (11%) Departments and a variety of hospital Consultants, Clinical Medical Officers and Health Visitors (11%).

Timing of Referrals. There were two peak referral times during the year: February/March (25%) and October/November (23%). These represent an increase in referrals occurring at the start of school terms beginning in September and January. The time lag in each instance reflect the time taken for the teacher to advise the parent to request a referral to the Clinic from the GP. The lowest rate of referrals occurred around Christmas over the months of December and January (8%). The remainder were spread relatively evenly across the year: April/May (13%), June/July (14%), August September (17%).

Waiting Lists and Intake Procedures. The majority of cases were seen within a month (64%) and the remainder (36%) were offered an appointment within three months. A small but significant group of patients (7%) were offered immediate crisis consultations. Crisis consultations were offered for cases of self-harm, acute psychotic states, urgent child abuse assessments and atypical paediatric cases where an urgent opinion on psycho-social factors was required.

Eight out of ten intake interviews were conducted at the main

Clinic in Thurlow House. One in ten were conducted at a Satellite Clinic in Wisbech. The remainder were carried out on a ward of the District General Hospital, at the Clients home or elsewhere in the community.

   Characteristics of Referrals. Cases were spread across the life cycle in the following way. About a quarter (23%) of the families referred were young couples or single parents with the identified patient being a child under 5. In 41% of cases families were established and had primary school-going children with the identified patient being in the 6-11 year old category. In 37% of cases families were dealing with the difficulties posed by having teenage children.

   Although the clinic has had a policy of operating from a family-systems orientation, virtually all referrals were described in individual terms. The male/female ratio for referred children was 2:1, a common finding in survey's of attendance's at Child Mental Health Clinics (Bailey & Garralda, 1989).

   At a systems level, cases were classified in terms of severity of psychosocial difficulties and the patterning of these difficulties within referred families. Only 50% of referrals presented with a single focal problem. The remainder presented with a range of severe psychosocial difficulties. The distribution of these within the cohort is described in Table 17.1. These cases are complex, difficult to manage and place heavy demands on clinic resources. What follows is a description of each of the categories contained in the table.

   Multiproblem families referred to families with two or more distinct problems. For example, a referred child presented with a conduct disorder, the mother suffered from depression and the father abused alcohol. In cases where families faced a major problem which was complicated by the fact that one of the children presented with specific reading retardation or mild mental handicap the case was classified as having psycho-educational difficulties. Families where there was one child who presented with three or more distinct problems such as an emotional disorder, a history of self-harm and a multiplacement experience were described as families with multiproblem children. Multiagency involvement refers to cases where three or more agencies or professionals were involved at one time. For example, in one such case a GP, a paediatrician, a community based social worker, a health visitor, an adult psychiatrist and two probation officers were involved when the case was referred to us. Cases where child abuse was strongly suspected or had occurred were classified as child abuse cases in Table 17.1. Foster care cases in Table 17.1 are those where a child was already in foster care or where assessment for suitability for foster care was requested.

Table 17.1. Family Psychosocial Difficulties

Family Difficulties	Frequency	%
Multiproblem family	106	33
Psycho-educational difficulties present in one child	91	29
Family contains a multiproblem child	60	19
Child Abuse	58	18
Multi-agency Involvement	52	16
In foster care	32	10

Note: N = 319. Percentages sum to more than 100 because categories are not exclusive.

Cases were also classified from a traditional psychiatric perspective. Table 17. 2 describes the main ICD- 9 diagnoses shown by identified patients using the first axis of Rutter's multiaxial system (Rutter et al, 1975). Mixed disorders of emotions and conduct, adjustment reactions, conduct disorders and emotional disorders account for more than four out of five cases. The predominance of these types of cases is consistent with the epidemiology of childhood disorders (Links, 1983).

Table 17. 2. ICD-9 Diagnosis

Diagnosis	ICD-9 Code	Frequency	%
Mixed Disorder of Emotions and Conduct	312.3	104	33.0
Adjustment Reaction	309	74	23.0
Conduct Disorder	312.0 &.1	44	14.0
Conduct Disorder	313	38	12.0
Psychosomatic Difficulties*		22	7.0
Child Psychosis	299.9	1	0.3
Normal Developmental Variation		36	12.0
Total		319	

*Includes anorexia (307.1), enuresis (307.6), encopresis (307.7), psychalgia (307.8), psychic factors associated with various physical illnesses (316), physiological malfunctioning arising from mental disorders (306).

A small but significant group of identified patients (n=22) presented with psychosomatic disorders. These included eating disorders, elimination disorders, psychogenic pain, and problems adjusting to long term illnesses like diabetes or cystic fibroses. More than one in ten cases were found to be in the normal range and were probably referred because of parental concerns about the normality of a child's development.

THE CONSULTATION PROCESS
Staffs' Perspective. The identified patient and significant family members from the child's household and/or network were invariably invited to an intake consultation. This preliminary consultation involved parents and siblings in the case of intact families. In child care cases or other complex cases with multi-agency involvement, social workers, foster parents, probation officers or other significant network members attended. We adopted this practice because failure to engage with significant network members early in the consultation process can often greatly compromise later therapeutic progress (Carr, 1990a). Following the intake consultation, a preliminary family formulation was drawn up and a plan for further involvement established, if this was required. One approach that we used in formulating family problems and some case examples are described elsewhere (Carr, 1990b)

In 11% of cases families were found to be functioning normally and their children were found to display normal developmental variation. These cases were not seen for further consultation and none were re-referred for consultation during the 16 month audit period. In 72% of cases further consultations occurred. Depending upon the formulation, these consultations occurred at one or more levels within the system including the interagency network, the family, the couple, the parents as individuals or the child. A number of such programmes have been previously described (Carr et al, 1989a; 1989c).

Our rationale for consulting to particularly complex cases involving families with adolescents and our programme for working with child protection cases have been documented elsewhere (Carr, et al, 1989b; Gawlinski et al, 1988). Both programmes provide a systemic framework for working with these complex and cases. They also outline the rationale used by our multidisciplinary team for dealing with family and professional network subsystems. In the 16 month period under review, 46 cases (14%) completed the Adolescent Programme. Four entered the programme and dropped out. Nine cases (3%) completed the Thurlow House Child Protection Programme. Here there was only one drop out.

A third of cases (34%) were active for 0-3 months; just over a third (39%) were active for 3-9 months and the remainder (27%) were active for between 9 months and two years. Apart from complex cases assigned to the Adolescent Programme and the Child Protection Programme, each case received an average of 6 hours consultation. This is congruent with the finding that brief therapeutic contact of between 6 and 10 hours has been reported in reviews of family therapy and a variety of other child therapies (Kazdin, 1991, Carr, 1991).

Clients' Perspective. Patient's opinions based on the Postal Survey (n = 45) about the services they received are set out in Table 17.3. On the positive side, more than two thirds of the patients surveyed felt that the therapist understood and sympathised with them, was moderately fair, gave practical advice and was helpful in the intake interview.

On the negative side, only 22% of patients knew what to expect when they first attended the clinic and only 15% of children liked attending the clinic a lot. Both of these issues will be addressed later in the Discussion section.

GP's Perspective. In Table 17.4, the results of the interviews with the GPs are summarised. GP were in strong agreement in describing the type of service they required from the clinic. More than 70% expected a service that ameliorated presenting problems, improved family functioning, reduced risk associated with child care cases and improved interagency management of complex cases. After treatment, they expected that their input into referred cases would decrease. They also stressed the importance of written or oral feedback from the clinic.

The need for patients to be better prepared before attending the Child and Family Centre was endorsed by 80% of the GPs. This is in keeping with the opinions of patients and the attitudes of children outlined in the previous section.

OUTCOME

Staffs' Perspective. In the bulk of families (60%) completed assessment and/or treatment programmes. In only 15% of cases were two or more consecutive appointments missed and contact discontinued. In 25% of cases, families partially completed treatment but withdrew with the team recommending further intervention.

Key staff involved with each case rated outcome on a four point scale (Good, moderate, poor and deterioration). Because such ratings are subject to error due to clinicians either over or underestimating outcome, two precautions were taken. First, operational definitions of each category were agreed at staff meetings. Second, in a subsample of 20 cases, rated by two clinic staff, inter-rater reliability was assessed. 90% agreement was obtained.

Table 17.3. Patients' Perspectives

Patient's Beliefs	Frequency	%
Consultation Process		
We felt completely or moderately understood	37	82
We felt that the therapist completely or moderately sympathised with us	36	80
We felt that the therapist was completely or moderately fair	35	78
We felt that the therapist gave some or a lot of practical advice	31	69
After the intake interview, we saw the clinic as helpful	31	69
We knew what to expect when we first attended the clinic	10	22
Our child liked the clinic a lot	6	15
Outcome		
After treatment there was some or much improvement in the main problem	25	56
The consultations were moderately or completely helpful	30	67
We have not sought further help since we attended the clinic	34	76
We would recommend the clinic to others with similar problems	37	82
We would definitely or probably return for treatment if the problem recurred	33	73
We would like to be able to refer ourselves for consultation	22	49

Note: N = 45. Percentages do not sum to 100 since categories are not exclusive

For the cohort as a whole, staff gave 57% of cases a rating of good outcome and 18% a rating of moderate outcome. Overall, therefore staff viewed 75% of interventions as being at least moderately successful. In the remaining 25% of cases poor outcome was recorded. No case was rated as deteriorated. Deterioration refereed to a reduction in psycho-social functioning between referral and discharge. Poor outcome refereed to minimal improvement during the same period.

Patients' Perspectives. From Table 17.3 it may be seen that just over half the parents surveyed (using 5 point likert scales) rated the service they received as leading to some or much improvement and about two thirds described the service as completely or moderately helpful.

These results in combination with the staff ratings of outcome suggest that the clinic offers a useful service to between a half and three quarters of its patients, a finding consistent with more tightly controlled research on family therapy outcome (e.g. Carr, 1991).

Table 17.4. GPs' Perspectives

GP's Beliefs	%
Consultation Process Treatment at the clinic should lead to...	
a reduction in the severity or intensity of the presenting problem	90
an improvement in overall family functioning	100
a reduction in risk to the child's well being in child care cases	90
an improvement in the interagency management of complex cases	80
a reduction in the number of attendance's of the patient at my surgery	70
It is very important to receive written or oral communication from the clinic about referred cases	90
Patients need better preparation before attending the clinic so that they will know what to expect	80
Outcome	
The clinic provides a good service to my patients	80
The formulation offered by the clinic is very helpful	70
Patients should be able to refer themselves to the clinic for treatment	20

Note: N = 10. Percentages do not add to 100 because the categories are not exclusive

It is noteworthy that staff rated outcome significantly more positively than patients (Chi Square ($1df$) = 7.92, p<.01).

To identify aspects of the consultation process associated with good outcome selected items from both the TESS sheet and the Postal Survey Questionnaire were correlated with patient's report's of improvement in the presenting problem (rated on a 5 point scale). Five meaningful items correlated significantly (p<.01) with patient reported outcome. Feeling understood (r = .49), feeling sympathised with (r = .62), seeing the therapist as fair (r = .43) and viewing the therapist's advice as practical (r = .62) were all positively correlated with good outcome. A positive outcome was also associated with seeing the therapist as helpful during the intake interview (r = .58). These results are consistent with widely obtained findings on therapist variables associated with therapeutic success in individual and family therapy, despite the diversity of rating scales used in this burgeoning literature (Carr, 1991; Keuhl et al, 1990, Kazdin, 1991).

About three quarters of patients sought no further help with their problems after discharge, would recommend the clinic to others with problems and would return if the problem recurred. This suggests that patients saw the clinic as offering a quality service.

Only about half of the patients surveyed thought that self referral was a desirable option.

GPs' Perspective. From Table 17.4, it may be seen that 8 of the 10 GPs surveyed rated the service offered by the clinic to patients as good or very good (points 4 or 5 on a 5 point scale).

7 out of 10 rated the formulation offered by the clinic as very helpful (5 on a 5 point scale).

In line with patients' views only 20% of GPs favoured the idea of patients being able to refer themselves for treatment rather than the GP making the referral. These findings are in stark contrast to those of Richards (1992). In a survey of 48 GP's in the Merton Child Guidance Clinic's catchment area, she found that 90% were in favour of self-referral. Self-referral has never occurred in our district, so patients have not experienced the benefit it first hand. In Merton, self-referral has been common practice for years and clients obviously would not want to loose this referral method.

DISCUSSION
A number of substantive and methodological issues deserve further discussion. The purpose of the audit was to systematically describe the referral and consultation processes and the outcome of consultation from the perspectives of staff, patients and referring GPs. The audit confirmed many impressions which the clinical team had formed, but also highlighted issues which otherwise would have gone unnoticed. First, we were surprised that half of the families we saw presented with multiple problems and represented a client group with serious and extensive therapeutic needs. We had not suspected that the proportion was so large. Second, we were pleased to note that despite the large proportion of our cases that fell into the multiproblem category, our successful outcome rate was in keeping with the results of controlled treatment outcome studies (e.g. Markus et al, 1990). This information along with the statistics on referral rate of one new family per day or over 1000 new people per year was useful in making a case to

management about increasing staffing levels.

Third, we were disappointed that many of the families that were referred to us felt ill-prepared for the consultation process. We have tried to rectify this situation by writing an extensive services prospectus and making this available to referring agents.

Fourth, we were also disappointed to learn that children found the consultation process unpleasant. However, it is probably inevitable that many youngsters labelled as identified patients experience the referral and consultation process as punitive. At a therapeutic level all team members remain committed to making the consultation process as benign as possible for children. A detailed account of the variety of strategies that have evolved are given elsewhere (Carr, In Press). These include making the waiting room and consultation rooms cosmetically attractive to children, correcting negative expectations in the first session, explaining the therapeutic process and systemic ideas in concrete rather than abstract terms, using dolls and drawings to help children explain their view of the family situation, teaching children turn taking and other social skills necessary for engaging in therapy, using stories and metaphors with a specific focus on helping children reframe their view of the family situation, and providing children with adjunctive play therapy and an advocacy relationship with the play therapist to support them in family therapy sessions.

The methods that were used in the audit (case note review; postal survey; interview survey) were adequate for achieving our objectives. They captured important data about the domains of interest (referral, consultation and outcome) from three key sources (staff, patients and referring GPs). The quality of the information was sufficient for making essentially managerial rather than scientific decisions about future service delivery. However, our methods for collecting data had their limitations and it is worth reviewing these.

First, the TESS sheet, the Postal Survey and the GP Interview Schedule had limited coverage. Only a small number of items was contained in each instrument. In audit, the dilemma is always to balance the comprehensives of the instruments used, against the likelihood that respondents will co-operate. In this audit, particularly with the TESS sheet, our decision to design a brief instrument was very successful. In the majority of cases staff completed this face and where data were missing, it was possible to extract it from case notes with limited difficulty.

Second, the reliability of the data furnished by the three instruments is largely unquantified. For the TESS data, interrater reliability information was calculated for outcome only. It is particularly important to rate this accurately, hence our decision to check reliability here. We did not calculate interrater reliability for variables like diagnosis or psychosocial difficulties because we were satisfied that the rules for giving a diagnosis or scoring a psychosocial difficulty as present were clear enough to lead to accurate and reliable use of the categories. However, we acknowledge that this is a major weakness of the study. Ideally the inter-rater reliability of all variables needs to be assessed so that the degree of confidence which may be placed in the obtained results can be accurately specified. Also, if variables are defined in a way that yields high interrater reliability, then the scales may be used by other investigators and results from all studies using the scales compared.

The reliability of patients' and GPs' responses are unknown. We have assumed that both patients and GPs have been as accurate as possible in letting us know their views. Ideally, test-retest reliability data should have been obtained on a subsample of cases to determine the stability of respondents views over time.

Third, the validity of the data in this audit is unquantified. For example, we do not know the extent to which ratings of outcome would correlate with well established criteria like changes on psychometric scales like the Child Behaviour Checklist (Achenbach & Edelbrock, 1983) or the McMaster Family Assessment Device (Miller et al, 1985).

These reliability and validity problems are not unique to our study and they typify many audits of clinical practice in the field. Frude & Dowling (1980) have argued that self-reports from consumers are valuable in their own right, even if their reliability and validity remains unquantified. They furnish information that clinicians may usefully bring to bear on the way in which clinical services are offered.

REFERENCES

Achenbach, T. & Edelbrock, P (1983). *Manual for the Revised Child Behaviour Checklist.* Burlington, VT.

Allman, P., Sharpe, M. & Bloch, S. (1989). Family therapy in adult psychiatry. Paper presented at AFT/IFT Conference: Family Research and Family Therapy: Marriage, Cohabitation or Divorce. Institute of Psychiatry, DeCrespigny Park, 20-21 April 1989.

Bailey, D. & Garralda, M. (1989). Referral to child psychiatry: Parent and doctor motives and expectations. *Journal of Child Psychology and Psychiatry,* 30, 449-458.

Carr, A. (1994). Involving Children in Family Therapy. *Journal of Family Psychotherapy,* 5(1), 41-59.

Carr, A. (1990a). A formulation model for use in family therapy, *The Australian and New Zealand Journal of Family Therapy,* 11, 85-92.

Carr, A. (1990b) Failure in family therapy: A catalogue of engagement mistakes. *Journal of Family Therapy,* 12, 271-386.

Carr, A. (1991). Milan systemic family therapy: A review of 10 empirical investigations. *Journal of Family Therapy,* 13, 237-264.

Carr, A. & Afnan, S. (1989a). Concurrent individual and family treatment of a case of elective mutism. *Journal of Family Therapy,* 11, 29-44.

Carr, A., MacDonnell, D. & Afnan, S. (1989b). Anorexia Nervosa: The treatment of a male case with combined behavioural and family therapy. *Journal of Family Therapy,* 11, 335-351.

Carr, A., Gawlinski, G., MacDonnell, D., Irving, N., & Docking, S. (1989c). Thurlow House Adolescent Assessment Programme. *Practice,* 2, 60-190.

Chase, J. & Holmes, J. (1990). A two year audit of a family therapy clinic in adult psychiatry. *Journal of Family Therapy,* 12, 229-242.

Dangan, D. & Fish, A. (1991). A satisfaction questionnaire for a child and adolescent psychology service. *Clinical Psychology Forum,* 35, 21-24.

Frude, N. & Dowling, E. (1980). A follow-up analysis of family therapy clients. *Journal of Family Therapy,* 2, 149-156.

Gawlinski, G., Carr, A., MacDonnell, D., (1988). Thurlow House Assessment Programme for Families with Physically Abused Children. Practice, 2 (3), 208-220.

Irving, N., Carr, A., Gawlinski, G., & MacDonnell, D. (1988). Thurlow House Child Abuse Programme: Residential family evaluation. *British Journal of Occupational Therapy,* 51, 116-119.

Kazdin, A. (1991). Effectiveness of psychotherapy with children and adolescents. *Journal of Consulting and Clinical Psychology,* 59, 785-798.

Keuhl, B., Newfield, N. & Joanning, H. (1990). A client based description of family therapy. *Journal of Family Psychology,* 3, 310-321.

Links, P. (1983). Community surveys with the prevalence of childhood psychiatric disorders. *Child Development,* 54(3), 531-547.

McDonnell, D. (1973). An evaluation of day centre care. *International Journal of Social Psychiatry* ,23 (2), 1-10.

Markus, E., Lang, A. & Pettigrew, T. (1990). Effectiveness of family therapy: A meta-analysis. *Journal of Family Therapy,* 12, 205-221.

Mashal, M., Feldman, R. & Sigal, J. (1989). The unravelling of a treatment paradigm: A follow up study of the Milan Approach to Family Therapy. *Family Process,* 28, 457-469.

Miller, I, Epstein, N., Bishop, D., & Keitner, G. (1985). The McMaster Family Assessment Device: Reliability and Validity. *Journal of Marital & Family Therapy,* 11, 345-356.

Parry-Jones, W. (1992). Management in the National Health Service in relation to children and the provision of child psychiatric services. *Newsletter of the Association for Child Psychology and Psychiatry,* 14 (1), 3-10.

Richards, H. (1992). Parent referrals to a child guidance clinic. *Newsletter of the Association for Child Psychology and Psychiatry,* 14 (4), 179-180.

Rutter, M., Shaffer, D., & Shepherd, M. (1975). *A multiaxial classification of Child Psychiatric Disorders.* Geneva. WHO.

Stallard, P. & Chadwick, R. (1991). Consumer evaluation: A cautionary note. *Clinical Psychology Forum,* 34, 2-4.

Thomas, H. & Hardwick, P. (1989). An Audit of a small child psychiatric clinic. *Newsletter of the Association for Child Psychology and Psychiatry,* 11 (1), 10-14

CHAPTER 18

MILAN SYSTEMIC FAMILY THERAPY: A REVIEW OF 10 EMPIRICAL INVESTIGATIONS

ABSTRACT

Ten empirical investigations of Milan Family Therapy (MFT)are reviewed in this paper. The studies include both single group and comparative group outcome trials; investigations of therapeutic process; clinical audit and consumer satisfaction surveys. Substantive findings and methodological issues are discussed in the light of family therapy and individual psychotherapy research generally.

INTRODUCTION

Within the field of family therapy and systems-consultation the impact of the Milan Approach has been widespread (Campbell & Draper, 1985; Jones, 1988). Despite this, little empirical research on the effectiveness of Milan Family Therapy (MFT) or the processes underpinning systemic and symptomatic change which arise from it has been conducted. While literature reviews and meta-analyses of family therapy as a generic form of intervention abound, to date, no comprehensive review of extant empirical research on MFT has been published in a major family therapy journal or handbook (Gurman & Kniskern, 1978, 1981; Gurman, Kniskern & Pinsof, 1986; Hazelrigg et al, 1987; Markus et al, 1990; Shoham-Salomon & Bice-Broussard, 1990). To remedy this situation the present review was conducted.

METHOD
A detailed manual literature search was conducted covering all major English language family therapy journals and edited handbooks published between 1975 and 1990. Major British and North American psychotherapy, clinical psychology and psychiatry journals were also examined. Finally a letter requesting both published and unpublished manuscripts describing empirical investigations of family intervention, including MFT was placed in a variety of widely read periodicals and newsletters, e.g. the Newsletter of the Association for Child Psychiatry and Psychology, the Bulletin of the Royal College of Psychiatry, The Psychologist, Context and Social Work Today. The letter was placed in these periodicals as part of a broader review of empirical research on family intervention generally in the UK and Ireland.

OVERVIEW OF 10 STUDIES
Only 10 studies were identified which met minimal methodological requirements. Four were comparative group outcome studies (Green & Hegert, 1989a, 1989b; Simpson, 1989; Bennun, 1986; Bennun, 1988). Two were process studies (Bennun, 1989;Vostanis et al, 1990). One was a single group outcome study(Manor, 1989, 1990, 1990). Two were consumer surveys (Fitzpatrick et al, 1990; Mashal et al, 1989) and one was, a clinical audit of a series of consecutive patients (Allman et al., 1989).

A summary of the main characteristics of the 10 studies is set out in Table 18.1. Most have been conducted in the past five years. Four features of these studies bear on their ecological validity and deserve mention. First, the studies come from four different countries. Second, in all cases identified patients sought treatment rather than being solicited as recruits for an analogue study. Third, identified patients included both adults and children. Fourth, all of the studies were conducted in regular outpatient centres.

Table 18.1. Context and design of 10 MFT studies

No	First Author	Year of Pub	Country of study	Design	N per gp	Symptom	System
1	Green	1989	USA	CO	MFT=11 ST=11	Adult PD, Childhood PD, Relationship P	Difficult cases with chronic problems. Mixed ethnicity. Mixed SES. MFT consultation offered by senior staff to junior colleagues at private institute.
2	Simpson	1989	UK	CO	MFT=45 ST=42	Childhood PD	Cases with home, school & community based chronic problems. Referred by GPs to NHS Child Psychiatry OPC. Mixed SES.
3	Bennun	1988	UK	CO	MFT=6 ST=6	Alcohol Problems	Mean history of alcohol problems of 9 years. All from two generational families. 8 men & 4 women with a mean age of 43y. Referred from various sources to NHS OPC.
4	Bennun	1986	UK	CO	MFT=10 ST=10	Alcohol Problems Depression Childhood PD	Difficult cases with chronic problems. Mixed SES. Referred from various sources to NHS OPC.
5	Bennun	1989	UK	P	MFT+ ST=35	Alcohol Problems Depression Childhood PD	Difficult cases with chronic problems. Mixed SES. Referred from various sources to NHS OPC.
6	Vostanis	1990	UK	P	MFT=12	Childhood PD	Mixed Cases. Referred by GPs to NHS Child Psychiatry OPC.
7	Manor	1989	UK	SO	MFT=45	Childhood PD Child abuse	Difficult cases with chronic problems. Mixed ethnicity. Low SES. Referred by Social Workers to Social Services Family Therapy Clinic
8	Fitzpatrick	1989	Ireland	CS	MFT=24 ST=26	Childhood PD	Mixed cases. Mixed SES. Referred from various sources to a General Hospital Child Psychiatry OPC containing a family therapy training programme.
9	Mashal	1989	Canada	CS	MFT=19	Early adulthood PD	Difficult cases. Average age of children was 21. Mixed ethnicity. Mixed SES. Referred from various sources to General Hospital Psychiatry OPC
10	Allman	1989	UK	CA	MFT=50	Adult PD	Difficult cases with previous history of therapy. Separation-individuation was key issued for most. Mixed SES. Referred by GPs to NHS OPC.

NOTE: NHS OPC = National Health Service Out Patient Clinic.; CO = Comparative outcome study; P = Process study; SO = Single group outcome study; CS = Consumer survey. CA =Clinical Audit. MFT = Milan Family therapy; ST = Standard therapy.

Table 18.2. Methodological characteristics of 10 MFT studies

Design Feature	Study Number									
	1	2	3	4	5	6	7	8	9	10
Comparison group	1	1	1	1	0	0	0	1	0	0
Controlled assignment to groups	1	1	1	1	0	0	0	0	0	0
Groups comparable on baseline variables	1	1	1	0	0	0	0	1	0	0
Diagnostic homogeneity	0	0	1	0	0	0	0	0	0	0
Pre-treatment assessment	1	1	1	1	0	1	1	0	0	0
Post-treatment assessment	1	1	1	1	1	1	1	0	0	0
Follow-up assessment (>3 months)	1	1	1	1	0	0	1	1	1	1
Client ratings	1	1	1	1	1	0	0	1	1	0
Therapist ratings	1	1	0	0	0	0	1	1	0	1
Researcher ratings	1	1	0	0	0	1	0	0	1	0
Symptom assessed	1	1	1	1	1	0	0	1	1	1
System assessed	1	1	1	1	1	1	1	0	1	1
Deterioration assessed	1	1	1	1	1	0	1	0	1	1
Engagement in further treatment assessed	0	1	0	1	0	0	0	1	1	1
Appropriate statistical analysis	1	1	1	1	1	1	1	1	1	1
Experienced therapists used for all treatments	1	1	1	1	1	1	1	0	1	1
Treatments equally valued by therapists	1	1	1	1	1	1	1	1	1	1
Quality control of treatment	0	0	0	0	0	0	0	0	0	0
Data on concurrent treatment given	1	0	0	1	0	0	0	0	0	1
Total	16	16	14	14	8	7	9	9	10	10

Note: 1=design feature is present. 0= design feature is absent.

A summary of the methodological features of the 10 studies is set out in Table 18.2. From this table it may be concluded that the four comparative group outcome studies were methodologically quite robust. The single group outcome study and the process studies were slightly less methodologically sophisticated. Finally the consumer survey's were less robust than the other types of investigations. Conclusions may be drawn from the first four studies with considerable confidence. Only tentative generalisations may be made on the basis of the findings from the remainder of the studies.

Detailed methodological criticisms of each study will not be given. Rather, in the case of each study, readers may refer to the methodological profile for that study contained in Table 18.2. However, for each study one or two noteworthy methodological strengths and important methodological refinements that could be introduced in future research are given under the heading *Comments*. A fuller consideration of methodological issues in family therapy research generally is available in Gurman and Kniskern's 1978 and 1981 papers.

REVIEW OF 10 STUDIES

STUDY 1. Green, R. & Herget, M. (1989a; 1989b)

Design. In this comparative outcome study, eleven therapists were asked to select 2 ongoing family therapy cases matched for difficulty. One case was randomly selected from each pair to participate in a Milan-systemic consultation to help resolve a therapeutic impasse. The remaining cases served as a comparison group. Therapists who submitted families to the study worked in a variety of clinics in California and used a variety of models of family therapy. The consultations all occurred at the Redwood Centre. The model of consultation used, drew on the ideas and practices of the original Milan Team but was more frankly goal directed than the position taken by Boscolo and Cecchin when the original Milan team split up (Boscolo et al, 1987; Cecchin, 1987;Selvin-Palazzoli et al., 1989). In the majority of cases the end-of-consultation-interventions involved framing the persistence or resolution of the family's presenting problem as a dilemma. The pro's and con's of persistence or resolution for each member of the family was typically specified. Paradoxical prescriptions were rarely used by this team. Assessment occurred before consultation, one month following consultation, and at 3 year follow-up. The follow-up assessment was conducted by phone. 11 families per group were followed up at one month and 8 families per group were followed up at 3 years.

Measures. Kiresuk's (1968) Goal Attainment Scale (GAS) was the principal measure used to assess movement towards the three main therapeutic goals identified by each family during a preliminary independent research interview. Secondary measures included family and therapist ratings of improvement on 5 point scales a month after consultation and Moos'(1981) Family Environment Scale. This was completed by literate family members before the consultation and one month later. On each occasion family members' scores were averaged to obtain a family score on this questionnaire.

       Results. On the GAS, average movement towards Goal #1 and for a composite of Goals #1 + #2+ #3 was significantly greater for families who received MFT at one month and 3 years follow up. At post-therapy and follow-up effect sizes for principal goals and composite goal scores ranged between d = 0.82 and d = 1.29. That is, the average MFT client showed more improvement than between 79% and 90% of clients in the control group after treatment and at follow up on principal goal and composite goal attainment indices.(These treatment effects were very large by psychotherapy research standards, where most meta-analyses of psychotherapies yield d values of about 0.7. Rosenthal, (1984) has classified d values less than 0.2 as small; d values between 0.2 and 0.8 as moderate; and greater than 0.8 as large.)

       MFT and ST groups did not differ on baseline measures, i.e. the Family Environment Scales or problem chronicity. On the GAS, for those families receiving MFT, 54% made moderate or good progress towards Goals #1+ #2+ #3 after 1 month and 88% made moderate or good progress after 3 years. For ST families the figures were 36% at one month and 63% at 3 years. On both therapist and client rating scales MFT families were rated as making significantly more progress towards goals than ST families after 1 month. Changes on the Family Environment Scales were not significant for either the MFT or ST group.

       Comments. Green's study shows that a 2 hour MFT consultation enhanced the immediate and long term outcome of a variety of forms of family therapy with difficult cases where a therapeutic impasse was hampering progress.

       A key strength of the study was the use of a robust individualized method for assessing change in symptomatology, i.e. the GAS. It is disappointing that a more sensitive measure of systemic change was not included in the assessment battery. Studies by Bennun (1986) and Vostanis et al (1990) reviewed below suggest that Shapiro's (1961) Personal Questionnaire and the Expressed Emotion Scales (Vaughan & Leff, 1976) are highly sensitive to systemic changes. These might fruitfully have been included in Green's study. The Family Environment Scale which was used in Green's study as an index of systemic change has one main drawback. It is one of the many family assessment instruments which, like the psychometric personality inventories on which it is modelled, taps perceptions of relatively enduring aspects of family functioning.

STUDY 2. Simpson, L., (1989)

Design. In this comparative outcome study 118 referrals to Royal Edinburgh Hospital for Sick Children's Department of Child and Family Psychiatry were randomly allocated to MFT or ST. MFT was conducted following the description and guidelines set out in early Milan publications (Selvini-Palazzoli et al., 1978, 1980).ST comprised standard individually oriented child assessment and therapy coupled with parental counselling. MFT was carried out by 2 psychiatrists and 2 social workers. ST was carried out by a traditional multidisciplinary child psychiatry team. 74% of recruited families participated in treatment, 45 in MFT and 42 in ST. 2 families dropped out of the study before the end of treatment and two dropped out between the end of treatment and 6 month follow up. Families were assessed before and after treatment and at 6 month follow-up. Therapists were also interviewed. An independent researcher carried out these assessments using instruments listed below.

Measures. The following assessment battery was administered: a semi-structured family interview which inquired about the symptom, the family system and the family's involvement in treatment; Rutter's (1970) A & B scales which obtain ratings of parent and teacher perceptions of behaviour problems in school-going children or Richman's (1982) Behaviour Checklist in the case of preschoolers; visual analogue scales assessing the family's perception of symptom severity and family system functioning; and a stressful life event inventory. For each case, a record of the nature and duration of the therapy was obtained from each therapist using a standardised form.

Results. MFT & ST groups did not differ on baseline or demographic variables with one exception. The MFT group had more severe symptomatology as rated by Rutter's Teachers Questionnaire. After treatment and at six month follow up MFT & ST groups did not differ on any absolute indices of problem severity, family functioning, satisfaction with treatment or involvement in further treatment. Both MFT and ST alleviated symptoms in about 3/4 of cases, and overall families were satisfied with such treatment.

MFT led to slightly greater improvement in family functioning than ST. In MFT symptomatic and systemic improvement were associated. This was not the case for ST. MFT was briefer than ST. The average duration of MFT was 3 sessions and for ST it was 5 sessions. Fewer failed appointments occurred with MFT. However, MFT was not less manpower intensive since in this study a full four person team consulted to each family at each appointment.

Comments. The central finding of this study is that in a child psychiatry setting MFT on the one hand and traditional individual child therapy with parent counselling on the other led to similar levels of symptomatic change. However, MFT differed from the more traditional approach in that it led to improvement in perceived family functioning and this correlated with symptomatic improvement.

In MFT this greater perceived change in family functioning associated with symptomatic improvement may have been due to families adopting the beliefs of their therapists, i.e. that for symptomatic improvement to occur concurrent systemic change is essential. Alternatively it may have been due not only to a change in the family's beliefs but also to a change in family behaviour. Unfortunately independent observations of family behaviour were not obtained in Simpson's study, so this question remains to be answered in further research.

The brevity of MFT and the reduced number of failed appointments may have been due to the increased efficiency with which teams offer clinical service when they share a common clinical model. This unity of commitment is by definition absent in traditional multidisciplinary child psychiatry teams where eclecticism predominates.

The strengths of this study include the use of large groups, the use of an extensive assessment battery which included a stressful life events scale, and the use of the service offered by a multidisciplinary child psychiatry team as a comparison group. It is disappointing that no attempt was made to specify precisely how the formulations and family intervention of the MFT and ST teams differed since both were clearly engaged in differing forms of family work.

STUDY 3. Bennun, I. (1988)

Design. In this comparative outcome study 16 families each containing a person with alcohol problems were randomly assigned to either MFT or ST. MFT conformed to the model outlined in the writings of the original Milan group (Selvini-Palazzoli, 1978,1980). ST was behaviourally based problem solving therapy. MFT on average lasted for 8 sessions and ST lasted for 9 sessions. MFT was conducted by IB and a team. 5 other therapists treated the ST group. Community mental health clinic and a specialist alcohol unit served as a base for the therapy. Assessments were conducted before and after therapy and at 6 months follow up. 4 families dropped out of the study.

Measures. Three self-report questionnaires were used to assess symptomatology and marital and family functioning at each evaluation point in the study: Stockwell's (1983) Severity of Alcohol Dependence Questionnaire (SADQ), Olson's (1983) Family Satisfaction

Rating and Kimmel's (1974) Marital Adjustment Test(MAT). All three instruments are reliable and valid standardized self-report inventories.

Results. MFT & ST groups were comparable on baseline measures of alcohol dependence and marital and family satisfaction. After treatment and at follow up both MFT and ST groups showed no difference in symptomatology or system functioning on the 3 dependent measures. Overall both groups showed significant improvement in symptomatology and system functioning. Despite this clients were still in the mild dependency range of the SADQ and the distressed range of the MAT. Improvement in marital satisfaction occurred more rapidly with ST, possibly because spouses hope that treatment would be effective was effected more immediately by the problem solving approach.

Comments. Both MFT and behavioural problem solving therapies had very similar effects on clients' perceptions of drinking patterns and family functioning in this study of problem drinkers from intact families.

The use of problem-solving therapy, an intervention of proven effectiveness with problem drinkers, as a comparison treatment against which to assess MFT is a key strength in the design of this study. The notable weaknesses are the small group sizes and the absence of observational measures.

STUDY 4. Bennun, I. (1986)

Design. In this comparative outcome study 27 families were randomly allocated to MFT or ST, the definitions of which were similar to those given in the Bennun (1988) study just reviewed. The families presented with a range of difficulties including alcoholism, depression, eating disorders, agoraphobia and childhood and adolescent emotional and conduct problems. Treatment ranged from 7-10 sessions and was conducted by experienced therapists. Therapy was provided in NHS Community Psychiatry outpatient clinics. Families were assessed before treatment, midway through treatment, after treatment, and at 6 month follow-up. 25% of the sample dropped out before the end of treatment. A six month telephone follow-up was carried out with 13 (65%) of the families who completed therapy.

Measures. Systemic changes were measured using the Sharpiro's (1961) Personal Questionnaire (PQ). Statements about the relationship between the symptom and the family system were drawn up with each family at intake and the families beliefs about changes in these statements rated before and after therapy and midway through treatment. Symptomatic change was assessed using symptom specific measures appropriate to the presenting problem. These included Stockwell's (1983) Severity of Alcohol Dependence Questionnaire;

Beck's (1967) Depression Inventory; Mark's (1979) Fear Questionnaire; tantrum frequency; weight; frequency of asthma attacks; and number of therapist scheduled tasks completed. These measures were used before and after therapy and mid way through treatment. Change in families' levels of concern about the presenting problem was assessed by interview after therapy. Satisfaction with treatment was assessed on a 5 point scale after therapy. Symptomatic recurrence was assessed by telephone interview six months after therapy.

Results. Both groups showed significant positive systemic change as assessed by the PQ over the course of therapy. However the MFT group showed significantly more systemic change than the ST group. All families in both treatment groups showed moderate or good symptomatic improvement immediately after therapy. There were no marked differences between the MFT & ST groups on indices of problem severity after treatment. 20% of MFT families and 50% of ST families reported no change in their initial concerns after therapy. The mean rating of satisfaction with therapy for both groups of families was 1.6 on a 5 point scale, indicating that both groups of families were highly satisfied with the therapy received. Of 7 MFT families followed up at 6 months 5 (75%) were asymptomatic, 2 (25%) reported occasional recurrences and none reported seeking further treatment. Of 6 ST families followed up at 6 months 2 (33%) were asymptomatic, 3 (50%) reported occasional recurrences and 1 (17%) sought 3 further sessions of family therapy.

Comments. This study shows that in the short term both MFT and ST led to moderate or good symptomatic improvement, improved systemic functioning and a high level of therapeutic satisfaction. However, MFT led to greater improvement in family systems functioning, a greater decrease in concern over the presenting problem and better symptomatic improvement at follow-up compared to ST.

The most noteworthy feature of the study is the use of a robust individualized measure of systemic functioning, i.e. the PQ. It is unfortunate that some equivalent measure of symptomatic status such as the GAS was not also used so that the correlation or covariation of symptomatology and systemic functioning over the course of treatment could be statistically analysed.

STUDY 5. Bennun, I. (1989)

Design. This single group process study is based on perceptions of the therapist furnished by members of thirty five families who participated the two Bennun studies just reviewed(Bennun, 1986, 1988). In 23 families an adult was symptomatic and in 12 the focus for concern was a childhood problem. There were 35 fathers; 35 mothers and 27 literate identified patients over the age of 13. Of these 10 were fathers, 13 were mothers and 4 were children. Half of the families included in this study had received MFT and half had received ST. Therapy lasted between 7 & 10 sessions. At the beginning of session 2 literate family members complete the therapist rating scale described below. At the end of therapy, patients completed assessments of satisfaction with treatment-outcome and symptomatic status on the instruments described in the next section. The correlation between family members perceptions of the therapist and outcome were calculated for the whole sample and for the subsample of cases who had alcohol problems. Both analyses yielded similar results.

Measures. Clients' perceptions of the therapist were assessed with Schindler's (1983) Therapist Rating Scale. This is a 29 item schedule on which patients rate the therapist for 3 main sets of characteristics: positive regard/interest; competency/experience; activity/direct guidance. Satisfaction with treatment-outcome was assessed on a 5 point scale. For the 18 patients with alcohol problems Stockwell's (1983) Severity of Alcohol Dependence Questionnaire was used to assess symptomatic change.

Results. The perceptions of the therapist held by the father of a family had a much stronger association with therapeutic outcome than those of the mother, except when the mother was the identified patient. If fathers perceived the therapist as competent and active in providing direct guidance then therapy was more likely to be successful. The more divergent the views of the mother and the father of the therapist, the more likely therapy was to be unsuccessful. Clients' perceptions of therapists were unrelated to the form of therapy they received, i.e. MFT or problem solving therapy.

Comments. The centrality of the role of father's perceptions of the therapeutic process in determining outcome suggests that the notion of family hierarchy being based on generational status alone without reference to gender may be erroneous. This point has been central to feminist analyses of family therapy (e.g. Goldner, 1990). From a clinical perspective these findings suggest that engaging fathers early in the therapeutic process through the adoption of a competent and directive style should be a priority. The impact on outcome of fathers' perceptions of the therapeutic process in the later stages of therapy is an important question for further research. Does therapy lead to a more equal distribution of influence within the family as it progresses or does it reinforce the status quo?

That divergent parental opinions concerning the therapeutic process is associated with poor outcome suggests that therapists should avoid escalating conflict and disagreement between parents concerning their views of the therapeutic situation without facilitating the resolution of this conflict in the early stages of therapy. The impact on outcome of divergent parental opinions in the later stages of therapy remains open for investigation.

Few service based studies and surveys of consumer views of therapy use standardized instruments to assess clients perceptions of therapists. The use of such a measure is the study's main strength. Its main weaknesses are that client perception were only measured at one point in the therapeutic process and no assessment of therapist behaviour was made so as to determine the precise behavioural correlates (from an outsider's perspective).

STUDY 6. Vostanis, P., Burnham, J., & Harris, Q. (1990)

Design. In this process study Expressed Emotion (EE) (Vaughan & Leff, 1976) was rated from unedited videotapes of the first, second and last sessions of the therapies of 12 families attending the Charles Burns Clinic in Birmingham. In 6 of the cases therapy was conducted by JB and QH was the therapist in the remaining 6 cases. During data collection, therapists were blind to the nature of the study. The clients were families with children who presented with conduct, emotional or relationship difficulties, 80% of whom were referred by the GP. Therapy lasted between 2 & 8 sessions.

Measures. EE comprises 5 subscales: emotional overinvolvement (EOI), critical comments, warmth, hostility and positive comments. A range of scores were obtained from rated videotapes for the first three of these scales. For the final two scales in most cases a score of nil was obtained.

Results. Both over-involvement and critical comments showed a significant reduction over the course of the first two sessions.
Warmth did not increase significantly between the first and second session but did show an overall increase between the first and last session.

Comments. High EE scores in the families of schizophrenics have been associated with a high relapse rate for this disorder. It has been shown that behavioural, psychoeducational and supportive family interventions can lower EE and reduce this relapse rate (Berkowitz, 1988). Vostanis's study shows that MFT can reduce EE, albeit in a different population. An important question for further research is how changes in the family belief system facilitated by MFT lead to changes in the emotional climate of the family as assessed by the EE scale. What follows are some detailed hypotheses, based on attribution theory (Forsterling, 1988), which deserve investigation.

Parents who attribute their children's symptoms to illness (or 'being sick') probably respond with a high level of emotional overinvolvement. Those who attribute their children's problem behaviour to disobedience (or 'being bad') probably respond with a high level of critical comments. MFT helps parents to see their child's symptomatic behaviour as part of a wider pattern of family interactions rather than as an intrinsic 'sick' or 'bad' characteristic of the child. This new way of construing the child's symptoms may empower the parents to explore new ways of alleviating the child's symptoms. Vostanis study suggests that this de-labelling or reframing process occurs early in MFT. Once the parent has consolidated the belief that the child's symptomatic behaviour is a function of the situation in which he finds himself and not an entrenched personal characteristic, it becomes possible for the parent to express warmth towards the child. Vostanis' study suggests that this process occurs later in therapy.

The key feature of this study is the use of a well validated observational measure of systemic functioning. It is unfortunate that parental attributional beliefs concerning the source of the index patients symptomatology were not assessed so as to test the more detailed hypotheses set out in the previous paragraph. It would also have been useful if some index of symptomatic change was included so that the covariation in symptomatology and systemic functioning over the course of therapy could have been documented.

STUDY 7. Manor, O. (1989, 1990a, 1990b)

Design. A cohort of 46 cases who received MFT informed services at Rownham's Centre for Families and Children were followed up in this single group outcome study. MFT theory and technique were used at Rownham's within the context of a range of social work services including family assessment, family treatment and consultation to social workers who had reached a therapeutic impasse in working with multiproblem families. In 19 cases referred children were placed at Rownham's Residential Unit for a brief period as an adjunct to outpatient MFT services. The average length of contact with the centre was about 7 months. The majority of cases were referred by social workers, and in most instances referrers were included in at least one MFT consultation. Data were gathered before and after treatment and at six month follow-up. It was not possible to follow up 4 families post-treatment and a further 2 cases were lost at 6 month follow up.

Measures. Referring social workers perceptions of the referred cases were assessed by a questionnaire, which was administered before treatment, after therapy and at 6 month follow-up. The questionnaire solicited data on presenting problems, current and previous family structure and functioning, and involvement with other services. Two principal outcome measures were also assessed by the questionnaire: perceived risk and perceived complexity. Both variables were assessed on four point scales. Risk referred to the social worker's perception that a member of the family, usually a child, was at risk of injury, disablement or death. Complexity referred to the social worker's perception of the complexity of the family situation in terms of the number of people or agencies involved with the presenting problem and their related patterns of social interaction.

Results. Outpatient MFT along with the use of adjunctive residential facilities as necessary was associated with a significant overall reduction in the referring social worker's ratings of the risk and complexity of referred cases. Risk reduction was associated specifically with the placement of a child in a residential unit temporarily while MFT occurred. The reduction in a social worker's perception of case complexity was specifically associated with the family's participation in MFT. Despite the differential effects of MFT and residential placement on perceived risk and complexity there was a significant positive correlation between the two variables. High risk families were perceived by social workers as complex. Low risk families were seen as less complex.

Comments. The following hypotheses which specify the processes which link MFT and residential placement to the reduction of perceived complexity and risk deserve further investigation. Residential placement probably reduced perceived risk in this study by containing the children of dysfunctional families while the parents of these families and the referring social workers had an opportunity to explore new ways of dealing with their family problems in MFT. MFT itself probably reduced the perceived complexity in two ways. First, it may have helped the referring social worker develop a more coherent systemic hypothesis within which to conceptualize the role of various agencies in the problem determined system. Second, this hypothesis may have provided a framework from which to negotiate the inclusion or exclusion of involved agencies in problem resolving system.

The outstanding features of this study is its focus on perceptions of referrers rather than those of family members and the identification of perceived risk and complexity as meaningful variables in this type of research. Allowing for the usual limitation of single group outcome studies (noted in Table 18.2) the principal shortcoming of this work is the indeterminate reliability and validity of the perceived risk and complexity measures. The refinement of these measures is an important task for the future.

STUDY 8. Fitzpatrick, C., NicDhomnaill, C., & Power, A. (1989)

Design. Of 68 families followed up in this consumer survey, 50 agreed to participate. 24 families had received MFT and 26 had received ST. MFT was offered by trainees on a 2 year Family Therapy Training Programme at the Department of Child Psychiatry in the Mater Hospital, Dublin. Experienced systemic therapists offered trainees live supervision using a one-way screen and telephone. The model of MFT employed drew on both the early ideas of the Milan team (Selvini-Palazzoli et al, 1978, 1980) and on Cecchin's later developments (Cecchin, 1987). ST, which was offered by a multidisciplinary child psychiatry team from the same hospital, involved individual assessment and treatment of the child and concurrent parent counselling. The MFT and ST groups were cohorts referred independently to either the Family Therapy Training Programme or the Child Psychiatry team from separate sections of the hospital's overall catchment area. Semi-structured family interviews were conducted 12-18 months after treatment by independent researchers. Each family's main therapist also completed a questionnaire. The families contained children under 18 most of whom were referred because of neurotic or conduct problems. Most were referred by the GP or the school. In most cases MFT and ST lasted for 2-6 sessions. MFT and ST groups were comparable on demographic variables.

Results. There was more frequent disagreement between therapist and family about the referral problem remaining a central focus of therapy in the MFT group than in the ST group. In the MFT group 42% of families said that their therapists disagreed with them about this matter. In the ST group disagreement occurred in only 16% of cases. Otherwise families opinions concerning the experience of MFT and ST and its effect on both symptom and system were comparable. In the case of both treatments about 3/4 of families reported sustained symptomatic improvement.

Comments. An important question arising from this study it the client's perceptions of the conditions under which disagreement between therapists and clients concerning the focus of therapy in MFT is perceived as useful in facilitating change. In MFT clients are offered a reframing of their presenting problems in systemic terms. If this difference is too small, the therapist's reframing of the situation will be assimilated into the clients original belief system without any alteration to it. If the difference is too large, the therapist's reframing will be rejected as irrelevant, outlandish or non-empathic. Reframings that are too similar or too different from the clients original belief system concerning the presenting problem will not facilitate therapeutic change. The difference between the client's original view of the problem and the therapists reframing of it must be sufficient to facilitate a therapeutic change in the client's belief system and related behaviour and feelings. The precise parameters of this difference from the client's perspective is a key question for future research in this area.

STUDY 9. Mashal, M., Feldman, R., & Sigal, J. (1989)

Design. In this consumer survey 76 individuals from 17 families who had received MFT at the Family therapy Department of the Jewish General Hospital were interviewed by telephone using a semi-standardized 12 item interview. The degree of psychopathology shown by family members and families as a whole was independently and reliably rated by two clinicians on the basis of information available in the case notes. MFT in this study was probably based on the early writing of the original Milan team (Selvini-Palazzoli et al., 1978, 1980). The average age of children in the families was 22 years, so the central lifecycle issue was 'leaving home' or individuation. All were difficult cases where previous therapy had been unsuccessful. Families attended for about 10 sessions on a monthly basis.

Results. Patients were more likely to view MFT as leading to positive personal and family change than parents. Just over 3/4 of patients describe MFT as effective but MFT was considered to be effective by just over 1/2 of parents. Almost 1/2 of all family members disliked MFT. For parents, this dislike was tied to a negative attitude towards the team behind the screen. For fathers, the long delay between sessions and the overall length of treatment also contributed to their dissatisfaction. Negative attitudes to MFT were not associated with videotaping consultations. Families who disliked MFT, particularly those containing a severely symptomatic member, sought other forms of further treatment.

Comments. A strength of this study is its empirical focus on factors that detract from client satisfaction. However, half o the families in this study found the use of a team and screen satisfying and also were satisfied with the way in which the schedule of therapeutic consultations was established. It is unfortunate that way in which the therapists managed these tasks successfully was not investigated in further detail. This is an important area for further research.

STUDY 10. Allman, P., Sharpe, M., & Bloch, S. (1989)

Design. In this clinical audit the case notes of the first 50 patients seen at the Warneford Hospital Family Clinic were reviewed by the clinical team using a standardized review form. Patients were adults (17-65 yrs) with histories of previous psychiatric intervention and 20% received concurrent pharmacological treatment during MFT. Most were single, living with their parents and had a diagnosis of neurosis. MFT lasted, on average, 4-5 sessions.

Results. In this study 2/3 of cases showed symptomatic improvement and 1/2 showed positive systemic change. Separation from family of origin was the most common systemic problem in a group of predominantly neurotic adults. The most common end-of session-intervention (EOSI) was to show non-specific positive respect for the family and to offer hope. Less common was the direct offering of an alternative view of the problem (in the form of a partial or complete systemic hypothesis). It was rare for the team to use paradox or ritual prescription. Because of small cell frequencies crosstabulations of diagnostic categories, systemic themes and frequencies of various EOSIs were not reliably interpretable.

Comments. An important feature of this study was the attempt made to quantify the family issues upon which systemic hypotheses were based and the characteristics of EOSIs. However, frequency counts of EOSI characteristics is not a research method which holds much promise. More important is the patterning of EOSI characteristics and types over the course of therapy and the exploration of the relationship of these patterns of interventions to case type and outcome. For example it is of little use to the clinicians who conducted this audit to know that positive connotation was used frequently and ritual prescription rarely. Most clinicians would wish to know at what point during the course of therapy with a particular type of case was it useful to couple positive connotation with ritual prescription.

DISCUSSION
   1. Symptomatic Change. A summary of the data on the therapeutic outcome for clients who have received MFT is contained in Table 18.3. MFT leads to symptomatic improvement in about 2/3 - 3/4 of cases. Deterioration occurs in under 1/10 of cases which have received MFT. MFT is helpful with a range of cases from routine adult and child psychiatric referrals to very difficult social work cases or chronic adult psychiatry cases. MFT is as effective in facilitating symptomatic change as problem focused family therapy and is sometimes more effective in facilitating positive systemic changes than problem focused therapy.

   These data on symptomatic outcome and deterioration for MFT are comparable to outcome data for other forms of family therapy (e.g. Gurman & Kniskern, 1981; Gurman Kniskern and Pinsof, 1986, Hazelrigg et al, 1987, Markus et al, 1990) individual adult therapy (Garfield, 1981; Parloff et al, 1986) and individual child therapy (Kazdin, 1988).

   2. Systemic Change. About 1/2 of cases show positive systemic change as a result of MFT. Improvement in marital and family functioning noted after therapy is sustained at 6 month follow-up and possibly longer. This finding is consistent across a variety of standardized and unstandardized self-report measures of systemic functioning.

Family Therapy and Systemic Practice

Table 18.3. Ratings of outcome after MFT from 9 studies

	Study Number								
	1	2	3	4	6	7	8	9	10
Symptomatic improvement after treatment									
Client	-	74	SI	80	-	-	-	-	-
Therapist	-	73	-	-	-	-	-	-	-
Researcher	54	-	-	-	-	-	-	-	-
Symptomatic improvement at follow-up									
Client	-	84	SI	100	-	-	71	67†	-
Therapist	-	-	-	-	-	70*	-	-	68
Researcher	88	-	-	-	-	-	-	-	-
Systemic improvement after treatment									
Client	0	CI	SI	CI	-	-	-	-	-
Therapist	-	-	-	-	-	70*	-	-	-
Researcher	-	-	-	-	SI	-	-	-	-
Systemic improvement at follow-up									
Client	-	CI	SI	-	-	-	-	73†	52
Therapist	-	-	-	-	-	-	-	-	-
Researcher	-	-	-	-	-	70*	-	-	-
Drop-out rate	28	30	25	25	-	13	26	22	-
Deterioration	-	7	-	0	-	-	-	6†	10
Sought further therapy	-	24	-	-	-	-	33	62	28

NOTE: CI = Comparative and significant improvement relative to control group.
SI = Significant improvement relative to pre-therapy status. *This is a 'perceived risk' rating.
†These scores have been averaged from mothers', fathers' and patients' responses.

Over the course of MFT family members observe changes in the frequency with which symptom related patterns of family interaction occur (as measured by the PQ). Parental criticism and over-involvement (as measured by the EE scale) decrease rapidly over the course of MFT and parental warmth towards the problem child increases more gradually as MFT progresses.

3. The Process of Engagement. The father's perceptions of the therapist in early sessions are more important than the mother's in determining the outcome of MFT. MFT is more likely to be effective where father's view the therapist as directive and competent, at least in the early sessions of therapy. More general reviews of the family therapy literature have yielded similar findings to these. Failure to engage the father in therapy correlates with therapeutic dropout and poor outcome (Gurman & Kniskern, 1978). The technical skills of family therapy alone are insufficient for effective treatment. The therapist must also have developed relationship building skills (humour, warmth etc.) and structuring skills which give family therapy sessions focus and direction (Gurman & Kniskern, 1981).

4. Treatment Duration. A notable feature of MFT is its brevity. In this review, most treatments lasted between 5 and 10 sessions. This brevity of treatment, however, is not unique to MFT. In general reviews of family therapy, it has been concluded that effective outcome is usually yielded by treatments that last between 10 and 20 sessions (e.g. Gurman & Kniskern, 1981). In adult psychotherapy 15% of patients show measurable improvement before the first appointment, 50% of patients are measurably improved by 8 sessions and this figure rises to 75% after 26 sessions (Howard et al, 1986). In reviews of individual child therapy average duration of treatment has been estimated at about 10 sessions (Kazdin, 1988, Chapter 3).

5. Consumer's Views. About half of client's dislike MFT and this dissatisfaction is in part linked to specific aspects of MFT practice, i.e. screens, teams and the scheduling of therapy. Such ambivalence is not unique to MFT, or indeed to psychotherapy. Over 50% of clients in a cohort that had received structural or strategic family therapy at the Family Institute in Cardiff described treatment as 'uncomfortable' but despite this 89% viewed therapy as helpful (Frude & Dowling, 1980). 68% of Sigurd Reimers (1989) cohort found their initial contact with his Structural Family Therapy Clinic uncomfortable, but 84% said they would return for further therapy. The concerns about the use of screens and teams in family therapy identified in this review are in line with those described by Howe (1989) and must be a stimulus for MFT practitioners to explore ways in which the technology of MFT can be used to empower clients rather than arouse dissatisfaction. A spate of recent papers have described such pioneering explorations (Pimpernell & Treacher, 1990; Birch, 1990; Hoffman, 1990; Anderson, 1990; Cade, 1990)

6. Consultation and Co-ordination. MFT consultation to cases where therapists and families have reached a therapeutic impasse leads to greater short and long term symptomatic change, than the absence of such consultation. MFT (along with adjunctive residential containment of children at risk where necessary) leads to a reduction in the referring worker's perception of case complexity and risk. MFT probably reduces case complexity. Residential containment probably reduces risk.

7. Measurement of Symptoms and Systems. In future outcome research the use of goal attainment scaling to assess symptomatic change and the use of the Sharpiro's personal questionnaire to assess systemic change is recommended. In future process research this review suggests that the use of the EE scales and client perception of therapist scales would be fruitful. Of particular interest would be the investigation of the differences on these measures between cases that show improvement and deterioration. Also of interest would be changes on these measures in relation to the occurrence of "critical therapeutic moments" or "highly valued micro-interventions".

REFERENCES

Allman, P., Sharpe, M., Bloch, S. (1989). Family therapy in adult psychiatry. Paper presented at the AFT/IFT Conference; Family Research & Family Therapy: Marriage, Cohabitation or Divorce, Institute of Psychiatry DeCrespigny Park, 20-21 April, 1989.

Andersen, T. (1990). Reflecting Teams. Paper presented at Cardiff Family Institutes International Conference: Developments in Systemic Approaches, St David's Hall Cardiff.

Beck, A. (1967). *Depression: Clinical, Experimental, and Theoretical Aspects.* New York: Harper Row.

Bennun, I. (1986). Evaluating family therapy: A comparison of Milan and Problem-solving approaches. *Journal of Family Therapy,* 8, 225-242.

Bennun, I. (1988) Treating the system or the symptom: Investigating family therapy for alcohol problems. *Behavioural Psychotherapy,* 16, 165-176.

Bennun, I. (1989) Perceptions of the therapist in family therapy. *Journal of Family Therapy,* 11, 243-255.

Berkowitz, R. (1988). Family therapy and adult mental illness: Schizophrenia and depression. *Journal of Family Therapy,* 10, 339-356.

Birch, J. (1990). The context setting function of the video consent form. *Journal of Family Therapy,* 12, 281-286.

Boscolo, L., Cecchin, G., Hoffman, L., & Penn, P. (1987). *Milan Systemic Family therapy. Conversation in theory and practice.* New York: Basic.

Cade, B. (1990). Demonstration interviews; Some questions and comments. *Journal of Family Therapy,* 12, 295-204

Campbell, D. & Draper, R. (1985). *Applications of Systemic Family Therapy.* London: Grune & Stratton.

Cecchin, G. (1987). Hypothesizing, circularity and neutrality revisited: An invitation to curiosity. *Family Process,* 26, 405-413.

Fitzpatrick, C., NicDhomnaill, C., & Power, A. (1990). Therapy - Views of families and therapists. *Newsletter of the Association for Child Psychology and Psychiatry,* 12, 9-12.

Forsterling, F. (1988). *Attribution Theory in Clinical Psychology.* Chichester: Wiley. Translated by Jonathan Harrow.

Frude, N. & Dowling, E. (1980). A follow-up analysis of family therapy clients. *Journal of Family Therapy,* 2, 149-161.

Garfield, S. (1981). Psychotherapy. A 40 year appraisal. *American Psychologist,* 36,174-183.

Goldner, V. (1990). A feminist perspective in systemic family therapy. Paper presented at Cardiff Family Institutes International Conference: Developments in Systemic Approaches, St David's Hall Cardiff.

Green, R. & Herget, M. (1989) Outcome of systemic/strategic team consultation: 1. Overview and one-month results. *Family Process,* 28, 37-58.

Green, R. & Herget, M. (1989) Outcome of systemic/strategic team consultation: 11. Three year follow-up and a theory of emergent design. *Family Process,* 28, 419-437.

Gurman, A. & Kniskern, D. (1978). Research on Marital and Family therapy: Progress, perspective and prospect. In S. Garfield & A. Bergin (Eds.) *Handbook of Psychotherapy and Behaviour Change* (Second edition). New York: Wiley.

Gurman, A. & Kniskern, D. (1981). Family therapy outcome research: Knowns and Unknowns. In a. Gurman & D. Kniskern (Eds.), *Handbook of Family Therapy.* New York: Brunner/Mazel.

Gurman, A., Kniskern, D. & Pinsof, W. (1986). Research on marital and family therapy. In S. Garfield & A Bergin. (Eds.) *Handbook of Psychotherapy and behaviour change* (Third edition). New York: Wiley.

Hazelrigg, M., Cooper, H., & Borduin, C. (1987). Evaluating the effectiveness of family therapy: An integrative review and analysis. *Psychological Bulletin,* 101, 428-422.

Hoffman, L. (1990). How I changed My Mind Again! Paper presented at Cardiff Family Institutes International Conference: Developments in Systemic Approaches, St David's Hall Cardiff.

Howard, K., Kopta, S., Krause., M., Orlinksy, D. (1986). The dose effect relationship in psychotherapy. *American Psychologist,* 41, 159-164.

Howe, D. *The Consumers' View of Family Therapy.* Aldershot. Gower.

Jones, E. (1988). The Milan method - quo vadis. Journal of Family Therapy, 10, 325-338.

Kazdin, A. (1988). *Child Psychotherapy.* New York. Pergamon.

Kimmel, D. & Van der Veen, F. (1974). Factors of marital adjustment in Locke's Marital Adjustment Test. *Journal of Marriage and the Family,* 36, 57-63.

Kiresuk, T., & Shirman, R. (1968). Goal attainment scaling: A general method for evaluating comprehensive mental health programmes. *Community Mental Health Journal,* 4, 443- 453.

Manor, O. (1989). Reducing risk through family work. *Social Work Today,* 21 (No.7), 29.

Manor, O. (1989). Effecting Family situation: A pilot study of the perceptions of referrers of a family work centre. Unpublished Manuscript, Middlesex Polytechnic

Manor, O. (1989). Family work at the front line: Exploring the referrers views. Unpublished manuscript, Middlesex Polytechnic.

Marks, I. & Mathews, A. (1979). Brief standard rating for phobic patients. B*ehaviour Research and Therapy,* 17, 263-267.

Markus, E., Lange, A., Pettigrew, T. (1990) Effectiveness of family therapy: A meta-analysis. *Journal of Family Therapy*, 12, 205- 221.

Mashal, M., Feldman, R., & Sigal, J. (1989). The unravelling of a treatment paradigm: A follow-up study of the Milan approach to family therapy. Family *Process*, 28, 457-469.

Moos, R. & Moos, B. (1981). *Manual for the Family Environment Scale*. Palo Alto, CA: Consulting Psychologist's Press.

Olson, D., & Wilson, M. (1982). *Rating of family satisfaction.* University of Minnesota, Department of Family Social Science.

Parloff, M., London, P., & Wolfe, B. (1986). Individual psychotherapy and behaviour change. *Annual Review of Psychology,* 37, 321-349.

Pimpernell, P. & Treacher, A. (1990). Using a videotape to overcome client's reluctance to engage in family therapy - Some preliminary findings from a probation setting. *Journal of Family Therapy*, 12, 59-71.

Reimers, S. (1989). A survey to examine clients' perceptions and experiences of a child and family guidance service. Unpublished Manuscript, Bath District Health Authority.

Richman, Stevenson, J. & Graham, P. (1982). *Preschool to school.* London: Academic press.

Rosenthal, R. (1984). Meta-analytic Procedures for Social Research. Beverley Hills. Sage. Rutter, M., Tizard, J., & Whitmore, K. (1970). *Education, Health and Behaviour.* London: Longman.

Schindler, L., Revensdorf, D., Hahleweg, K. & Brengelman, J. (1983). Therapeutenverhalten in der verhaltenstherapie entwicklung eines instruments zue beurteilung durch den klienten. *Partnerberatung*, 20, 149-157.

Selvini-Palazzoli, M., Boscolo, L., Cecchin, G., & Prata, G. (1978). *Paradox and Counterparadox.* New York: Aronson.

Selvini-Palazzoli, M., Boscolo, L., Cecchin, G., & Prata, G. (1980). Hypothesizing-neutrality-circularity: three guidelines for the conductor of the session. *Family Process*, 19, 3-12.

Selvini-Palazzoli, M., Cirillo, S., Selvini, M., & Sorentino, A. (1989). *Family Games: General Models of Psychotic Processes in the Family.* New York: Norton.

Shoham-Salomon, V. & Bice Broussard, D. (1990). The state of the art and the progression of science in family therapy research. *Journal of Family Psychology*, 4, 99-120.

Shapiro, M. (1961). A method of measuring changes specific to the individual psychiatric patient. *British Journal of Medical Psychology*, 34, 151-155.

Simpson, L. (1989). The comparative efficacy of Milan Family Therapy for disturbed children and their families. Unpublished Manuscript, Department of Child & Family Psychiatry, Royal Hospital for Sick Children, Edinburgh.

Stockwell, T., Murphy, D., & Hodgson, R. (1983). The severity of alcohol dependence questionnaire: its use, reliability and validity. *British Journal of Addiction*, 78, 145-155.

Tomm, C. (1984a). One perspective on the Milan Approach. Part 1. Overview of development theory and practice. *Journal of Marital and Family Therapy*, 10, 113-135.

Tomm, C. (1984b). One perspective on the Milan Approach. Part 2. Description of session format, interviewing style, and interventions. *Journal of Marital and Family Therapy*, 10, 253-271.

Vaughan, C. & Leff, J. (1976). The measurement of expressed emotion in the families of psychiatric patients. British *Journal of Social and Clinical Psychology*, 15, 157-165.

Vostanis, P., Burnham, J., & Harris, Q. (1990) Changes in Expressed Emotion in Systemic Family therapy. Unpublished Manuscript. Charles Burns Clinic, Birmingham.

CHAPTER 19

PSYCHOTHERAPY RESEARCH

ABSTRACT
In this paper research methods for studying the process and outcome of psychotherapy are described along with a summary of the major substantive findings of current psychotherapy research. Such research has indicated that about 2/3 of cases benefit from therapy. The provision of social support, the facilitation of belief system exploration and consulting to behavioural change are three factors common to many forms of psychotherapy that contribute to a positive outcome. These factors are optimally effective at different stages of the change process, with support being important during the early transition from the precontemplation to the contemplation stage; a focus of belief system exploration being central to the transition from contemplation to planning; and consultation to behavioural change being critical during the action and maintenance stages of the change process. Specific therapeutic approaches that research has shown to be uniquely effective with various types of problems are also described with particular reference to depression, anxiety, alcohol and drug abuse, schizophrenia, marital problems and child-focused difficulties. Research findings on the contribution of client and therapist characteristics to therapy outcome are summarized. Work on the impact of therapy duration on outcome is also considered along with factors that contribute to deterioration. Finally, knowledge claims that may be made about the findings of psychotherapy research are considered.

THREE TYPES OF QUESTIONS
Questions about research on psychotherapy may be divided into three categories:

- Methodological questions like *What methods may be used to find reliable answers to questions about if and how psychotherapy works?*
- Substantive questions like *Does psychotherapy work and if so how does it work?*
- Philosophical questions like *What knowledge claims may be made for the results of psychotherapy research?*

In this paper questions in each of these categories will be posed and some answers offered. The answers to these questions are of interest to a variety of stakeholders in the wider system of psychotherapy service development and practice. These include clients, therapists, psychotherapy trainers and supervisors, psychotherapy researchers and those involved with the development of health and social services in the public and private sectors.

METHODOLOGICAL QUESTIONS
A broad distinction may be made between psychotherapy *outcome studies* which aim to determine if therapy works and *process studies* where the central question is the way in which psychotherapy works (Kazdin, 1994; Beutler & Crago, 1991; Barker, Pistrang, & Elliott, 1995).

Outcome studies
In a typical psychotherapy outcome study, clients with similar problems are randomly assigned to two groups. Clients in the first group receive treatment and those in the second group do not. Before and after the first group receive treatment clients' problems are assessed using reliable and valid measures of client problems. Six months or a year following the end of treatment clients complete a follow-up assessment. If the treatment group show a greater reduction in problems over the course of therapy in comparison with the control group, it may be concluded that the gains were due to treatment rather than to the passage of time, and if these gains are sustained at six months or a year follow-up, it may be concluded that the therapy led to lasting benefits. The change in average levels of symptoms before and after treatment may be compared, and the statistical significance of this improvement determined. However, often such statistically significant improvement is of little clinical significance. Many researchers therefore also report the number of cases that showed clinically significant improvement. This basic design is the cornerstone of all psychotherapy outcome research and all other designs are refinements or modifications of it. A diagram of this design is presented in Figure 19.1.

Figure 19.1. Basic two group design for a treatment outcome study

PRE-THERAPY ASSESSMENT	PRE-THERAPY ASSESSMENT
TREATMENT GROUP	CONTROL GROUP
POST-THERAPY ASSESSMENT	POST-THERAPY ASSESSMENT
6 MONTH OR 1 YEAR FOLLOW-UP PERIOD	6 MONTH OR 1 YEAR FOLLOW-UP PERIOD
FOLLOW-UP ASSESSMENT	FOLLOW-UP ASSESSMENT

Refinements that increase the confidence with which conclusions may be drawn from such studies deserve mention. First, the homogeneity of the client groups may be enhanced by using explicit inclusion and exclusion criteria and widely accepted diagnostic systems such as the DSM-IV (APA, 1994). For example, in most outcome studies of cognitive behaviour therapy, cases with brain damage are excluded and all included cases meet the DSM IV diagnostic criteria for major depression. Second, specific measures of clients problems such as clearly defined individualised therapy goals in addition to general measures of client functioning such as the SCL-90 (Derogatis, 1983) are used to permit specific and general improvement to be assessed. Third, to prevent therapists' expectations and biases from influencing the results of the assessments, the evaluation of clients' problems and symptoms may be carried out by someone other than the therapist who is unaware of whether or not the client is in the treatment or control group. Fourth, to insure treatment integrity and purity, the precise nature of the therapy offered may be specified in a therapy manual and audiotapes of therapy checked by an independent researcher to determine the degree to which the therapist offered the type of therapy being tested in the study. For example, if a therapist is participating in a study of family therapy, a manual such as *Positive Practice: A Step-by-Step Guide to Family Therapy* (Carr, 1995) may be used and audiotapes of therapists' sessions checked against a list of therapist and client activities such as maintaining a focus on interactional aspects of the problem, permitting all family members to contribute to the session and so forth.

The basic two group outcome design may be modified to answer questions other than whether cases receiving therapy improve more than those who do not. One important question is the degree to which improvements shown by a therapy group are due to some specific technical aspect of the therapy, over and above visiting a therapist and talking to him or her. To answer this question, an attention-placebo control group may be used. Here, clients attend a therapist who allows them to an opportunity to discuss their problems or other issues but does not actively engage them in therapy. Where clients in therapy groups have better outcomes than clients in attention placebo groups, it may be concluded, that some specific technical aspect of the therapy, over and above visiting a therapist and talking to him or her, led to improvement. Where the central question is which of two or more therapies are more effective for a particular problem, cases may be randomly assigned to two or treatment groups and their outcomes compared. In other instances, the question may be with which of two or more problems is a particular treatment effective. Here, groups of cases with different problems may be offered the same therapy and their outcomes compared.

Process studies

While outcome studies are concerned with the overall effectiveness of therapy, process studies are concerned with identifying features of the client, the therapist and the interaction between clients and therapists that contribute to positive changes within therapy sessions, between therapy sessions and improvement at the end of therapy (Kazdin, 1994; Beutler & Crago, 1991; Barker, Pistrang, & Elliott, 1995). In many of these studies, therapist characteristics (such as age, gender and so forth); client characteristics, and therapist-client interactions (such as provision of warmth, empathy and so forth); and structural features of the sessions such as the duration of therapy are assessed and correlated with positive changes in the clients' adjustment within sessions, after sessions or at the end of therapy. Traditional descriptive case study methods are typically used to generate hypotheses about important psychotherapy processes which are subsequently tested in quantitative or qualitative process studies.

Meta-analysis
Thousands of psychotherapy process and outcome studies have been conducted. Meta-analysis is a quantitative method for synthesizing the results of these many studies (Cooper & Hedges, 1994). In its simplest form, meta-analysis involves obtaining an average improvement rate from a large number of studies. Smith, Glass and Miller (1980) conducted the first major meta-analysis of psychotherapy outcome studies and concluded that broadly speaking a person receiving psychotherapy was better off than 80% of those in control groups who did not receive therapy. There have been many criticisms of meta-analysis, the most important of which is that only similar studies using similar client groups, similar treatments and similar measures should be combined in meta-analyses.

Methodology problems
Current psychotherapy studies are very sophisticated (Beutler & Crago, 1991). In most good studies, cases with specific diagnoses are randomly assigned to groups, independent assessors are used and manualized therapies are employed. However, in the US where most research is done, recruited rather than referred patients are treated often by inexperienced therapists in university rather than community based clinics in typical psychotherapy research studies (e.g. Weisz & Weiss, 1993). These factors may limit the generalizability of results to community settings. A second major problem is that the results of psychotherapy research are rarely translated into user-friendly terms and disseminated to therapists or those involved in service development.

SUBSTANTIVE QUESTIONS
Among the many important substantive questions, to which the psychotherapy research literature offers some answers are the following:
- Does psychotherapy work?
- What factors contribute to therapeutic change?
- What factors common to all forms of therapy are appropriate at various stages of the change process?
- What factors or techniques specific to particular types of therapy are appropriate for particular problems?
- What impact do client or therapist characteristics have on therapy outcome?

- What impact does the duration of therapy have on therapy outcome?
- Can psychotherapy be harmful?

In subsequent sections tentative answers to these questions will be offered based on the psychotherapy research literature much of which has been reviewed and summarized in the following sources: Bergin & Garfield, 1994; Beutler & Crago, 1991; Pinsof & Wynne, 1995; Weisz & Weiss, 1993; Giles, 1993; Norcross & Goldfried, 1992.

Effectiveness of psychotherapy
Results of meta-analyses show that a person receiving psychotherapy shows greater improvement in presenting problems at the end of therapy than 80% of the cases in control groups who received no treatment and about 66% of adults presenting for outpatient psychotherapy benefit from the experience (whereas only about 34% of those in waiting list control groups show some improvement) (Lambert & Bergin, 1994). In most of the hundreds of studies underpinning these conclusions the principal problems were anxiety, depression or interpersonal difficulties and the principal treatment techniques were therapies arising from the cognitive-behavioural, psychodynamic, humanistic and family therapy traditions. There is a growing body of evidence which suggests that a majority of clients maintain treatment gains at follow-up. However, relapse rates are high for particular problems such as alcohol and drug abuse or recurrent episodic depression (Lambert & Bergin 1994).

These broad conclusions, while widely accepted by psychotherapy researchers of various theoretical orientations, continue to be disputed by a minority of scientists, notably Eysenck, who first argued that there was no difference between improvement due to psychotherapy and improvements due to spontaneous remission over 40 years ago (Eysenck, 1952). The interested reader may wish to consult Eysenck's 1993 paper for an update on his position.

Common factors that contribute to therapeutic change
From Figure 19.2, which is adapted from Lambert's (1992) literature review, it may be seen that 40% of change during therapy may be attributed to factors outside treatment and the remainder to features of the therapy situation. While specific therapeutic techniques (such as graded exposure to feared situations) and clients' expectations of improvement each account for about 15% of change, non-specific therapeutic factors are by far the most important determinants of therapeutic change and these account for about 30% of improvement during therapy.

Figure 19.2. Factors which contribute to the improvement of clients during psychotherapy.

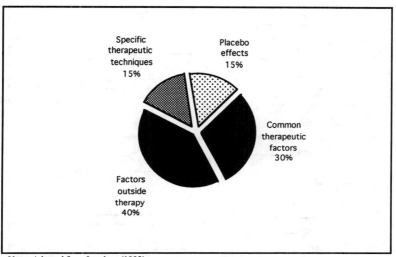

Note: Adapted from Lambert (1992).

These non-specific factors fall into three broad clusters:
- provision of social support
- facilitating exploration of belief systems about the problem and its impact
- consulting to behavioural change

With respect to the provision of emotional support, it has been found that the quality of the therapeutic alliance, in particular accurate empathy, respect, warmth, genuineness and a collaborative approach are positively related to outcome (Orlinsky, Grawe & Parks, 1994). With respect to belief system exploration, the following specific factors have been found to be associated with a positive outcome: clients' openness; clients' level of affective experiencing within therapy; clients' insight experiences within therapy; clients' exploration of life problems and significant relationships within therapy; therapists' confrontation of inconsistencies in clients' accounts and experiences and therapists' interpretation of clients' accounts (Orlinsky, Grawe & Parks, 1994). Therapists' encouraging exposure to feared intrapsychic material or external situations; therapist modelling of adaptive behaviour; and therapists giving corrective feedback on practice are the features of consulting to behavioural change that have been found to be associated with positive outcome across a range of therapeutic models (Orlinsky, Grawe & Parks, 1994; Lambert, 1992).

Figure 19.3. Common therapeutic factors which facilitate movement through the stages of change

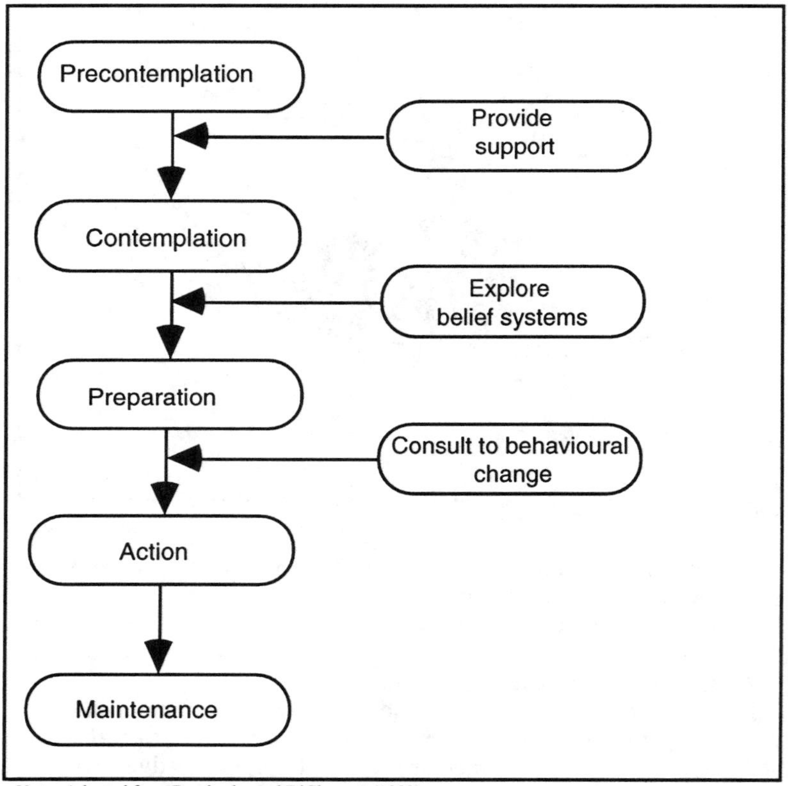

Note: Adapted from Prochaska and DiClement (1992).

Common factors and the stages of therapy

Prochaska and DiClement (1992), from an analysis of 24 schools of therapy, identified five stages of therapeutic change. These were: pre-contemplation, contemplation, preparation, action and maintenance. They also found by surveying clients and therapists engaged in therapy, that specific techniques were maximally effective in helping clients make the transition from one stage of change to the next in the manner set out in Figure 19.3. The list of a dozen techniques identified by Prochaska and DiClement fall into the categories of support, belief exploration and consulting to behavioural change which have been mentioned in the previous section. In the precontemplation stage, the provision of support by the therapist provides a climate within which clients may ventilate their feelings and express their views about their problem or life situation. Such support may help clients move from the pre-contemplation phase to the contemplation phase. By facilitating an exploration of belief systems about the evolution of the problem and its impact on the client's life, in addition to providing support, the therapist may help the client move from the contemplation to the planning stage. In the transition from planning to action, the most helpful role for the therapist to adopt is that of consultant to the clients' attempts at problem solving. In addition to providing support and an opportunity to explore belief systems, the therapist helps clients examine various action plans that may help disrupt destructive behavioural patterns. The therapist also facilitates the development of an emotional commitment to change. This role of consultant to the clients' attempts at behavioural change is also an appropriate for therapists to adopt in the transition from the action phase to the maintenance phase where the central concern of the client is relapse prevention. Prochaska and DiClement (1992) noted that different schools of therapy place particular emphasis on one or more of these common change processes, but most schools of therapy have something to say about each and in practice therapists tend to move through a progression from support to belief-system exploration to behavioural change consultation with their clients.

Specific factors
In Figure 19.2, it was noted that while 30% of client change may be attributed to common factors, 15% may be attributed to specific factors: that is, to particular therapeutic techniques. A central idea within the psychotherapy integrationist movement is that modules which research has shown to be effective with particular problems may be incorporated in most forms of psychotherapy practice (Norcross & Goldfried, 1992). What follows is a summary of some of the more important research on specific therapeutic approaches that have been shown to be effective with particular presenting problems.

For depression, cognitive therapy or interpersonal therapy coupled with antidepressant medication have been shown to be more effective than other treatments (Hollon & Beck, 1994). Cognitive therapy helps patients to alter their mood by providing them with skills for changing their negative thinking style and weaken the link between negative thoughts and low mood. Interpersonal therapy aims to provide clients with the skills to understand and change those aspects of their relationships which maintain their negative moods. Both forms of psychotherapy are as effective as antidepressant medication in alleviating depressive symptoms but in conjunction with antidepressant medication are far more effective in preventing relapse than medication alone.

For anxiety that is associated with specific stimuli, various behavioural procedures where clients undergo controlled *exposure* to feared stimuli are maximally effective (Emmelkamp, 1994). These stimuli may be external (as in the case of agoraphobia) or internal (as in the case of trauma related memories). In vivo exposure for phobias is more effective than imaginal exposure and the longer the exposure and the more therapist support is provided the more effective the treatment tends to be. For obsessive compulsive disorders exposure to the stimuli that lead to anxiety (such as dirt) must be coupled with response prevention, so that the person learns to tolerate anxiety without engaging in compulsive rituals.

For alcohol and drug problems, the most effective treatment is a multimodal programme which includes the following elements: brief client-centred motivational counselling to reduce denial and facilitate treatment engagement; self-control training to help develop skills necessary to manage high risk situations where alcohol or drug abuse are probable; social skills and assertiveness training to help clients develop skills for making and maintaining supportive interpersonal relationships; and family therapy to enhance family communication and problem-solving skills and increase the rate at which the family reinforce the client for reducing drug and alcohol consumption (Hodgson, 1992; Edwards & Steinglass, 1995; Liddle & Dakof, 1995).

For schizophrenia, family education and therapy coupled with neuroleptic medication is the treatment most likely to reduce a pattern of chronic relapsing (Goldstein & Miklowitz, 1995). Florid positive symptoms may be controlled with neuroleptic medication. Family education should focus on the multifactorial nature of the disorder and the importance of stress reduction in the prevention of relapse . Family therapy should aim to help family members reduce their expression of negative or intrusive emotions towards the person with schizophrenia. This in turn will reduce the exposure of the client to unnecessary stress which might precipitate a relapse.

For marital problems, marital therapy in which communication and problem-solving skills training occurs, where behavioural exchange skills are learned; and in which couples gain insight into the factors that contribute to their marital difficulties is the most effective treatment (Bray & Jouriles, 1995). For psychosexual problems such as vaginismus or erectile dysfunction behavioural interventions designed specifically to reduce sexual anxiety coupled with marital therapy focusing on enhancing communication is the most effective intervention (Emmelkamp, 1994).

For child focused problems, particularly internalizing and externalizing behavioural problems individual work with the child coupled with family interventions which actively involve both parents and the child is treatment of choice (Estrada & Pinsof, 1995; Chamberlain & Rosicky, 1995). Effective family interventions aim to improve parent-child communication and provide parents with the skills to work together in supporting their children and consistently monitoring and explicitly discouraging antisocial behaviour while encouraging and rewarding prosocial behaviour.

Client and therapist characteristics
In addition to the common and specific factors in therapy, various characteristics of clients and therapists have an important bearing on outcome. Clients with more severe symptomatology and more comorbid diagnoses respond less well to therapy (Garfield, 1994). For both adults and children, clients from families where there is excessive criticism or overinvolvement or family problems are more likely to make poorer therapy gains and to relapse (Kavanagh, 1992). For married couples, marital conflict has a negative impact on therapy outcome for other problems such as depression or alcohol abuse (Alexander, Holtzworth-Munroe & Jameson, 1994). For children, parental mental health problems, parental discord, stress, and lack of parental support are all associated with poor outcome (Chamberlain & Rosicky, 1995).

A variety of demographic and psychological characteristics of therapists have been found to contribute to a positive therapeutic outcome (Beutler, Machado & Neufeldt, 1994). Where therapists are similar to clients in terms of age, gender and ethnicity, it is more likely that clients will stay in therapy rather than drop out. Where clients perceive therapists to have a high level of expertise, to be trustworthy and to be attractive, they are more likely to have a positive outcome following therapy. Where therapists and clients place similar value on wisdom and honesty a positive therapeutic outcome is more likely. In contrast if clients place less value on interpersonal intimacy in friendship than their therapists, greater therapeutic progress occurs and this often involves change in relationship related values. Interpreting these findings, Beutler et al (1994) argue that humanistic values (such as valuing wisdom and honesty) may lead clients to engage in therapy to solve problems associated with difficulties in making and maintaining psychologically intimate relationships and over the course of therapy there may be a convergence of therapist and client values in the relationship domain.

Therapist level of professional experience influences both the process and outcome of therapy in quite specific ways (Beutler, Machado & Neufeldt, 1994). In comparison with less experienced therapists, those with more experience tend to develop better working alliances; to help more of their clients reach more favourable outcomes; and to have fewer clients who deteriorate. Fewer clients drop out of therapy when their therapist is experienced, and more severely distressed clients make therapeutic gains with experienced compared with inexperienced therapists.

The use of detailed structured therapy manuals and adherence to the guidelines set out within the manuals is associated with positive outcome, although differing manualized therapies such as cognitive behaviour therapy or interpersonal therapy have been found in some studies to have similar effects (Beutler, Machado & Neufeldt, 1994). It seems to be that adherence to a coherent structured approach, rather than specific aspects of the approach that is important for a positive outcome.

Therapy duration and dropout
Within the psychodynamic tradition which has probably had the most widespread influence on our way of thinking about the therapy process, psychotherapy evolved into a long-tern intervention. However, surveys of outpatient clinic attenders shows that most adult and child clients attend for only 6-10 session for individual and family or marital therapy (Garfield, 1994; Carr 1991; Weiss & Weisz, 1993). This is not surprising given that by 8 sessions 50% of adult clients have shown improvement and by 26 sessions 75% have made significant gains (Lambert & Bergin, 1994). Thus, it is clear that earlier sessions (the first 8-10) make a major contribution to improvement and thereafter, each the contribution of each session to improvement decreases.

In order for clients to benefit from the critical first 8-10 sessions, they must be engaged in therapy. Not all clients engage in therapy with equal facility. Clients from lower socio-economic groups, with lower educational levels and inaccurate treatment expectations are more likely to drop out of therapy (Garfield, 1994). Clients who participate actively in early sessions by talking freely and clients who have a positive emotional response to the therapeutic situation are more likely to stay in therapy. Therapists can prevent dropout by explicitly stating what the client and therapist's roles entail, by giving a clear rationale for adopting these roles and by offering a brief a therapy contract for 8-10 sessions, which may be reviewed in the light of progress (Orlinsky, Grawe & Parks, 1994).

Harm caused by therapy
Approximately 10% of patients are harmed by therapy. Client characteristics, therapeutic techniques and therapist characteristics which contribute to deterioration have been identified (Lambert, 1994). Clients with diagnoses of borderline personality disorder or

schizophrenia are particularly susceptible to deterioration. For clients with these problems, deterioration is more likely to occur in therapy which focuses on breaking down habitual coping strategies and defenses. People with schizophrenia or borderline personality disorder tend to benefit from supportive structured approaches to therapy rather than approaches involving confrontation. Coldness, disrespect and lack of empathy on the part of the therapist have been shown consistently to lead to deterioration.

PHILOSOPHICAL QUESTIONS
Two main viewpoints concerning the knowledge claims that may be made about findings from research on psychotherapy may be identified (Gergen, 1994). These are the positivist position which argues that the accumulated results of studies lead to the development of a grand narrative which has universal truth; and the social constructionist position which argues that the findings of psychotherapy research projects provide no more than local knowledge shared by highly specific communities. Ken Gergen (1994) has persuasively argued that the latter position is probably the most tenable. Within the field of psychotherapy quantitative and qualitative, process and outcome research will not lead to a grand narrative about how change always occurs in therapy or which therapies will always lead to problem resolution. However, this type of research may lead to many useful conclusions about which types of therapies work with which types of clients in particular socio-cultural contexts. The more rigorous this research is, the more useful and the less ambiguous the local narratives will be. Evaluation of therapeutic change from multiple-perspectives including the views of clients, therapists referring agents and so forth is an important emphasis for such research. This is because it may throw light on how constructs such as improvement or deterioration are socially constructed by the community of people who are involved in the social venture we call psychotherapy. This community includes clients, therapists, insurance companies, service managers and so forth.

THE FUTURE
Psychotherapy outcome research provides useful information about the proportion of clients that benefit from therapy under particular circumstances. In Ireland today this information is critical in making a case for the development of a public psychotherapy service. Psychotherapy process research provides information about how therapy works. This information is of particular interest to practitioners who wish to refine their practice so that they may offer their clients the type of therapy that is most likely to lead to improvement.

Conducting large scale psychotherapy research projects,

requires funding and an extaordinary amount of co-ordination and co-operation among therapists, clients, researchers, and funding agents. In Ireland today, with the recognition that the majority of the people that consult their GP do so because of psychological problems (McKeown & Carrick , 1991); the recent publication of the first major book on psychotherapy in Ireland (Boyne, 1993); and the recent publication of the Psychotherapy Register, the climate is just about right for such work to blossom.

REFERENCES

Alexander, J., Holtzworth-Munroe, A., Jameson, P. (1994). The process and outcome of marital and family therapy. In A. Bergin & S. Garfield (eds.), *Handbook of Psychotherapy and Behaviour Change* (pp. 595-630). New York: Wiley.

American Psychiatric Association (1994) *DSM -IV* Washington, DC: APA.

Barker, C., Pistrang, N. & Elliott (1995). *Research Methods in Clinical and Counselling Psychology.* New York: Wiley.

Bergin, A. & Garfield, S. (1994). *Handbook of Psychotherapy and Behaviour Change.* New York. Wiley.

Beutler, L. & Crago, M. (1991). *Psychotherapy Research. An International Review of programmatic Studies.* Washington: American Psychological Association.

Beutler, L. Machado, P. & Neufeldt, S. (1994). Therapist variables. In A. Bergin & S. Garfield (eds.), *Handbook of Psychotherapy and Behaviour Change* (pp.229-269)New York. Wiley.

Boyne, E. (1993). *Psychotherapy in Ireland.* Dublin. Columba Press.

Bray, J. & Jouriles, E. (1995). Treatment of marital conflict and prevention of divorce. *Journal of Marital and Family Therapy* , 21, 461-473.

Carr, A. (1991). Milan Systemic Family Therapy: A review of 10 empirical investigations. *Journal of Family Therapy,* 13, 237-264.

Carr, A. (1995). *Positive Practice: A Step-by-Step-Guide to Family Therapy.* Reading, UK: Harwood.

Chamberlain, P. & Rosicky, J. (1995). The effectiveness of family therapy in the treatment of adolescents with conduct disorders and delinquency. *Journal of Marital and Family Therapy* , 21, 441-459.

Cooper, H. & Hedges, L. (1994). *The Handbook of Research Synthesis.* New York: Sage.

Derogatis, L. (1983). SCL-90. Scoring and Procedures Manual for the Revised Version. Baltimore: Clinical Psychometric Research.

Edwards, M. & Steinglass, P. (1995). Family therapy treatment outcomes for alcoholism. *Journal of Marital and Family Therapy,* 21, 475-509.

Emmelkamp, P. (1994). Behaviour therapy with adults. In A. Bergin & S. Garfield (eds.), *Handbook of Psychotherapy and Behaviour Change* (pp. 379-427). New York: Wiley.

Estrada, A., Pinsof, W. (1995). The effectiveness of family therapies for selected behavioural disorders of childhood. *Journal of Marital and Family Therapy* , 21, 403-440.

Eysenck, H. (1952). The effects of psychotherapy: An evaluation. *Journal of Consulting Psychology*, 16, 319-327.

Eysenck, H. (1993). Forty years on: The outcome problem in psychotherapy revisited. In R. Giles (ed.), *Handbook of Effective Psychotherapy* (pp. 3-20). New York: Plenum

Garfield, S. (1994). Research on client variables in psychotherapy. In A. Bergin & S. Garfield (eds.), *Handbook of Psychotherapy and Behaviour Change* (pp.190-228)New York. Wiley.

Gergen, K. (1994). *Realities and Relationships. Soundings in Social Constructionism.* Cambridge, MA: Harvard University Press.

Giles, R. (1993). *Handbook of Effective Psychotherapy* . New York: Plenum

Goldstein, M. & Miklowitz, D. (1995). The effectiveness of psychoeducational family therapy in the treatment of schizophrenic disorders. *Journal of Marital and Family Therapy*, 21, 361-376.

Hodgson, R. (1992). Alcohol dependence treatments: The Research and Policy connections. In British Psychological Society Division of Clinical Psychology (eds.), *On advising Purchasers. Part 2. Section 11. Reprints* (pp. 78-86). Leicester: BPsS.

Hollon, S. & Beck, A. (1994). Cognitive and cognitive behavioural approaches. In A. Bergin & S. Garfield (eds.), *Handbook of Psychotherapy and Behaviour Change* (pp. 595-630). New York: Wiley.

Kavanagh, D. (1992). Recent developments in expressed emotion and schizophrenia. *British Journal of Psychiatry,* 160, 601-620.

Kazdin, A. (1994). Methodology, design and evaluation in psychotherapy research. In A. Bergin & S. Garfield (eds.), *Handbook of Psychotherapy and Behaviour Change* (pp.19-71). New York. Wiley.

Lambert, M. & Bergin, A. (1994). The effectiveness of psychotherapy. In A. Bergin & S. Garfield (eds.), *Handbook of Psychotherapy and Behaviour Change* (pp.143-190). New York. Wiley.

Lambert, M. (1992). Psychotherapy outcome research: Implications for integrative and eclectic therapists. In J. Norcross & M. Goldfried (eds.). *Handbook of Psychotherapy Integration* (pp. 94-129). New York: Basic.

Liddle, H. & Dakoff, G. (1995). Efficacy of family therapy for drug abuse: Promising but not definitive. *Journal of Marital and Family Therapy*, 21, 511-543.

McKeown, P. & Carrick, S. (1991). Public attitudes to depression: A national survey. *Irish Journal of Psychological Medicine*, 8, 116-121.

Norcross, J. & Goldfried, M. (1992). *Handbook of Psychotherapy Integration* . New York: Basic.

Orlinsky, D., Grawe, K. & Parks, B. (1994). Process and outcome in psychotherapy - Noch Einmal. In A. Bergin & S. Garfield (eds.), *Handbook of Psychotherapy and Behaviour Change* (pp. 270-238.). New York: Wiley.

Pinsof, W. & Wynne, L (1995). *The effectiveness of Marital and Family Therapies. Journal of Marital and Family Therapy Volume 2. Special Edition.* Washington, DC: AAMFT.

Prochaska, J. & DiClement, C. (1992). The transtheoretical approach. In J. Norcross & M. Goldfried (eds.). *Handbook of Psychotherapy Integration* (pp. 300-334). New York: Basic.

Smith, M., Glass, G. & Miller, T. (1980). The Benefits of Psychotherapy. Baltimore: Johns Hopkins University Press.

Weisz, J. & Weiss, B. (1993) *Effects of Psychotherapy with Children and adolescents.* London: Sage.

Wells, R. & Gianetti, V. (1990). *Handbook of the Brief Psychotherapies.* New York: Plenum.

CHAPTER 20

FAMILY PSYCHOLOGY: THE EMERGENCE OF A NEW FIELD

ABSTRACT

Family psychology is a field of study that takes the family and not the individual as the basic unit of inquiry. In this paper the way in which developments in nine of areas of academic and clinical psychology, along with related developments in other social sciences and helping professions have contributed to the emergence of family psychology, are outlined. A preliminary attempt to define the field is made and some important landmarks in the historical development of family psychology are identified.

INTRODUCTION

Traditionally, introductory texts in both general psychology and many specialist subfields have entailed an unquestioning individualism. By that I mean that the authors of these texts have assumed that the individual is the primary unit of analysis. For example, general introductory texts such as Gleitman's (1981) include chapters on perception, cognition, learning, motivation and emotion. An account of each of these functions is given in individualistic terms and the role of family members are considered only insofar as they make unidirectional inputs at a genetic or environmental level to the individual's execution of these functions.

Introductory texts in the field of developmental psychology such as Mussen et al's (1990) have traditionally given great weight to individualistic stage-wise theories of cognitive or language development. Chapters on socialization, which address the child's development within a family context, have usually been accorded a relatively minor position within such texts.

Figure 20.1. Contributions from nine areas to family psychology.

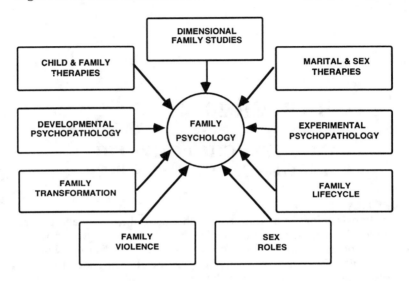

The same trend is present in North American social psychology where traditional texts focus on attitudes, social influence, behaviour in groups and so forth, as if the individual functioned independently of his or her immediate familial social context (Steiner, 1979). (It is worth mentioning, however, that European social psychology has avoided this rampant individualism (Hewstone et al., 1988).

Nowhere is the problem of unquestioning acceptance of individualism as an appropriate framework for inquiry more prevalent than in the field of abnormal psychology (e.g. Carson & Butcher, 1992). It is accepted without question that problems such as anxiety, depression conduct disorders and so forth are best conceptualised as intrinsically individual in aetiology and course. Granted, the role of family factors in the development of these disorders is given consideration. However, the conceptualisation of abnormal behaviour (following widely used classification systems such as DSM 111-R (APA, 1987) and ICD-10 (WHO, 1988) is fundamentally individualistic.

Family psychology has evolved as a reaction against the

intellectual and pragmatic constraints entailed by this uncompromising individualism. It is a new field. Officially, it was first recognised in the USA in the Mid 80's when Division 43, the Division of Family Psychology of the American Psychological Association was established and the first edition of Journal of Family Psychology was published. However, family psychology has a long history and is constituted by theory and research from a variety of areas within psychology as a whole. In this essay the way in which developments in the nine of areas of academic and clinical psychology noted in Figure 20.1 along with related development in other social sciences and helping professions have contributed to the emergence of family psychology will be outlined. Some important landmarks in the historical development of family psychology will be identified. Directions that future research in family psychology may take will also be mentioned.

ABNORMAL PSYCHOLOGY AND EXPERIMENTAL PSYCHOPATHOLOGY

The rigorous study of family interaction and communication within a laboratory setting began with early investigations of individuals with a diagnosis of schizophrenia. Three noteworthy research programmes in the US aimed to uncover the social origins of psychosis. They spawned the Double Bind Theory (Bateson et al., 1956), the concept of Communication Deviance (Singer & Wynne, 1965) and the marital schism/marital skew models of family functioning (Lidz et al., 1957). Bateson's (1956) double bind theory entailed the view that when children were given a primary injunction to act in one way, and a secondary covert injunction to act in a contradictory manner, they would behave bizarrely if they were prohibited from commenting on this conflict or leaving the field. The laboratory-based observation that communication in the families of schizophrenics resembled the thought disorder which typified psychotic individuals led Singer and Wynne(1965) to argue that this disjointed and unclear communication in families of schizophrenics caused the disorder.

Focusing less on family process and more on structural characteristics of families, Lidz et al. (1957) classified the marital relationships of parents of individuals with schizophrenia as being characterized by a schism or a skew. Skewed marriages were dominated by one parent with the other colluding in what was often a bizarre world view. A marital schism on the other hand occurred when parents continued to cohabit despite a deep hostile ongoing conflict. These marital styles were posited to have an etiological role in cases of schizophrenia.

The exploration of the role of the family in schizophrenia and other major psychological problems lost favour during the 1960's while researchers and funding agencies concentrated their efforts on genetic and drug treatment studies. This was largely due to the apparent efficacy of the phenothiazines as a treatment for schizophrenia and the failure of the early crossectional family studies to yield substantial evidence of important differences between the families of schizophrenics and the families of individuals without this diagnosis. However, in the 70's it became apparent that the phenothiazines do not offer a permanent solution to the problem of schizophrenia and more than a third of cases on medication relapse. The possibility that family factors played a role in relapse required exploration. It also became clear from genetic studies that the role of heredity in the aetiology of schizophrenia was complex and that gene-environment interactions probably offered the most coherent avenue for understanding aetiology of this disorder (Goldstein & Strachan, 1987)

          These events of the 70's led to two very important lines of research focusing on the role of the family in the aetiology and course of schizophrenia respectively. Both lines of research used longitudinal designs and reliable and valid indices of family interaction. Vaughan and Leff (1976) found that the relapse rate for schizophrenics stabilized on phenothiazines depended upon the quality of relationships that the schizophrenics had with other family members and the amount of time they spent with them. Schizophrenics who lived in families where other family members were excessively critical towards them or who became emotionally overinvolved with them were more likely to relapse, especially if they had more than 35 hours contact per week. Tienari et al (1985) in the Finnish adoption study compared the prevalence of schizophrenia in children of schizophrenic mothers and normal mothers adopted away into families with varying levels of dysfunction. They found that children of schizophrenic mothers although genetically vulnerable to schizophrenia, did not develop the disorder if they were adopted away into families who functioned at or above the normal range on well standardized family health scales (Beavers & Hampson, 1990). A small proportion of children of normal parents adopted away into extremely dysfunctional families, on the other hand, did develop schizophrenia.

          Tienari et al.'s (1985) and Vaughan and Leff's (1976) data suggest family psychology has an important role to play in building models to account for the aetiology and course of psychological problems. However, these models must be broad enough to account for the interaction between family interactional variables and genetic factors. Such models are currently being articulated by researchers exploring a variety of psychological difficulties including delinquency, alcohol abuse and depression (Jacob, 1987). The most important application of this type of family psychology is the modification of patterns of family interaction associated with the aetiology and course of psychological disorders. Ian Falloon's (1985) project is an outstanding example of this type of work. He showed that high levels of criticism and overinvolvement may be reduced through behavioural family therapy and that this is associated with a reduction in medication usage and risk of relapse.

DEVELOPMENTAL PSYCHOLOGY & PSYCHOPATHOLOGY
Within mainstream developmental psychology the study of mother-child attachment (Bretherton & Waters, 1985) parenting style (Maccoby & Martin, 1983), the role of fathers in child care (Lamb et al., 1987), and the social ecology of the child's environment (Bronfenbrenner, 1986) have all contributed to the emergence of a body of theory and research which is now being integrated into a family systems psychology of child development in both the UK (White & Woollett, 1992) and the US (Ford & Lerner, 1992). A number of broad generalizations may now be made which sketch the outline of this developmental family systems psychology.

The type of attachment that a child forms with its primary caretaker early in life, be it secure or anxious, has an impact on later development with secure attachment being associated with better adjustment in later life (Bretherton & Waters, 1985). Mother's childhood experiences of parent-child attachment probably serve as a template for their attachments to their own children (Grossman et al., 1988; Fonagy et al., 1991). Patterns of attachment are also influenced by the amount of stress in the caretaker's environment and the available level of social support (Teti et al., 1991). Influence in parent-child relationships is bidirectional and parents are more likely to develop favourable relationships with children who have easy rather than difficult temperaments (Belsky et al, 1986,1987) . That is, children who respond with a positive mood or in a predictable way with a moderate level of intensity to new situations and who maintain regular patterns of feeding and sleeping.

Beyond infancy, the ways in which parents relate to their children appear to vary on the two orthogonal dimensions of warmth and control (e.g. Herbert, 1991, p.91). Reviews of the extensive literature on parenting suggest that by combining these two dimensions of warmth and control, four parenting styles may be identified and each of these is associated with particular developmental outcomes for the child (Baumrind, 1982; Herbert, 1991; Maccoby & Martin, 1983; White & Woollett, 1992). First, authoritative parents who adopt a warm child-centred approach coupled with a moderate degree of control which allows children to take age-appropriate responsibility provide a context which is maximally beneficial for children's development as autonomous confident individuals. Second, children who grow up with authoritarian parents who are warm but controlling tend to develop into shy adults who are reluctant to take initiative. Those that grow up with permissive parents who are warm but lax in discipline in later life lack the competence to follow through on plans and show poor impulse control. Children who have experienced little warmth from their parents and who have been either harshly disciplined or had little supervision develop adjustment problems.

In our culture, the greater the quantity and quality of time the father spends with children the better the overall adjustment of children is in the long term. Children from families with high levels of father involvement show greater instrumental and interpersonal competence and higher self esteem (Lamb et al., 1987).

Increased father involvement, the use of an authoritative parental style and the provision of a secure attachment relationship in early life are facilitated by the presence of a good marital relationship and supportive relationships between family members and the wider social network within which the family is embedded (Belsky et al., 1984). The degree to which parents can provide an optimal social environment for their children may be compromised by psychological disturbance in either parent and family or work related stress (Werner, 1985)

The approach to family psychology illustrated by the findings reviewed here holds promise for building up complex multifactorial models of how children develop within a family context and the complex patterns of mutual influence that underpin this developmental process.

CHILD AND FAMILY THERAPIES

The child guidance movement in the US the UK and Ireland was based on a multidisciplinary model of practice where the psychologist assessed the child and furnished the psychiatrist with the results as an aid to individual psychodynamically oriented child therapy. Concurrently, the social worker assessed the mother's capacity to meet the child's physical and psychological needs and offered counselling where deficiencies were noted. Only occasionally were father's involved in the consultation process.

The exclusion of fathers from successful individual child therapy and maternal counselling therapy in some cases led to a deterioration in their functioning. Two other important observations were also being widely made round about 1950. First, that in many cases marital difficulties accompanied childhood psychological problems and second that in many cases where fathers were uninvolved in the consultation process therapeutic gains were not made. These factors together underlined the need for an approach to practice and a theory that addressed the interconnectedness of family members (Broderick & Schrader, 1991).

Over the decade from 1950 to 1960 family therapy evolved as one solution to these two problems. A surprising feature of family therapy is that it emerged in many places at the same time with little communication between various pioneers. For example in 1949, John Bowlby at the Tavistock, breaking all the rules of his psychoanalytic training, conducted a series of interviews with the family of a difficult adolescent who had not responded to two years of weekly individual therapy which resulted in a dramatic therapeutic breakthrough (Bowlby, 1949). Concurrently Gregory Bateson assembled the famous Palo Alto group which included Haley, Weakland and Jackson and they began a series of studies of paradox which included a therapy programme with the families of schizophrenics and which led to the development of the famous double-bind hypothesis mentioned above (Bateson et al., 1956). Jackson, a member of the Palo Alto group was co-founder with Nathan Ackerman, a New York based psychoanalytic family therapist, of *Family Process* in 1961. This continues to be the key American organ of the family therapy movement. The major UK based *Journal of Family Therapy* was not developed until 1970.

In the 60's and 70's family therapy in both the US and the UK involved conjoint family interviews as a method of practice and systems theory as an over-arching conceptual framework. In particular the following ideas were imported into family therapy from General Systems Theory as articulated by von Bertalanffy (1968) and Buckley (1968) (Guttman, 1991). First, the family system is more than the sum of the attributes of its individual members. The rule-governed patterns of communication and interaction between members are central to an understanding of family members' health or pathology. Second, relatively stable homeostatic patterns of interaction develop within families to preserve the family's integrity. These are recognizable in healthy families as the organized routines carried out to meet family members' needs for survival, education, belongingness, independence and so forth. Third, when an individual is referred for treatment, often his or her symptomatic behaviour is embedded in homeostatic, change-resistant, patterns of family interaction. A typical example of this is a depressed woman whose condition is in part maintained by her husband and daughter's continual futile attempts to cheer her up. Fourth, as open systems, families are capable of change or morphogenesis. The routines that families develop for dealing with new information, new people or new circumstances subserve the process of morphogenesis. Fifth, where families have poorly developed routines for morphogenesis, they may have difficulty adjusting to the tasks associated with family development and also with benefiting from therapy by dealing usefully with new information provided within a therapeutic context. Sixth, where families have overly developed routines for morphogenesis, the integrity of the family may continually be threatened by members' attempts to change the family structure of the way the family functions on a day to day basis. Seventh, the process of therapy involves joining the family system, mapping out the homeostatic and morphogenic routines that characterize it (notably those in which the presenting problem is embedded) and facilitating change in these routines so that the presenting problem is resolved and the family system evolves a healthy balance between homeostatic and morphogenic routines.

While this core set of ideas was shared by most family therapists, subgroups of professionals led by charismatic clinicians developed variations on the core ideas. Schools of systemic, structural, strategic, functional, problem-solving, psychodynamic, contextual and symbolic-experiential family therapy emerged and are detailed in Alan Gurman and David Kniskern's (1981,1991) *Handbook of Family Therapy,* Volumes 1 & 2. These volumes are an important contribution to the emerging field of family psychology.

During the 50's and early 60's the application of behaviour therapy and behaviour modification to children's problems became widespread (Falloon, 1988). Therapists trained parents to conduct home based behavioural programmes. Practice involved conjoint family interviews, parent and child interviews and detailed observational assessment. Gerry Patterson (1982), the most outstanding contributor to this field, found that factors such as parental mental health, marital discord and social isolation compromised the efficiency with which parents could be trained to implement behavioural programmes. He also noted that while parents tried to implement programmes, aggressive children tried to shape parental behaviour to ensure that the programmes would fail. His detailed analysis of behaviour in families with aggressive boys led him to develop a complex model of family functioning based on both systems theory and social learning theory. His landmark publication summarizing work from this period was *Coercive Family Process*. The application of social learning theory to a variety of child and family problems followed the trail blazed by Patterson. These are characterized by the functional analysis of presenting problem and the patterns of family interaction in which they are embedded, the development of specific intervention programmes for specific problems, the involvement of family members in the implementation of these programmes and a commitment to methodologically rigorous treatment evaluation. The *Journal of Child and Family Behaviour Therapy* provides an outlet for these developments. Ian Faloon's (1988) *Handbook of Behavioural Family Therapy* contains a good summary of the current status of the field.

As the fields of behavioural and non-behavioural family therapy have matured, process and outcome research in this area has proliferated (Carr, 1991). Extant reviews indicate that for a variety of child, adult and family problems, brief family therapy leads to symptomatic improvement in two thirds to three quarters of cases and to adaptive family changes in 50% of cases. These changes are maintained over time. In contrast, there is some evidence that families of conduct disordered children who participate in individual therapy deteriorate following their children's treatment(Szapocznik et al., 1989). Also there is evidence that late teenage anorexics benefit more from individual than from family therapy (Russell et al, 1987). The challenge for family psychology is to begin a systematic exploration of the therapeutic processes that give rise to these global findings.

MARITAL AND SEX THERAPIES
The marriage guidance and counselling movement developed in the US in the 30's 40's and in the UK in the 50's using a predominantly psychodynamic framework in a climate where mainstream psychoanalysis frowned on both conjoint marital therapy and simultaneous analysis of both members of couple by the same therapist (Broderick & Schrader, 1991). The major contribution of this movement in the US to family psychology was the *Journal of Marriage and Family Therapy* which was named in 1979 and evolved from the *Journal of Marital and Family Counselling.* This is now, along with the journal *Family Process* one of the most prestigious American journals in the field.

In the UK a landmark work in the development of marital therapy was Dicks (1967) *Marital Tensions* . This book describes pioneering work in marital therapy based on object relations theory which was developed at the Tavistock in the 1950's. A central theme of this work is that marital dissatisfaction occurs when couples maintain unresolved transference relationships with each other. Marital harmony depends upon couples recognizing that the version of their partner that they fell in love with was largely a projection based on a model of their relationship with their primary caretaker early in life. Marital satisfaction requires that couples discard this mutual projective system and accept each others actual strengths and limitations. If this does not occur, marital partners will continue to respond to each other as if they were responding to the negative aspect of their primary caretaker that frustrated them during their earliest months of life.

In a manner similar to family therapy, many marital therapists on both sides of the Atlantic adopted the practice of conjoint interviewing and looked to systems theory as a conceptual framework for organizing their work. Of course, there were variations on this central theme.   Both psychodynamic and behaviourally oriented models emerged as the main variants with the behavioural model, based on social learning theory, generating more research and better quality empirical research than the rest of the field.

While marital therapy was evolving from the marriage guidance movement, sex therapy was evolving from the scientific study of the human sexual response by Master's and Johnson (1966, 1970). The team began their work in the mid 50s and were given confidence by the acceptability of Alfred Kinsey's survey research on sexual practices (Kinsey et al., 1948;1953). The sex therapy movement made two very important discoveries (Mason, 1991). First, many sexual difficulties such as premature ejaculation, impotence, disparunia and anorgasmia may have a profoundly negative effect on an otherwise viable marriage. In such cases if sexual difficulties are treated with brief behaviourally oriented therapy in a majority of cases the sexual difficulties resolve with a consequent positive effect on the overall relationship.   The second discovery of the sex therapy movement was that some sexual difficulties are a symptom of serious relationship difficulties. In such cases, brief behaviourally oriented treatment of the sexual difficulty will be of little value unless coupled with marital therapy . The sex therapy and marital therapy movements have now begun to merge with an acceptance that marital distress and sexual difficulties in many instances are inextricably linked. An important journal this field, reflecting the integration of marital and sex therapy is the *Journal of Sex and Marital Therapy.*

As marital and sex therapy has evolved two related research trends have emerged. On the one hand there are studies of therapy process and outcome. On the other there is the investigation of the characteristics of intimate relationships and an exploration of the difference between distressed and non-distressed couples. Interestingly, the results of this empirical research on distressed couples, outlined below, is consistent with the clinical insights of the early psychoanalytic investigations.

Research on differences between distressed and non-distressed couples is well summarized by Holtzworth-Munroe & Jacobson (1991) and allows the following broad conclusions to be drawn. Distressed couples tend to selectively attend to their partners negative behaviour and to operate on a short-term quid pro quo basis whereas non-distressed couples tend to operate on long term good will. Distressed couples tend to control each other through punishment whereas non-distressed couples tend to control each other less and when they do use positive reinforcement. Distressed couples tend to avoid each other as a way of managing conflict rather than negotiating a solution. Negotiating a solution is more aversive in the short term (particularly for men who experience far higher physiological arousal levels during verbal conflict than women) but in the long term this approach to conflict resolution leads to greater marital satisfaction than withdrawal. These behavioural patterns associated with marital distress appear to occur because distressed couples tend to employ a negative attributional style whereby they attribute global, stable negative intentions to their partners. Many of the apparently diverse disagreements in which distressed couples engage appear to cluster around a core conflict over the desired level of intimacy. Usually husbands are demanding greater psychological distance and wives greater psychological intimacy. These positions reflect distressed husbands' wishes to retain the power and benefits of traditional gender roles and the distressed wives' wishes to evolve more egalitarian marriages. It is therefore not surprising that husbands are less likely to seek marital therapy and that when distressed couples participate in therapy only 50-60% can benefit (Gurman & Kniskern, 1978). A continuing project for family psychologists in this field is the identification of factors that distinguish successful from unsuccessful cases.

FAMILY VIOLENCE

Major surveys in the USA have shown that marital violence or physical child abuse occurs in about one in ten families (Gelles, 1987). Preliminary investigations into various forms of family violence fell into three categories. One research strategy aimed to identify the unique psychological characteristics of the perpetrators. These studies provided psychological or psychiatric profiles of violent husbands or abusive parents (e.g. Wolfe, 1985; Roy, 1982) . A second group of studies focused on unique attributes of the victims. Psychological, psychiatric and medical characteristics which rendered women and children vulnerable to abuse within the family were sought in these investigations (e.g. Herrenkohl et al., 1979; Hilberman & Munson, 1978). A third research strategy was to document the broader social context within which family violence occurred (e.g. Straus & Gelles, 1986). These psychosocial studies profiled the stresses and supports that impinged on families where marital or child abuse occurred. In hindsight it is easy to recognise that all three approaches have limitations and that a coherent investigative framework must take account of the characteristics of the victim, the perpetrator, the relationship between these two and other family members and the broader social context within which the family is embedded. Such multidimensional systemic frameworks are now commonplace in research on family violence (Cicchetti & Carlson, 1989; Gelles &

Loseke, 1993). As illustrative examples of such frameworks Niel Frude's (1990) model of marital violence and Jay Belsky's (Belsky & Vondra, 1987) model of physical child abuse will be described in some detail.

Niel Frude (1990) following an extensive literature review has integrated extant empirical research on marital violence into the following model. High levels of stress and low levels of social support place couples at risk for marital violence. Social isolation, unemployment, poverty, or major life transitions such as the birth of a child or caring for an aged relative are some of the factors that more commonly lead distressed couples to escalate from verbal abuse to marital violence . The risk of marital violence is potentiated by a number of cognitive factors, notably beliefs which violent husband's hold. These include the view that physically threatening or aggressive strategies are the most appropriate ways to solve interpersonal problems. Often this belief in aggression as problem solving strategy has its roots in early socialization experiences where violent marital partners witnessed marital violence or experienced child abuse as children. Such beliefs inhibit the development of other conflict management strategies such as negotiation. Beliefs underpinning low self esteem also contribute to male marital violence. In particular men who believe that their own socio-economic status is below that of their wife's and who take this as an indication of personal inadequacy or those that view sexual performance problems as a reflection of personal inadequacy are more likely to abuse their wives. Finally, beliefs such as these are more likely to lead to violence when inhibitions against aggression have been dulled by alcohol or by the presence of an impulse control disorder such as borderline or antisocial personality disorder. Frude's model of marital violence comprehensively integrates findings from social, cognitive, situational and psychiatric studies spouse abuse and offers a framework for further integrative research.

A further example of a framework for comprehending another form of family violence is Jay Belsky's model of physical child abuse (Belsky & Vondra, 1987). The model integrates empirical research findings (sell summarized in Belsky & Vondra, 1987) from a wide variety a variety of aspects of this form of family violence. Situational factors lie at the heart of the model. Non-accidental injuries occur, according to this model, following an escalating spiral of negative interaction between parent and child. Children who place special demands on their parents, especially those with a history of prematurity, illness, low birthweight or difficult temperament are particularly at risk for becoming involved in such patterns of interaction. Parents are at risk for involvement in such escalating spirals of negative interaction if they have developed particular belief systems or cognitive styles:

specifically, those which lead them to view corporal punishment as a regular means for imposing discipline, those which lead them to expect more self-control from the child than is age appropriate and also those which lead them to attribute global, stable negative intentions to the child when he or she places caregiving demands upon the parent. Such belief-systems and cognitive styles are more common among parents who themselves have been abused as children, who come from chaotic families and who have low levels of educational attainment. These belief-systems and cognitive styles are more likely to lead to violence when parents face high levels of life stress and have low levels of social support. Anger and arousal associated with the high levels of stress in the absence of support may be displaced onto the child. Low levels of support and high levels of stress are typically due to such factors as marital discord, social isolation, cramped housing conditions, poverty , unemployment and the management of major life events such as the birth of a child.

The family psychology of violence and abuse is now widening the aperture of its lens to focus on the positive and negative impact of state intervention in detected cases. The overriding question is how may the state intervene in families in a way that offers the child maximal protection and opportunities for growth, healing and a satisfying family life while minimizing further abuse within the family and at the hands of the state's judicial procedures.

DIMENSIONAL STUDIES OF FAMILIES

The marital and family therapies along with experimental studies of child and adult psychopathology have led to the articulation of cross-sectional dimensional models of family functioning and developmental models of the family lifecycle.

Dimensional studies of families have set as their goal the identification of significant dimensions or continua along which families may be classified. In many respects the search for dimensions of family functioning that can be validly and reliably assessed parallels the project undertaken by Eysenck (1990), Cattell (1990) and other personality theorists who adopted a trait model as an avenue to account for individual differences between people (rather than families).

Numerous methods for classifying families have been developed (McCubbin & McCubbin, 1988). Three frameworks are currently very prominent. These are the McMaster Model (Epstein & Bishop, 1981), Olson's Circumplex model (Olson et al, 1989) and the Beaver's Timeberlawn Model (Beavers & Hampson, 1990). While there are differences between these models, they are outweighed by their similarities. All three models contain both an instrumental or task oriented dimension and an affective dimension which reflects the degree of emotional cohesion within the family. Reliable self-report questionnaires and observational rating scales have been developed to assess a family's status with respect to each of the three models. Studies exploring the validity of these models will be a key task for family psychology in the coming decade. One such study which investigates the sensitivity and specificity of the three models mentioned here is currently in progress in UCD (Drumm, Carr & Fitzgerald, 1993).

A further important question which may be addressed by researches using dimensional models is the extent to which particular family structures are associated with particular individual diagnostic categories, particular prognoses or therapeutic response patterns. In short the task is to answer the structuralist's question: what types of dysfunctional social systems lead to psychological difficulties for members of that system and how may these be changed?

THE FAMILY LIFE CYCLE
If dimensional models of family functioning have looked to trait theory as a methodological forerunner for their research programme, then lifecycle models of family functioning draw their inspiration from developmental stage theories of individual growth. These lifecycle models start from the premise that families evolve over time and that at each stage of the lifecycle there are particular tasks that need to be completed (Carter & McGoldrick, 1980). A summary of important tasks that families complete at various stages of the lifecycle is presented in Figure 20.2.

Dimensional models of family functioning provide useful assessment tools, such as rating scales and self-report instruments, for family assessment and description. Lifecycle models, on the other hand draw our attention to specific transitions and stresses that families must face as they evolve over time. A useful project for family psychology will be the integration of these two frameworks by evaluating families that cope and those that have difficulties with various lifecycle transitions and stresses using dimensional assessment scales. An interesting preliminary study of 1000 families in the USA using precisely this strategy has been completed by David Olson and his colleagues at Minnesota University (Olson et al, 1983). Among the many results from this project, it was found that families varied in the levels of adaptability, cohesion, family stress and family satisfaction as they moved through the family lifecycle.

An important feature of elaborating a psychology of the family lifecycle and the ways in which families manage change over time will be the exploration of how families cope with the stress of the very young, the very old, the ill and the disabled.

Figure 20.2. Stages of the family lifecycle

STAGE	TASKS
1. Family of origin experiences	• Maintaining relationships with parents, siblings and peers • Completing school
2. Leaving home	• Differentiation of self from family of origin and developing adult to adult relationship with parents • Developing intimate peer relationships • Beginning a career
3. Premarriage stage	• Selecting partners • Developing a relationship • Deciding to marry
4. Childless couple	• Developing a way to live together based on reality rather than mutual projection • Realigning relationships with families of origin and peers to include spouses
5. Family with young children	• Adjusting marital system to make space for children • Adopting parenting roles • Realigning relationships with families of origin to include parenting and grandparenting roles
6. Family with adolescents	• Adjusting parent-child relationships to allow adolescents more autonomy • Adjusting marital relationships to focus on midlife marital and career issues • Taking on responsibility of caring for families of origin
7. Launching children	• Negotiating adult to adult relationships with children • Adjusting to living as a couple again • Adjusting to including in-laws and grandchildren within the family circle • Dealing with disabilities and death in the family of origin
8. Later life	• Coping with physiological decline • Adjusting to the children taking a more central role in family maintenance • Making room for the wisdom and experience of the elderly • Dealing with loss of spouse and peers • Preparation for death, life review and integration

Note: Adapted from Carter & McGoldrick (1989).

There is a growing consensus reflected in recent major review papers (e.g. Tunali & Power, 1993; Beresford, 1994) that families which adjust well to the stress imposed by coping with vulnerable dependants, such as ill or handicapped children, have certain characteristics. These include high quality social support networks, although often these networks contain only a few close friends or extended family members; robust supportive marriages where emphasis is placed on parenting rather than marital intimacy; good negotiation and communication skills; and individual coping strategies where parents seek professional information and services and redefine the ways in which their own needs may be met so that the burden of care they face does not compromise their own sense of self-fulfilment.

The clinical literature is replete with case studies of families who have been referred to therapy when children present with psychological problems which coincide with the transition from one stage of the family lifecycle to another. Elective mutism is a good example of a syndrome that typically occurs when the family is moving from a stage where there are toddlers at home to where children begin school (Carr & Afnan, 1989). Anorexia nervosa, on the other hand typically occurs as families move into that phase where they have teenage children at home or at the transition to the empty nest stage of the lifecycle (Carr, McDonnell & Afnan, 1989). More detailed empirical research on the relationship between lifecycle transitions and the psychological adjustment of children will be an important future project for family psychology.

SEX-ROLES

In recent times major changes in roles adopted by men and women within families have stimulated much research and an ethical sensitivity within psychology to gender issues. These studies suggest that couples' attempts to move from a traditional patriarchal family power system towards an egalitarian family structure may pose a number of unforseen obstacles (Gilbert, 1993). Women in dual career families suffer more role strain than their partners (Aldous, 1982). This is in part due to the fact that housework and child care tasks are rarely distributed equitably across both marital partners despite verbal commitments on the part of both partners to a fair division of labour.

However, growing up in a dual career family does not appear to have adverse effects on children and may in many cases have a beneficial impact (Lamb et al., 1987). Father's in dual career families have higher levels of contact with their children compared with fathers from families where they are the sole earners and increased father involvement is associated with positive development on a variety of indices. Also, girls who grow up in dual career families are more likely to make high status vocational choices and to value an independent career as much as or more than a homemaking role (Aldous, 1982).

Balancing the personal satisfactions and costs of evolving new family roles will continue to be a particular challenge for both men and women over the coming decades. The analyses of the intrapsychic and interpersonal processes underpinning this process will be an important area of study for family psychology.

FAMILY TRANSFORMATION

Dimensional models of family functioning assume that there is an acceptable way to define family membership, for example two generations of blood relatives living in a household. Lifecycle models of family functioning, traditionally assumed that normative stages could be identified through which all families pass. Of course both assumptions are valid for only a subset of families. The membership and developmental trajectory of, what may well be called, the post-modern family is not clearly defined (Cheale, 1993). The postmodern family takes many forms and may be formed or transformed by many processes including divorce, abortion, adoption, fostering, single-parenting, blending, heterosexual co-habiting and homosexual or lesbian cohabiting. Family members may define the membership of their families in legal terms, in religious terms, in biological terms, in terms of household composition, or in terms of psychological criteria such as the socialization of children or the provision of social support to all members. These are complexities with which family psychology has only begun to grapple.

A major contribution to the psychology of family transformation has come from the study of divorce (Carr, 1993). Divorce is not a rare event . It occurs in one in three families in industrialised countries and one in five children come from a family where divorce has occurred (Emery, 1988). Children from families where divorce has occurred, on average, are less well adjusted than those from intact families. However, recent meta analysis of 95 studies found that the mean effect size for such differences is small (ES = -.19 (Amato & Kieth, 1991)) with the majority of children showing no long term ill effects (Heatherington, 1989).

Where marital issues do not contaminate parents negotiation and execution of parenting duties and where good parent-child relationships are maintained, children's long-term adjustment is not compromised (Emery, 1988). On the other hand, children exposed to long-term marital conflict in families where parents stay together for the sake of the kids often suffer serious psychological consequences including delinquency and drug abuse (Rutter, 1985)

The impact of divorce is best conceived in bi-directional

systemic terms. Not only do parents effect children but the way children respond to their parents following divorce effect overall family functioning. For example, some daughter's develop highly supportive relationships with their mothers and so protect them from depression. This in turn protects the integrity of the functioning of the family as a whole (Heatherington, 1989).

Studies such as those conducted by Mavis Heatherington's team offer a useful template for future research on the transformation of the post-modern family (Heatherington et al, 1985). First, multiple self-report and observational measures were obtained in various contexts including the home, the laboratory and the school. Second, families were followed up over time within the context of a case-control longitudinal design. Third, univariate and multivariate analyses were used to test simple unidirectional hypotheses and to explore bidirectional patterns of influence.

CONCLUDING COMMENTS

The emerging field of family psychology is informed by the nine subfields outlined in this essay, fields which are united by a disenchantment with the selection of the individual rather than the family as the appropriate unit of analysis. The nine fields suggest fruitful directions for future research.

From the subfields of adult psychopathology, family violence and child development it is clear that a multifactorial approach to family studies is particularly useful. Both lifecycle and dimensional models of family functioning offer complimentary longitudinal and cross-sectional frameworks for such multifactorial research projects. From studies of family transformation and sex-roles, it is clear that family psychology must accept a broad definition of the family and various roles within the variety of family types. Studies of these non-traditional families will provide much needed normative data on new family configurations. This data will compliment results of future research on marital and family therapy with non-traditional families. The critical questions in the study of marital and family therapy will be *What types of family can benefit from intervention?* and *How does therapy help families?* These questions require investigators to change their emphasis away from research on therapy outcome and to focus on the process that occur during successful marital and family therapy. This type of process research will probably require the articulation of micro-models of the therapeutic system: That is, models which explain how systems that include both the therapist and the family function when they interact.

REFERENCES

Aldous, J. (1982). *Two Paycheques: Life in Dual Earner Families.* Beverley Hills: Sage.

Amato, P & Kieth, B. (1991). Consequences of the effects of divorce for the well-being of children: A meta-analysis. *Psychological Bulletin, 110,* 26-46.

American Psychiatric Association (1987). *Diagnostic and Statistical Manual of the Mental Disorders (3rd. ed. revised). (DSM 111 - R)* . Washington, DC: APA.

Bateson, G., Jackson, D., Haley, J. & Weakland, J. (1956). Toward a theory of schizophrenia. *Behavioural Science,* 1, 252-264.

Baumrind, D. (1982). Are androgenous individuals more effective persons and parents? *Child Development,* 53, 44-75.

Beavers, W. & Hampson, R. (1990). *Successful Families: Assessment and Intervention.* New York: Norton.

Belsky, J., Robins, E. & Gamble, W., (1984). The determinants of parental competence: Towards a contextual theory. In M. Lewis (Ed.). *Beyond the Dyad.* New York: Plenum.

Belsky, J. & Vondra, J. (1987). Child maltreatment: prevalence, consequences, causes and prevention. In D. Crowell, I. Evans, & C. O'Donnell (Eds.) *Childhood Aggression and Violence: Sources of Influence, Prevention and Control.* New York: Plenum.

Belsky, J., Ward, M., & Rovine, M., (1986). Prenatal expectations, postnatal experiences and the transition to parenthood. In R. Ashmore & D. Brodzinsky (Eds.) *Thinking about the Family: Views of Parents and Children.* Hillsdale, NJ: Lawrence Erlbaum.

Beresford, B. (1994). Resources and strategies: How parents cope with the care of a disabled child. *Journal of Child Psychology and Psychiatry,* 35, 171-210.

Bowlby, J. (1949). The study and reduction of group tension in the family. *Human Relations,* 2, 122-128.

Bretherton, I. & Waters, E. (1985). Growing points of attachment theory and research. *Monographs of the Society for Research in Child Development,* 50, No 1-2, Serial No. 209.

Broderick, C. & Schrander, S. (1991). The history of professional marriage and family therapy. In A. Gurman and D. Kniskern (Eds.) *Handbook of Family Therapy.* New York. Brunner Mazel.

Bronfenbrenner, U. (1986). Ecology of the family as a context for human development: Research perspectives. *Developmental Psychology,* 22, 723-742.

Buckley, W. (1968). *Modern Systems Research for the Behavioural Scientist: A Sourcebook.* Chicago: Aldine.

Carr, A. (1993). The Effects of Divorce. *Irish Psychologist,* 19, 133-135.

Carr, A. (1991). Milan Systemic Family Therapy: A review of 10 empirical investigations. *Journal of Family Therapy,* 13, 237-264.

Carr, A. & Afnan, S. (1989). Concurrent individual and family therapy in a case of elective mutism. *Journal of Family Therapy,* 11, 29-44.

Carr, A. MacDonnell, D., & Afnan, S. (1989). Anorexia Nervosa: The treatment of a male case with combined behavioural and family therapy. *Journal of*

Family Therapy, 11, 335-351.

Carson, R & Butcher, J. (1992). *Abnormal Psychology and Modern Life* (9th. Edition). New York: Harper/Collins.

Carter, E. & Mc Goldrick, M. (1980). *The Family Lifecycle.* New York. Gardner Press.

Cattell, R. (1990). Advances in Cattellian personality theory. In L Pervin (Ed). *Handbook of Personality: Theory and Research.* New York. Guilford Press.

Cheale, D. (1993). Unity and difference in post-modern families. *Journal of Family Issues,* 14, 5-19.

Cicchetti, D. & Carlson, V. (1989). *Child Maltreatment.* Cambridge: Cambridge University Press.

Dicks, H. (1967). *Marital Tensions.* London: Routledge & Kegan Paul.

Drumm, M., Carr, A., & Fitzgerald, M. (1993). *The sensitivity and specificity of three approaches to family evaluation.* Research in progress at UCD & the EHB.

Emery, R. (1988). *Marriage, Divorce and Children's adjustment.* Newbury Park, CA: Sage.

Epstein, N. & Bishop, D. (1981). Problem centred systems therapy of the family. In A. Gurman, & D. Kniskern, (Eds). *Handbook of Family Therapy.* New York. Brunner Mazel.

Eysenck, H. (1990). Biological dimensions of personality. In L Pervin (Ed). *Handbook of Personality: Theory and Research.* New York. Guilford Press.

Falloon, I. (1985). *Family Management of Schizophrenia: A study of Clinical, Social, Family and Economic Benefits.* Baltimore: Johns Hopkins University Press.

Falloon, I. (1988). *Handbook of Behavioural Family Therapy.* New York: Guilford.

Fonagy, P., Steele, M. & Steele, H. (1991). Intergenerational patterns of attachment: maternal representations during pregnancy and subsequent infant-mother attachments. *Child Development,* 62, 891-905.

Ford, D. & Lerner, R. (1992). *Developmental Systems Theory: An Integrative Approach.* Newbury Park, CA: Sage.

Frude, N. (1990). *Understanding family Problems.* Chichester: Wiley.

Gelles, R. (1987). *The Violent Home: Updated Edition.* Beverley Hills, CA: Sage.

Gelles, R. & Losekem D. (1993). *Current Controversies on Family Violence.* London: Sage.

Gilbert, L. (1993). *Two Careers, One Family.* London: Sage.

Gleitman, H. (1981). *Psychology.* New York: Norton.

Goldstein, M. & Strachan, A. (1987). The family and schizophrenia. In T. Jacob (Ed.) *Family Interaction and Psychopathology.* New York: Plenum.

Grossman, K., Fremmer-Bombik, E., Rudolph, J. & Grossman, K. (1988). Maternal attachment representations as related to patterns of infant mother attachment and maternal care giving during the first year. In R. Hinde & J. Stevenson-Hinde (Eds.) *Relationships Within Families: Mutual Influences.* Clarendon: Oxford.

Gurman, A. & Kniskern, D. (1978). Research on marital and family therapy:

Progress, perspective and prospect. In S. Garfield & A Bergin (Eds.). *Handbook of Psychotherapy and Behaviour Change* (2nd. Ed.) New York: Wiley.

Gurman, A. & Kniskern, D. (1981). *Handbook of Family Therapy*. New York. Brunner Mazel.

Gurman, A. & Kniskern, D. (1991). *Handbook of Family Therapy, Volume 11*. New York. Brunner Mazel.

Guttman, H. (1991). Systems theory, cybernetics and Epistemology. In A. Gurman and D. Kniskern (Eds.) *Handbook of Family Therapy. Vol 2*. New York. Brunner Mazel.

Herbert, M. (1991). *Clinical Child Psychology: Social Learning, Development and Behaviour*. Chichester: Wiley.

Herrenkohn, E., Herrenkohl, R. (1979). A comparison of abused children and their non-abused siblings. *Journal of the Academy of Child Psychiatry, 18,* 260-269.

Hetherington, M. (1989). Coping with family transitions: Winners losers and survivors. *Child Development, 60,* 1-14.

Heatherington, M., Cox, M. & Cox, R. (1985). Long-term effects of divorce and remarriage on the adjustment of children. *Journal of the American Academy of Child Psychiatry, 24,* 518-530.

Hewstone, M., Stroebe, W., Codal, J., & Stephenson, (1988). *Introduction to Social Psychology*. Oxford. Blackwell.

Hilberman, E. & Munson, K. (1978). Sixty battered women. *Victimology: An International Journal, 4,* 460-470

Holtzworth-Munroe, A. & Jacobson, N. (1991). Behavioural marital therapy. In A. Gurman and D. Kniskern (Eds.) *Handbook of Family Therapy. Vol 2..* New York: Brunner Mazel.

Jacob, T. (1987). *Family Interaction and Psychopathology*. New York: Plenum.

Kinsey, A, Pomeroy, W. & Martin, C. (1948). *Sexual Behaviour in the Human Male*. Philadelphia: W.B. Saunders.

Kinsey, A, Pomeroy, W., Martin, C. & Gebhard (1953). *Sexual Behaviour in the Human Female*. Philadelphia: W.B. Saunders.

Lamb, M., Pleck, J., Charnov, E. & Levine, J. (1987). A biosocial perspective on paternal behaviour and involvement. In J. Lancaster, J. Altman, A. Rossi & L. Sherrod (Eds.) *Parenting Across the Lifespan: Biosocial Perspectives*. Hawthorn, NY: Aldine.

Lidz, T., Cornelison, A., Fleck, S. & Terry, D. (1957). The intrafamilial environment of schizophrenic patients 2. Marital schizm and marital skew. *American Journal of Psychiatry,* 114, 241-248.

Maccoby, E. & Martin, J. (1983). Socialization in the context of the family: Parent-child interaction. In P. Mussen & M. Heatherington (Eds). *Handbook of Child Psychology. Vol 4. Socialization, Personality, and Social Development*. New York. Wiley.

Mason, M. (1991). Family therapy as the emergent context for sex therapy. In A. Gurman and D. Kniskern (Eds.) *Handbook of Family Therapy. Vol 2.* New York. Brunner Mazel.

Masters, W. & Johnson, V. (1966). *Human Sexual response*. Boston: Little Brown.

Masters, W. & Johnson, V. (1970). *Human Sexual Inadequacy.* Boston: Little Brown.

McCubbin, M. & McCubbin, H. (1988). Family Systems Assessment. In P. Karoly (Ed.) *Handbook of Child Health Assessment.* New York: Wiley.

Mussen, P., Conger, J., Kagan, J. & Huston, A. (1990). *Child Development and Personality (7th. ed.).* New York: Harper Collins.

Olson, D., McCubbin, H., Barners, H., Larsen, S., Muxen, M. & Wilson, M. (1983). *Families: What makes them work?* Beverley Hills, CA: Sage.

Olson, D., Russell, C. & Sprenkle, D. (1989). *Circumplex Model: Systemic Assessment and Treatment of Families.* New York: Haworth.

Patterson, G. (1982). *Coercive Family Process.* Eugene, OR: Castalia.

Roy, M. (1982). *The Abusing Partner: An Analysis of Domestic Battering.* New York: Van Nosrand Reinhold.

Russell, G., Szmukler, G., Dare, C. & Eisler, I. (1987). An evaluation of family therapy in anorexia nervosa and bulimia nervosa. *Archives of General Psychiatry,* 44, 1047-1056.

Rutter, M. (1985). Family and school influences on behavioural development. *Journal of Child Psychology and Psychiatry, 26,* 349-368.

Singer, M. & Wynne, L. (1965). Thought disorder and family relations of schizophrenics. 4. Results and implications. *Archives of General Psychiatry,* 12, 201-212.

Steiner, (1979). Social Psychology. In E. Hearst (Ed.) *The First Century of Experimental Psychology.* Hillsdale, NJ: Lawrence Erlbaum.

Straus, M., & Gelles, R. (1986). Societal change and marital violence from 1975 to 1985 as revealed by two national surveys. *Journal of Marriage and the Family, 48,* 445-479.

Szapocznik, J., Riom A., Murray, E., Cohen, R., Scopetta, M., Rivas-Vazquez, A., Hervis, O, Posada, V. & Kurtines, W. (1989). Structural family versus psychodynamic child therapy for problematic Hispanic boys. *Journal of Consulting & Clinical psychology,* 57, 571-578.

Teti, D., Nakagawa, M., Das,, R. & Wirth, O. (1991). Security of attachment between preschoolers and their mothers: Relations among social interaction, parenting stress and mothers' sorts n the attachment Q-set. *Developmental Psychology,* 27, 440-447.

Tienari, P., Sorri, A., Lahti, I., Naarala, M., Wahlberg, K., Pohjola, J. & Moring, J. (1985). Interaction of genetic and psychosocial factors in schizophrenia. *Acta Psychiatrica Scandinavia,* 71, 19-30.

Tunali, B. & Power, T. (1993). Creating satisfaction: A psychological perspective on stress and coping in families of handicapped children. *Journal of Child Psychology and Psychiatry,* 34, 945-957.

Vaughan, C. & Leff, J. (1976). The measurement of expressed emotion in the families of psychiatric patients. *British Journal of Clinical and Social Psychology,* 15, 157-165.

von Bertalanffy, L. (1968). *General Systems Theory.* New York: Brazziler.

Werner, E. (1985). Stress and protective factors in children's lives. In A. Nicol (Ed.) *Longitudinal Studies in Child Psychology and Psychiatry.* Chichester: Wiley.

White, D. & Woollett, A. (1992). *Families: A context for development.* London:

Falmer.
Wolfe, D. (1985). Child abusive parents: an empirical review and analysis. *Psychological Bulletin, 97,* 462-482.
World Health Organization (1988). *International Classification of Diseases: 10th. Edition (ICD-10).* Geneva: WHO.